'In Spain with Orwell'

'In Spain with Orwell'

George Orwell and the
Independent Labour Party Volunteers
in the Spanish Civil War, 1936-1939

Christopher Hall

"'In Spain with Orwell' - George Orwell and the Independent Labour Party Volunteers in the Spanish Civil War, 1936-1939"
Copyright © 2009, 2012 Christopher Hall. All rights reserved.

The right of Christopher Hall to be identified as the author and of the Work has been asserted by him in accordance with the Copyright, Designs and Patents Act 1988.

First published 2009 under the title "Not Just Orwell" by Warren & Pell Publishing
This second revised edition published and copyright 2013 by
Tippermuir Books Limited, Perth, Scotland
www.alternative-perth.co.uk
tippermuirbooks@blueyonder.co.uk

No part of this publication may be reproduced or used in any form or by any means without written permission from the Publisher and the author except for review purposes.

ISBN-10: 0956337457
ISBN-13: 978-0-9563374-5-0
A CIP catalogue record for this book is available from the British Library.

Design and artwork by Bernard Chandler,
Glastonbury, England. www.graffik.co.uk
Text set in ITC Cheltenham with titling in Perpetua.

Front cover photograph:
On Parade at the Lenin Barracks
(Orwell Archive, UCL Special Collections)

Printed and bound by CPI Group (UK) Ltd,
Croydon, CR0 4YY

DEDICATION

To all British and Irish
anti-Fascist volunteers who served
in the Spanish Civil War.

ACKNOWLEDGEMENTS

MANY PEOPLE HAVE HELPED and encouraged me in this venture, and they all deserve my thanks. Firstly, Paul Philippou, Rob Hands and Tippermuir Books for agreeing to publish this book and seeing the need for the story of Orwell's fellow volunteers to be acknowledged and remembered. Secondly, Barry Winter of Independent Labour Publications willingly photocopied and posted articles from the ILP newspaper the *New Leader* for me and allowed me to use pictures from their archive, as well as being an excellent host when I visited the ILP rooms in Leeds. Thirdly, thanks to Archie Potts for allowing me to use his photographs of John McNair and Bob Smillie and McNair and the ILP Contingent at Victoria Station. Fourthly, thanks to the International Brigade Memorial Trust for allowing me to use the picture of ILP member and International Brigader, Lance Rogers. Fifthly thanks to Bernard Chandler for his professionalism and hard work in organising and designing this book. My wife Melanie has, as ever, been a highly efficient editor, turning my enthusiastic writing into English that people will understand.

I would also like to thank Philip Mahon for his translation of a Catalan article for me and to Amanda Smith who translated a Spanish article.

Particular thanks go to Jim Carmody, the chief researcher of the International Brigade Memorial Trust, who sent me much useful information about British and Irish Volunteers in the Spanish militias; and to Dan Payne who told me about a Liverpool volunteer previously unknown to me. My thanks also go to Andy Durgan, who very kindly sent me a copy of his new edition of 'International Volunteers in the POUM', and to Michael Eaude who sent me his notes on the ILP Contingent. In addition both Andy and Michael were invaluable sources of advice on all things Catalan. Thanks also to Richard Baxell for information about the volunteer David Wickes.

I am especially grateful to former ILP and 'Spanish Aid' activist Sidney Robinson for writing the foreword. Also Roma Marquez Santo, a POUM activist and Spanish Civil War veteran who spoke to me about his militia experiences and came to Britain to unveil the commemorative plaque in honour of the ILP Contingent in the Salford Working Class Movement Library in 2009. Roma was a passionate man who taught himself English and was always amazed that British people recognised and honoured the anti-Fascist fight in the Spanish Civil War. He died peacefully in 2010.

A special mention goes to my children, Rosa and Alexandra, who generally behaved well when Dad was using the computer, especially when they wanted to use the Internet.

A final thanks goes to a generous and brave gentleman who served in Spain and who died in 1999. I was fortunate to meet Stafford Cottman in 1993 and to correspond with him for several years. It is Staff's story, and those of his comrades, which inspired me to write this book.

Christopher Hall

Contents

Acknowledgements	vi
List of Illustrations	viii
Foreword by Sidney Robinson	xi
Introduction	1
1. The ILP from Foundation to Disaffiliation	7
2. The ILP in the 1930's	19
3. The Spanish Republic and the Formation of the POUM 1931-36	37
4. The POUM and the Spanish Civil War 1936-37	45
5. The ILP and the Spanish Civil War	61
6. The Revolutionary Militias and the POUM	81
7. The ILP Contingent	103
8. Leaders of the ILP Contingent	127
9. British and Irish Members of the ILP Contingent	171
Conclusion	245
Selected Bibliography	253
Index	262

LIST OF ILLUSTRATIONS

Illustration number / title   Page

1. They did not pass. *(ILP Archive)*   21
2. Hunger Marchers led by Bob Edwards. *(NL)*   24
3. James Carmichael, James Maxton and John McGovern. *(NL)*   30
4. Lance Rogers, ILP Merthyr Activist and International Brigader *(IBMT)*   60
5. Ambulance drivers. *(NL)*   62
6. Maurin Ambulance. *(NL)*   63
7. John McNair. *(ILP Archive)*   64
8. John McNair with POUM members in Barcelona. *(courtesy of A. Potts)*   64
9. Food ship for Bilbao cartoon. *(NL)*   66
10. House in Street (Somerset) for Basque Refugee Children. *(NL)*   67
11. Basque Refugee Children. *(NL)*   68
12. Fenner Brockway. *(ILP Archive)*   70
13. Milicianos fortify a position in the Sierra de Alcubierre, 1936 to 1937. *(Fototeca, Diputación de Huesca)*   82
14. POUM miliciano in the Sierra de Alcubierre, 1936 to 1937. *(Fototeca, Diputación de Huesca)*   85
15. POUM position in the Sierra de Alcubierre, 1936 to 1937. *(Fototeca, Diputación de Huesca)*   85
16. Milicianos of the Lenin Column and Macias Company Column resting after a meal. 1936 to 1937. *(Fototeca, Diputación de Huesca)*   90
17. Milicianos of the Lenin Column and Macias Company Column in the Sierra de Alcubierre, 1936 to 1937. *(Fototeca, Diputación de Huesca)*   91
18. Front line in the Sierra de Alcubierre, 1936 to 1937. *(Fototeca, Diputación de Huesca)*   95
19. Miliciano serving wine in a shelter in the Sierra de Alcubierre, 1936 to 1937. *(Fototeca, Diputación de Huesca)*   96
20. Milicianos of the POUM and Macia Company Column in the Sierra de Alcubierre, 1936 to 1937. *(Fototeca, Diputación de Huesca)*   97

LIST OF ILLUSTRATIONS

21. Miliciano in the Sierra de Alcubierre, 1936 to 1937. *(Fototeca, Diputación de Huesca)*	97
22. Milicianos by the entrance to a shelter at a position in the Sierra de Alcubierre, 1936 to 1937. *(Fototeca, Diputación de Huesca)*	97
23. ILP Volunteers leaving London. *(NL)*	104
24. ILP Contingent at Victoria Station en route to Spain. *(courtesy of A. Potts)*	105
25. ILP Volunteers in the 'Lenin Barracks'. *(NL)*	108
26. Part of the ILP Contingent; and the ILP Soldiers' Committee. *(NL)*	108
27. Georges Kopp. *(NL)*	132
28. Bob Edwards. *(ILP Archive)*	138
29. Arthur Chambers. *(NL)*	157
30. George Orwell and Eileen O'Shaughnessy on the Aragon Front. *(UCL)*	171
31. Stafford Cottman. *(NL)*	181
32. Frank Frankford. *(NL)*	191
33. Reg Hiddlestone. *(NL)*	197
34. Philip Hunter. *(NL)*	199
35. Urias Jones. *(NL)*	200
36. Charles Justessen. *(NL)*	202
37. Hugh McNeil. *(NL)*	202
38. Bob Smillie. *(NL)*	207
39. Bob Smillie and John McNair in the POUM offices,	208
40. Letchworth Summer School 1937. (L - R top row: Stafford Cottman, George Orwell, John Braithwaite. L - R bottom row: Douglas Moyle, Ted Fletcher, John McNair.) *(Photograph lent by Stafford Cottman to author)*	246
41. The commemorative plaque of the ILP Contingent (design by Les Cartlidge) in the Reading Room of the Salford Working Class Movement Library near Manchester.	250
42. The author and Roma Marquez, one of the last surviving militia men of the 29th POUM Division who went to Zaragoza in August 1936 discussing the Huesca battlefield in October 2008.	251
43. Roma Marquez, having a cup of coffee in Huesca on March 22nd 2009, almost seventy-three years late!	251

Foreword
by Sidney Robinson

AS I AM SURE YOU WILL APPRECIATE due to the passing of almost seventy years since the end of the Spanish Civil War, memories of much detail have become faded. Due to my work I left Newport in 1939 and gradually lost active contact. My present age of ninety-three does not help. Although I make occasional visits to Newport, I do not know of any survivors from the 1930's decade who were active at that time in the political and other organisations in Newport. I was a member of the ILP through the 1930's.

The Newport ILP was a small branch, which met weekly; most members were middle aged and tended to have small business backgrounds rather than manual occupations. There was also an active Communist Party Branch most of whose members were connected with shipping and Newport Docks. The Labour, Liberal and Conservatives formed the large parties. As the Civil War continued a large party (about four-hundred) of Basque children were brought to Newport, were accommodated at nearby Caerleon and most returned home after the war.

The ILP and the local Communist Party took the lead in establishing a broad front to assist the suffering of the civil population in Spain and I was appointed Secretary of the newly formed Spanish Relief Committee. We raised a considerable amount of finances, food, medical supplies etc and had the co-operation of most of the political parties, trade unions, Co-ops, churches and chapels etc. Apart from the military assistance given by the then German and Italian Governments to the Franco Army, we had to contend with the unsympathetic attitude of the British Government and a section of the British daily press. The three national papers, *Daily Herald*, *News Chronicle* and *Reynolds News* were helpful as well as the Newport daily, *The South Wales Argus*.

There was a small Spanish community living in Newport at the time, who were anxious over their relatives in Spain, and we worked closely with them.

Members of the Relief Committee also contacted the crews of Spanish ships coming to Newport, and on many occasions were invited to their homes in Newport. This was a very strong link as there were regular cargoes of iron ore from northern Spain for the Ebbw Vale steelworks.

I had a good friend at the time, Edwin Williams: he was a member of the Newport Branch of the Communist Party who joined the International Brigades but sadly lost his life.

I am very pleased to see that finally a book has been published that tells the full story about ILP involvement in the Spanish Civil War. The story of those men and women who served in the ILP Contingent is a story that needs to be told. Chris Hall has written a book that should be read by all persons interested in British involvement in the Spanish Civil War.

Sidney Robinson
ILP Activist and Secretary,
Spanish Relief Newport Committee
(2009)

Introduction

IN 2006 NUMEROUS EVENTS WERE HELD throughout Britain and Ireland to commemorate the 70th anniversary of the outbreak of the Spanish Civil War. These events were a tribute to the British and Irish anti-Fascist volunteers who fought and served in the International Brigades on the side of the Spanish Republican Government against the Fascist rebels in the Civil War of 1936-39. As a member of the International Brigade Memorial Trust (IBMT) I was heavily involved in designing commemorative china, helping to organise the Annual General Meeting in Manchester and in producing a concert headlined by the singer Billy Bragg. Events in Britain and Spain celebrated the selfless heroism and anti-Fascism of the men and women who served in the International Brigades. Later, when I sat down to reflect on the past year, it dawned on me that, throughout all the events commemorating anti-Fascist British and Irish volunteers who fought in Spain, one group of volunteers had been omitted. This group of volunteers were a small group of men who fought in a military unit raised by the Independent Labour Party.

Since the end of the Civil War many International Brigades veterans have recounted their experiences in Spain, and academics, amateur historians and family members have written many biographies of International Brigades veterans. There have been five works on the British and Irish International Brigades volunteers in Spain written by Bill Rust, Bill Alexander, John Hopkins and most recently two excellent scholarly accounts by Richard Baxell.[1] It has been estimated that more books have been written about the Spanish Civil War than World War II, and interest in the Spanish Civil War appears to be increasing as many more books are published on the subject; even, in the case of Anthony Beevor's book, becoming a bestseller![2]

However there is one aspect of the story of British and Irish anti-Fascist volunteers in Spain which has received little or no coverage. Approximately forty British and Irish Volunteers served in a unit raised by the Independent Labour Party and fought briefly in the militia of the Spanish Marxist Party called the POUM. The best-known written account of this group of volunteers was George Orwell's description of his experiences in this unit in *Homage to Catalonia*.[3] Precious little has been written since then, although the director Ken Loach made a highly-acclaimed dramatised account of one British volunteer's experiences with the POUM in his 1995 film 'Land and Freedom'.[4] Twenty-five years ago Peter Thwaites wrote a journal article on the ILP volunteers [5] and more recently Tom Buchanan wrote about the death of the ILP volunteer Bob Smillie.[6] In 1993 I interviewed Stafford Cottman, an ILP volunteer, and included him in my book, *Disciplina Camaradas* along with three members of the International Brigades.[7] Three ILP volunteers have been interviewed by the Imperial War Museum and the historian Hywel Francis interviewed a Welsh ILP volunteer.[8] But as yet there has been no book written specifically about the British and Irish ILP volunteers and, except for George Orwell, no ILP veteran has written an account of his experiences in Spain.

Why would this be? The main reason was that the Independent Labour Party in Britain supported the political party in Spain, the POUM. The POUM supported the Spanish Revolution, which had erupted in Catalonia and Aragon in the summer of 1936 and continued into the following summer. Revolutionary militias took over the reins of government and, while they opposed the Fascist forces at the Front, they also refused to surrender power to the (legally elected) Spanish Republican Government. The volunteers of the International Brigades, some academics and many more people on the Left believe that the Spanish Revolution undermined the war against the Fascists. They believed that the Revolution made it more difficult to centralise resources and set up a trained army. The POUM and the Anarchists - the largest political group in Catalonia - joined together in armed rebellion to resist attempts by the Central Government to overturn the Revolution in Catalonia, and were derided as no better than Fascists. The POUM were also critical of Russia's leader, Stalin, who was the major supplier of arms to the Spanish Republican Government. The Anarchists were too powerful a political force to destroy; however the much smaller POUM was vulnerable and it was

INTRODUCTION

declared illegal in June 1937 by the Spanish Government. The POUM was crushed and its militants executed or imprisoned.

Many books have been written supporting the Spanish Revolution and the POUM position. They like to portray the Communist Party as a 'puppet master', pulling the strings of the Spanish Republican Government. The thrust of this work is to find out about the ILP volunteers themselves rather than to argue about the rights and wrongs of the Spanish Revolution versus the Republican Government. The policies and the role of the ILP and the POUM must be considered in order to give readers an insight into the background to the ILP volunteers' presence in Spain. But I have tried to be dispassionate as far as is possible in a debate that can still cause controversy over seventy-five years later. I have also tried to use, wherever possible, non-partisan academic sources, but on many occasions I have had to include source materials written by writers who are sympathetic to the POUM and/ or the ILP.[9] The ILP newspaper the *New Leader* is a major source of information about the ILP volunteers and I have made extensive use of it, as in some cases it is the only source material that covers the subject in any detail. I accept that these sources will present the POUM and the ILP in a good light and I have tried to take this into account when using them.

The main focus of this book is to look at the organisation, actions and individual members of the ILP Contingent in Spain. I have attempted to provide a definitive list of those men who served in the unit in order to give a brief biography of each volunteer. In some cases this has led to quite detailed studies, in other cases only a few lines are possible. This is the first time that any publication has attempted to tell the story of the individuals who fought in the ILP Contingent in Spain.

The efforts of the ILP in supporting Republican Spain have always been coloured by their support of the POUM. The Communist Party's support of the International Brigades and its leading role in the 'Aid Spain' movement has overshadowed the ILP's role in the Spanish Civil War to the extent that it has been largely ignored. This publication intends to redress the balance a little to show that the ILP were a committed anti-Fascist political party throughout the Civil War, even supporting the Spanish Republican Government after it had suppressed the POUM.

The ILP's support for the Revolution and the POUM meant that it was ostracised by the rest of the British Left who supported the Spanish Republican Government. However I hope to show in this study that the ILP and its volunteers played an honourable and, given its limited resources, a not insubstantial role in supporting the anti-Fascist cause in Spain.

Because of its size and position in British politics, the ILP's efforts could not compare to those of the Communist Party and rest of the British Left in terms of the amount of money raised and the number of volunteers serving in Spain, including those killed and wounded. The ILP volunteers who served with the POUM served on a quiet Front and were involved in only one minor action. They were also sucked into the 'May Days' events when the POUM and Anarchists resisted the Government's attempts to suppress the Revolution by launching an armed uprising. After the 'May Days' several ILP volunteers joined non-POUM units, and after the POUM was declared illegal most ILP volunteers were forced to flee Spain and return to Britain.

After the 70th anniversary of the outbreak of the Spanish Civil War the time is ripe to tell the story of the ILP volunteers in Spain. To find out about these men, their background, politics, experiences in Spain and what happened to them afterwards. Were they so very different from International Brigades volunteers? This book aims to tell the story of these men in a straightforward manner while being as impartial as possible. The author respects all anti-Fascist volunteers who served in Spain and hopes this account will be accepted in this spirit.

Notes

[1] William Rust, *Britons in Spain: The History of the British Battalion of the XVth International Brigade* (London, Lawrence and Wishart, 1939 and Abersychan, Warren & Pell, 2003), Bill Alexander, *British Volunteers for Liberty: Spain 1936-39* (London, Lawrence and Wishart, 1982), James K. Hopkins, *Into the Heart of the Fire: The British in the Spanish Civil War* (Stanford, Stanford Univ. Press, 1998), Richard Baxell, *British Volunteers in the Spanish Civil War: The British Battalion in the International Brigades, 1936-1939* (London, Routledge, 2004 and Abersychan, Warren & Pell, 2007) Richard Baxell, *Unlikely Warriors: The British in the Spanish Civil War and the Struggle against Fascism* (London, Aurum Press, 2012)

[2] Antony Beevor, *The Battle for Spain: The Spanish Civil War 1936-1939* (London, Weidenfeld & Nicolson, 2006)

[3] George Orwell, *Homage to Catalonia: And Looking Back on the Spanish War* (London, Penguin, 1988). First published 1938.

INTRODUCTION

[4] 'Land and Freedom' directed by Ken Loach, 1995, Artificial Eye.

[5] Peter Thwaites, The Independent Labour Party in the Spanish Civil War, *Imperial War Museum Review*, 1987, p50-61

[6] Tom Buchanan, *The Impact of the Spanish Civil War on Britain: War, Loss and Memory* (Brighton, Sussex Academic Press, 2007), p98-121. Reproduces his article from the *Historical Journal*.

[7] Christopher Hall, *'Disciplina Camaradas': Four English Volunteers in Spain 1936-39* (Pontefract, Gosling Press, 1994)

[8] The Imperial War Museum interviewed Bob Edwards, Frank Frankford and Stafford Cottman. Hywel Francis interviewed Urias Jones.

[9] Orwell's account is obviously favourable to the volunteers and the POUM position, as are most works on Orwell. Interviews with Bob Edwards and Stafford Cottman support the ILP/POUM position, but those with Jones and Frankford do not. Three works I have used for background information that support the ILP/POUM position include: Barry Winter, *The ILP: Past and Present* (Leeds, Independent Labour Publications, 1993). Barry Winter was an ILP member. Victor Alba and Stephen Schwartz, *Spanish Marxism Versus Soviet Communism: A History of the P.O.U.M.* (Oxford, Transaction Books, 1988), Victor Alba was a member of the POUM. Pierre Broue and Emile Temime, *The Revolution and the Civil War in Spain* (London, Faber and Faber, 1970). These two authors were French Trotskyites. Biographies or autobiographies of leading figures in the ILP and POUM have often been written by the individuals themselves or by admirers within the same party.

CHAPTER 1

The ILP From Foundation to Disaffiliation

THE INDEPENDENT LABOUR PARTY (ILP) was founded in 1893 and acted as the Socialist conscience of the Labour Party until 1932. Between 1893 and 1900 the ILP was a separate political party. In 1900 the ILP joined the Labour Representation Committee, which became the Labour Party in 1906. Before World War I the ILP supported many causes, including votes for women and the protests against the Boer War (1899-1902). Its members were at the forefront of spreading the Socialist message through outdoor meetings, rallies and publications.

During World War I the divisions between the Labour Party and the ILP began to grow. The ILP viewed the leaders of the Labour Party as happy merely to increase their share of the vote, make deals with the Liberal Party and support gradual reforms for the working class at the expense of the Socialist message. Many Labour Party and trade union members supported the Great War, whereas the majority of ILP members were hostile to the war, either because they were pacifists or because they saw it as an imperialist war. Many ILP members went to prison rather than serve in the armed forces. This included many leading figures in the ILP including such men as Ramsay MacDonald the future Labour Party Prime Minster and James Maxton and Fenner Brockway leading figures in the ILP at the time of the Spanish Civil War.[1]

After World War I the Labour Party's vote continued to grow and they formed minority Governments in 1924 and 1929-31. In both cases the ILP was frustrated by the lack of Socialist policies put forward by the Labour Government. The ILP had strongly supported the 1926 General Strike [2] and perceived that the Labour Party was reluctant to support the strikers. By 1932 the Labour Party was in disarray; they had suffered a huge election defeat in 1931 and their major statesmen had defected to a National Government.[3] Under the Labour Government of 1929-31 the 'Depression' had struck and this caused unemployment to rise to 2,700,000, this was 22% of the workforce.[4] A small group (seventeen MPs) within the one hundred and forty ILP MPs had been the sternest critics of the Labour Government. After the General Election defeat the ILP were ordered to vote the same way as the Labour Party in the House of Commons regardless of ILP policy. When the ILP refused to accept this they formally disaffiliated or left the Labour Party in 1932 to become a separate political party.[5]

The founding conference of the Independent Labour Party (ILP) took place in Bradford in January 1893. Bradford was one of the major textile manufacturing cities in Britain and in recent years had seen a very bitter mill strike. Unskilled workers fighting against wage cuts at Manningham Mill were on strike for five months until they were defeated. During the dispute local Liberal Councillors refused to support the strikers. Socialists in Leeds and Bradford supported the strikers, arranging mass meetings and raising funds. The leaders of the strike decided they could no longer count on support from the local Liberal Party and formed the Bradford Labour Union in 1891, which became in 1892 the Bradford Independent Labour Party. Strikers elsewhere found the Liberal Party unsympathetic to their plight and Independent Labour Parties were set up in many other areas.

In January 1893 one hundred delegates met in Bradford to set up the ILP. The famous Socialist Keir Hardie[6] was the Chairman of the conference. Most of the delegates were young working-class men, mostly from northern England and Scotland. There were representatives from the Marxist Social Democratic Federation (SDF), the Scottish Labour Party, independent Socialist groups, some trade unionists and trade council members. Many of the trade unionists had been involved in the 'New Unionism' of the 1880's and 1890's. This involved unionising unskilled workers for the first time. They had found the Liberal Party was only interested in supporting the craft unions and had no desire to support any militant strike action.

From the middle of the nineteenth century the Liberal Party had supported craft unions and had sponsored some trade union leaders, enabling them to become MPs. This process was known as 'Lib-Labism'. Many individual trade unionists saw the Liberal Party as the best guarantor of working-class needs and were hostile to the ILP, who they saw as weakening the Liberal vote. Ironically, the Miners' Union was very hostile to the ILP and was one of the last unions to break its connections with the Liberal Party. The first person to successfully challenge the Liberal Party was Keir Hardie, who in 1892 was elected MP for West Ham North in London as an Independent Labour candidate.

The name of the new party did not include the word 'Socialism', as the delegates wanted it to be a party of labour rather than Socialism. Its end goal was:

> "... to secure the collective ownership of all the means of production, distribution and exchange."[7]

Its short-term goals were to win elections and to be represented on all elected bodies, and by doing so, to help alleviate the suffering of the working class. Its long-term aims were to create a Socialist society. This was to be done by propaganda and education rather than by revolutionary means. At its foundation the ILP was a democratic Socialist party, rather than a revolutionary one.

From its foundation the ILP grew in influence, but only steadily. In the 1895 General Election all ILP candidates, including Keir Hardie, were defeated. As the nineteenth century came to a close recession struck Britain and trade unionists found that the Liberal Party did not oppose unfavourable court rulings against trade unions, and supported the employers. On the other hand, the ILP did support the trade unions by raising funds and being active within the unions. This led to the Trades Union Congress (TUC)[8] severing its links with the Liberal Party in 1899 and resolving to aim to have separate working class representation in Parliament.

In 1900 the Labour Representation Committee (LRC) was founded at a conference in London. Over one hundred trade unions were represented at this conference, along with the Fabian Society,[9] the SDF and the ILP. The Marxist SDF soon left when the conference rejected the idea of 'Class War' and the 'Socialisation of the means of production, distribution and exchange'. The LRC followed closely the principles of the ILP and agreed that it should aim to elect MPs to Parliament. To become a member of the LRC you had to be a member of a trade union or of a Socialist society. In 1906 the LRC became the Labour Party and the ILP was now no longer isolated from the trade unions. However the trade unions had a small majority on the National Executive Committee of the new Labour Party and could dominate the national conferences through its block voting rights.

Members of the ILP were often evangelical and crusading in their approach to carrying the Socialist message to the working classes, adopting the style of the evangelical or non-conformist Christian traditions that many had grown up with. The Socialist message was delivered from Meeting Halls which were also used for social and cultural events. Many ILPers were devout Christians and melded their Christianity and Socialism together by forming Labour churches.[10] Groups of ILPers toured villages and towns spreading the Socialist word on cycles and in Clarion vans.[11] ILP orators were famous for their open-air meetings, which usually took place on Sunday evenings. Many ILP members believed in equality for women and supported the campaigns to get women the vote [12] and equality in the household. ILP members were not afraid to support unpopular causes like 'Votes for Women' if they believed they were just causes. This was in complete contrast to the tactics of the Labour Party, which believed it was more important to win the votes of the working class than persuade them of the benefits of Socialism.

At the 1906 General Election the Labour Party reached an agreement with the Liberal Party (the 'Lib-Lab pact'), which allowed Labour candidates to stand unopposed by the Liberal Party in certain seats. The result was that, for the first time, the Labour Party had a bloc of thirty MPs in Parliament. However, the performance of these MPs disappointed many ILP supporters, who saw their efforts as meagre and in some cases as merely supporting the 'capitalist' Liberal Party. At a by-election in Colne Valley in Lancashire in 1907 a young ILP member, Victor Grayson,[13] defied national trade unions and the Labour Party by standing and winning the seat as a Labour and Socialist candidate. His only support came from several local ILP branches. By this time many ILP members had become disillusioned with the Labour Party, believing it to be controlled by the trade unions. ILP supporters were also unhappy with the Labour Party's electoral pact with the Liberals and wanted to contest the Liberal-held seats too. In 1910 the 'Green Manifesto' was published, which condemned deals with the Liberals and stated that the Labour Party should fight for Socialism equally against both capitalist parties (the Conservative and the Liberal parties).

The ILP were unique in pre-World War I politics in its support for women's suffrage. The ILP leader, Keir Hardie, had long had contacts with prominent members of the women's suffrage movement, in particular Sylvia Pankhurst [14] and Isabella Ford.[15] Many middle-class women joined the ILP for this reason, and ILP women influenced local branches to support the 'Votes for Women' campaign. In contrast, at a national level the Labour Party supported only partial gains for women's suffrage since not all men had gained the vote yet. Relations became strained between the ILP and the Women's Social and Political Union (WSPU) who were campaigning for female suffrage. The ILP opposed the WSPU tactics of using any means to try and gain votes for women as this included courting powerful men to help them while neglecting their working-class supporters. In some cases the WSPU even attacked Labour Party candidates at elections. At local and grassroots level some women continued to be in the ILP and WSPU and continued working with working-class women. In 1918 women over thirty were given the vote and ten years later all women over twenty-one gained the franchise.

1914 saw the beginning of World War I, with most of the Socialist parties in Europe supporting their governments and the war. The European Socialist parties, including the ILP, were part of the Second International,[16] which had earlier agreed that if war broke out each Socialist party would call a general strike and paralyse their country to prevent it.[17] Many ILP members opposed the war; some were pacifists and others refused to fight in what they saw as an imperialist war. This led many ILPers to be jailed as conscientious objectors for refusing to serve in the British Army after the introduction of conscription in 1916.

The divergence between the ILP and the labour movement was accelerated during the First World War. Many trade union leaders supported the war and encouraged their members to join the armed forces. They also agreed to 'no strike' agreements and the worsening of conditions of work to support the war effort. Several Labour MPs served in Coalition Government War Cabinets and gained experience of government.

In 1918 the Labour Party changed its organisation to make it a more organised election-winning machine. Individual members did not now need to join affiliated groups but could join a local branch. The National Executive was enlarged but no places were available for affiliated Socialist societies. The famous 'Clause IV' was adopted, calling for the collective ownership of the means of production, distribution and exchange. But the real intention was to make the Labour Party appeal not just to the working-class manual worker but to have a wider appeal and to become the party of government. The effect on the ILP was that it lost its seat on the National Executive of the Labour Party and many party activists left to join local Labour Party branches instead.

With its position in the Labour Party greatly weakened, the ILP needed to re-think its role. An upper-class London pacifist intellectual called Clifford Allen [18] transformed the fortunes of the ILP. Using contacts with many ILP middle-class pacifist supporters he was able to secure much financial support and so kept the party solvent. He saw the ILP as a body which could influence the decisions of the Labour Party, creating policies and moving the Labour leaders towards Socialism. Allen became leader (Chair) of the ILP and gathered many intellectuals together at the party's new HQ in London. He set up a Research and Information Department and re-vitalised the party's newspaper, the *Labour Leader* with a new editor. The *Labour Leader* was re-named the *New Leader* in 1922. The summer schools [19] for party members became less working class and more middle class.

Allen was friendly with Ramsay MacDonald, the Labour Party leader, and when MacDonald became Prime Minster in the 1924 Labour minority Government, Allen visited him several times at Downing Street. But Allen had earlier failed to persuade MacDonald to set up commissions to prepare detailed schemes for Socialist construction. The ILP set up one on agriculture and called for the nationalisation of the land.[20] This was accepted at the Labour Party Conference. Another ILP commission did not win Labour party support; this was called 'Socialism in our time or the living wage'. It called for a fixed minimum wage for all industries, and for family allowances. Banks, mines, land, electricity and transport were to be nationalised to provide the money to do this. The failure of Allen's commissions to become Labour Party policy hastened his demise and moved the ILP more leftwards. Allen's demise came about because of the rise of Jimmy Maxton, disillusionment amongst working-class ILP members at the middle-class bias of the leadership and a general mood that wished to challenge the gradualism of the Labour Party.

Jimmy Maxton and John Wheatley,[21] Glasgow ILP MPs, desired a more confrontational approach to dealing with the leadership of the Labour Party. Like many ILP activists, Maxton believed the Labour Party and the trade unions were obstacles to Socialism. During the 1926 General Strike the Labour Party did little to support the strikers. The ILP published the *The Miner* for the bankrupt miners union, selling 90,000 copies a week. After the failure of the strike, Maxton and the miners' leader, Arthur Cook,[22] published a joint manifesto that denounced all forms of class collaboration. The Cook-Maxton manifesto, along with 'Socialism in our Time' campaign was making the ILP very unpopular with Labour Party leaders.

In 1929 the Labour Party was the biggest party in Parliament for the first time, but it did not have an overall majority. Ramsay MacDonald wanted to show the Labour Party was 'fit to govern', which in practice meant not offending their Liberal supporters. This, coupled with the beginnings of the great 1930's 'Depression', meant that the Labour Party introduced no Socialist policies and were forced to cut public expenditure as unemployment soared and the cost of supporting the out-of-work increased. It seemed to many ILP members that the working class was suffering from the 'Depression' by losing jobs and having unemployment relief cut, whereas the capitalists were not suffering at all.

The ILP position was that the Labour Party should put radical popular measures before Parliament; if these were opposed the Government should campaign for them under the slogan, 'The people versus the banks'. The Labour Party leaders refused to support such a policy. A small core of ILP MPs criticised Government measures that were against ILP policy, and refused to support them. But most ILP-sponsored Labour MPs (140 in all) supported the Labour minority Government. When the ILP Executive ordered its MPs to vote against the Government on policies which the 1930 ILP conference had not agreed to, only 18 MPs agreed. Tension between the ILP and the Labour Party grew and the Labour Party refused to support ILP candidates in by-elections and in the 1931 General Election.[23]

The 'Depression' worsened and in 1931 the Labour Prime Minster, Ramsay MacDonald, and his Chancellor of the Exchequer, Philip Snowden,[24] defected from the Labour Party to form a National Government that was dominated by the Conservative Party. In the 1931 General Election the National Government won a landslide victory and the Labour Party were reduced to a mere 46 MPs with only one former Cabinet Minster surviving the election debacle. Of those MPs only five were ILP-endorsed. The huge Labour Party defeat in the 1931 General Election did not heal their relations with the ILP. The new Labour Party leadership insisted that ILP sponsored MPs must take the same Parliamentary whip and obey the same 'Standing Orders' as Labour MPs - i.e. vote the same way. The ILP refused to agree to this and they formally disaffiliated from the Labour Party in 1932.

Some writers see the decision to disaffiliate as political suicide; others see the bigger party deliberately pushing the smaller party to its political death. At the July ILP conference in Bradford, ILP members supported their leaders' decisions and voted to disaffiliate from the Labour Party by 241 to 142 votes. The Chairman at this conference, Fenner Brockway, spoke to delegates of the need to break away from the non-Socialist reformism of the Labour Party and move towards revolutionary Socialism. Many writers have seen the revolutionary rhetoric of the likes of Brockway as reasons why the ILP disaffiliated from the Labour Party, but the real causes were more mundane:

> "The issue of Standing Orders has been presented by some commentators as being of relatively minor importance to the disaffiliation of the ILP. Yet it is clear that to contemporaries within the ILP, especially the Parliamentary ILP, the issue was fundamental." [25]

Before the Bradford conference, the annual ILP conference had been reluctant to disaffiliate from the Labour Party. Two options were rejected in favour of an impossible option. The first motion was unconditional affiliation to the Labour Party which was heavily defeated, the second, disaffiliation, was narrowly defeated and the third, re-opening talks with the Labour Party about 'Standing Orders', was supported with a large majority. Most ILP members hoped the Labour Party might find a compromise, refusing to accept that the Labour Party would never allow a 'Party within a Party'. When the Labour Party refused to budge on the 'Standing Orders' question disaffiliation was the only option left to the ILP. To the majority of ILP members the decision to disaffiliate was logical and justified and not an act of insanity as is often portrayed.[26] The major problem for the disaffiliated party was that different groups within the party had different reasons for supporting disaffiliation. Those divergences would rip the party apart in the 1930's.

Notes

[1] Ramsay MacDonald (1866-1937) One time leader of the ILP and the Labour Party. Labour Party Prime Minster 1924, 1929-31 and National Government Prime Minster 1931-35.
James Maxton (1885-1946) see chapter 2 for brief biography.
Fenner Brockway (1888-1988) see chapter 5 for brief biography.

[2] General Strike 1926. The largest strike in British history in support of the miners whose pay was to be cut and hours of work increased. It lasted only a few days. But the miners battled on alone for over six months before being starved back to work.

[3] National Government. This was a coalition Government of Conservatives, Liberals and a few Labour Party men that was formed in August 1931 to tackle the 'Depression'. It won a landslide election victory in 1931 winning 554 out of 615 MPs. It became ever more Conservative dominated and lasted until 1945.

[4] The Depression. Began in the late 1920's and lasted well into the mid 1930's. A collapse in the world markets led to mass unemployment throughout the western world. The British unemployed statistics are from, Robert Skidelsky, *Politicians and the Slump: The Labour Government of 1929-1931* (London, Papermac, 1994), p399

[5] Most of this chapter is based on Barry Winter's book, *The ILP past and present*, (Leeds, Independent Labour Publications, 1993), p3-23

[6] Keir Hardie (1856-1915). Scottish-born Socialist MP, founder member of the ILP, and first leader of the Labour Parliamentary Party.

[7] Winter, op cit., p5

[8] Trades Union Congress (TUC). Founded in 1868, the central organising body of all the major trade unions.

[9] Fabian Society. Founded in 1884 a body of middle-class Socialist thinkers who believed in a gradual and democratic road to a Socialist-style state.

[10] Labour Churches. Were like churches but the preaching was on Socialism. They also included Socialist Sunday schools for children and they had their own ten commandments.

[11] Clarion Vans. These were part of the Clarion Movement and began in 1896 to visit remote communities and their speakers spoke from the vans spreading the message of Socialism.

[12] Votes for Women campaign. This covered roughly the period 1903-14 and involved many demonstrations, much political lobbying, and acts of civil disobedience including window breaking. One campaigner (Emily Wilding Davison) was killed when she threw herself in front of the

King's horse at 'The Derby' race meeting. Many campaigners were imprisoned and some died when force-fed during hunger strikes. The major capaign for 'Votes for Women' was called off during World War I. Most women were given the vote in 1918.

[13] Victor Grayson (1881-1922). Charismatic independent Socialist MP for Colne Valley 1907-10. He disappeared from politics after losing his seat.

[14] Sylvia Pankhurst (1882-1960). She was one of the leaders of the 'Votes for Women' campaign. Supported the cause of working-class women in London and formed her own Communist Party after the Russian Revolution of 1917. She refused to join the British Communist Party as she disagreed with fighting elections and spent the rest of her life supporting the rights of Abyssinia (Ethiopia) where she died.

[15] Isabella Ford. Like Sylvia Pankhurst supported working-class women's right to vote. She campaigned among the female textile workers in Leeds.

[16] Second International (1889-1914). The International was the organising body of the various Socialist parties throughout the world. The ILP was a member of this International. It effectively ceased to exist in its original form when World War I broke out.
Spanish Socialists and Anarchists had both been members of the Second International and had been involved in the arguments over which political doctrine was the correct one to follow. The Spanish Socialist representative at the 1891 Conference Pablo Iglesias the founder of the Spanish Socialist Party managed to get the Spanish Anarchist delegates expelled from the International. James Joll, *The Second International 1889-1914* (London, Routledge & Kegan Paul, 1974), p18, 24, 62, 68

[17] The 'Stuttgart Resolution' of 1907, agreed by the Second International, was a resolution whereby all Socialist parties were to do their utmost to prevent war by any means possible. Most Socialist parties did little and in Germany and France they actually voted to support the war.

[18] Clifford Allen (1889-1939). He was a pacifist during World War I and became the leading figure in the ILP in the 1920's. Became Lord Allen of Hurtwood in the 1930's.

[19] Summer Schools. Once a year in the summer the ILP held a one-week educational, political and social gathering for members.

[20] Nationalisation. A Socialist Government's management of the major industries of the state.

[21] John Wheatley (1869-1930). He was an ILP member and Minster of Health in first Labour Government. In post he passed a Housing Act that greatly increased the number of Council Houses available for local councils.

[22] Arthur Cook (1883-1931). He is better known as A. J. Cook, the charismatic

miners' leader. His constant efforts to protect miners' conditions of work led to his early death.

[23] Gidon Cohen, *'The Failure of a Dream'. The Independent Labour Party from Disaffiliation to World War II*, (London, Tauris, 2007), p20

[24] Philip Snowden (1864-1937). Leading member of the ILP and Chancellor of the Exchequer in the Labour Governments of 1924 and 1929-31. Joined the National Party in 1931 along with MacDonald.

[25] Cohen, op cit., p19

[26] Winter, op cit., p21-23, Ibid, p15-28, Robert E. Dowse, *'Left in the Centre': The Independent Labour Party 1893-1940* (London, Longmans, 1966), p179-184

CHAPTER 2

The ILP in the 1930's

BY 1932 THE DISAFFILIATED ILP was free to follow and develop its own policies and was very confident of becoming a major left wing party. By 1939 these dreams had been shattered. During the 1930's any attempts by the ILP to involve the Labour Party in any joint ventures was rejected. This meant the only natural ally for the ILP on the Left was the Communist Party of Great Britain (CPGB); however any association with the Communists meant the Labour Party would never work with the ILP. An attempt by a group within the Labour Party called the Socialist League to work with the ILP and CPGB led to them being threatened with expulsion from the Labour Party. Membership of the ILP fell by three quarters in this period and its influence in the trade unions had virtually disappeared at one point. The ILP had problems with factionalism and lost members because of this. There was an anti-Communist group, a pro-Communist group and a Trotskyite group; all were part of the ILP and all eventually left. The ILP was actively involved in the hunger marches of the 1930's,[1] the campaigns against the rise of Fascism in Britain and abroad and in attempts to form a united left. By 1939 the ILP was totally isolated and only kept in the public eye by their small group of MPs in Parliament led by the charismatic James Maxton. When offered a chance to rejoin the Labour Party the majority of the leaders were in favour but the outbreak of World War II postponed the decision indefinitely.[2]

Gidon Cohen describes the political situation faced by the disaffiliated ILP in his book on the ILP in the 1930's:

"...approximately one-third of the Party's membership was lost, with Scotland, where the ILP was particularly strong, worst affected. The decision was taken as a statement of fundamental incompatibility with the Labour Party. It also led to a reorientation internationally, as the ILP also disaffiliated from the Labour and Socialist International [3] and a fundamental rupture with the trade unions." [4]

The disaffiliated ILP had around 16,700 members in 1932 and was sure that it would become the dominant party of the Left now that it was no longer shackled by the Labour Party and the trade unions. With the 'Depression' getting worse the ILP was confident that a revolutionary route to Socialism was possible. The ILP broke all links with the Labour Party, the Co-Operative Movement [5] and trade unions, but in so doing they were forced into closer links with the small British Communist Party. After disaffiliation there was a major purge of ILP branches that had been opposed to disaffiliation and 203 branches out of a total of 653 - almost a third - were expelled. Many were in ILP heartlands. The number of ILP branches fell further to 284 by 1935.[6]

The ILP re-organised its ruling body in 1934. Firstly, a place on the National Administrative Council (NAC) was reserved for a member of its youth body 'The Guild of Youth'. Secondly, an Inner and Outer Executive were formed from leading members of the NAC, which effectively centralised power amongst the leading members of the ILP. The Inner Executive became dominated by the parliamentary MPs and on occasions they forced their own policies on the ILP.[7]

The Communist Party of Great Britain CPGB) sent a letter to the ILP in March 1933 suggesting a United Front against the growth of Fascism. The meeting took place and it was agreed to hold a series of meetings together highlighting the Fascist danger. Many ILP members supported Soviet Russia but were sceptical about working jointly with the CPGB. The ILP invited the Labour Party to join the United Front but this invitation was rejected. The link with the Communist Party greatly weakened the ILP in two ways:

The Labour Party would have nothing to do with the ILP if they were allied with the CPGB.
and
The Communists saw the link as a way to recruit ILP members for the CPGB.

As part of the Unity Campaign, members of the ILP and its 'Guild of Youth' played an active role in opposing Sir Oswald Mosley's [8] British

Union of Fascists (BUF). At the invitation of the CPGB members of the ILP and the 'Guild of Youth' were present at Mosley's notorious Olympia rally in London in June 1934, where hecklers were brutally beaten up and thrown out. Thanks to the violence against the anti-Fascist protesters, the BUF lost powerful supporters, in particular Lord Rothermere and his *Daily Mail* newspaper, and became more and more isolated politically.

1. 'They did not pass' pamphlet. *(ILP archive)*

The ILP were heavily involved in the most famous anti-Fascist event in the 1930's: the 'Battle of Cable Street'. Led by Mosley, the BUF planned to march through the predominantly Jewish East End of

London. By this stage the BUF's main support lay in London and its policies had become openly anti-Semitic. On October 3rd 1936 the *Star* (London newspaper) ran a headline appealing to workers to prevent Mosley's march through the Jewish East End. Fenner Brockway of the ILP claimed that every East End newsagent had an ILP poster in the window of their shop calling on workers to stop Mosley. The ILP hired a van with a loudspeaker and toured around East London appealing for support to block Mosley's march. The ILP convened a mass meeting at Hackney Town Hall to publicise further resistance to Mosley's planned march. Thousands of leaflets were duplicated by the ILP and distributed around the East End. On October 4th Mosley's BUF were successfully stopped by thousands of protesters, and violence only occurred when the police attempted to force a way through the protesters. The ILP stressed that working-class solidarity had won the day and produced a penny pamphlet which sold in its thousands, called 'They did not pass: 300,000 workers say no to Mosley'.

The pamphlet concluded:

"The Fascists did not pass...we must not be content with this. Mosley is the advance guard of Capitalism. We must now carry the offensive against Capitalism itself and against the National Government which represents it." [9]

The phrase 'they did not pass' is the English translation of the Spanish, 'No Pasaran' which was the battle cry of the Spanish Republicans in their successful defence of Madrid in November 1936 against the Spanish Fascist forces. Many British anti-Fascists saw parallels between repelling Mosley at Cable Street and the Spanish Republicans repelling the Spanish Fascists before Madrid a month later.

The ILP played a major role in blocking Mosley's attempt to march through the East End of London. The 'Battle of Cable Street' has become a fabled event that led to the demise of the BUF. Membership figures of the BUF after 1936 show that its support actually went up slightly but the anti-Fascist solidarity shown at Cable Street showed Mosley he could not march into Jewish areas without being resisted. [10]

Another aspect of the Unity Campaign with the CPGB was the ILP's involvement in fighting for jobs and better rates of relief for the unemployed; the hunger marches of the 1930's were the most symbolic aspect of this campaign. Hunger marches were where unemployed men and women marched from all areas of Britain to London to protest about unemployment and rates of relief. The hunger marches, especially the 'Jarrow Crusade',[11] are a potent symbol of unemployment in the 1930's.

Most hunger marches to London were organised by the Communist dominated (National Unemployed Workers Movement (NUWM) led by the Communist Wal Hannington. Because of this the trade unions and Labour Party often opposed the hunger marches, although local activists frequently ignored this opposition and supported the marchers anyway. During the 1929-31 Labour Government the ILP MPs opposed any move by the Labour Government to reduce unemployment payments and criticised its failure to restore higher rates of relief, which had been reduced in 1928 by the Conservative Government. At the October 1930 Labour Conference, the ILP had received 300,000 votes for its motion to tackle unemployment by Socialist methods, although the motion was heavily defeated.

In 1932 a major hunger march was organised involving over 1500 marchers converging on London from many different areas. During this march the marchers found little support from the Labour Party, trade unions and little sympathy from local authorities. At the Warrington workhouse[12] the Lancashire contingent of the marchers refused to hand over their belongings and also refused to be searched under the normal regulations. They were refused admittance to the workhouse and were left with nowhere to sleep. The local ILP branch allowed them to sleep at their club. Individual ILP members and branches helped the marchers on the way to London.

Violence between unemployed protesters and the police occurred several times in London and the heavy handedness of the police was criticised in Parliament by the ILP MP George Buchanan.[13] ILP MPs Maxton and McGovern[14] tried to persuade the Prime Minster to grant an audience to the hunger march leaders but he refused. John McGovern offered to present the petition of the hunger marchers to the Prime Minster but the hunger march leaders rejected this, so McGovern then denounced the marchers in Parliament for refusing to accept constitutional means. Maxton also appealed to the Government to pay to send the hunger marchers home and to promise that the hunger marchers would not lose their unemployment benefits (as they had been unavailable for work). This plea was rejected.

As well as long marches from all areas of the country to London there were also shorter local marches protesting against unemployment. In the Edinburgh march of 1933 the unemployed marchers were led by the ILP MP John McGovern.

The next major national hunger march was in 1934. This march was organised jointly by the CPGB and the ILP. During the march John McGovern was able to persuade one workhouse to give improved rations to the marchers. At Dunstable the local ILP branch marched into town with the marchers and helped to supply them with food.

2. Hunger Marchers led by Bob Edwards. *(New Leader)*

The marchers reached London on February 25th where around 50,000 protesters were assembled in Hyde Park. At the same time, a United Front Congress was taking place with 1492 delegates and the ILP MPs among its sponsors. James Maxton was attending the United Front Congress and led its delegates in procession to Hyde Park, accompanied by the left wing Labour MP Ellen Wilkinson. In Parliament, John McGovern presented the hunger marchers' petition to the Government. The ILP MPs pressed the Government to allow the leaders of the hunger march to be heard, being supported in this by the Labour Party leader Clement Attlee.[15] The motion was put to the vote in Parliament but sadly it was rejected by 270 to 52 votes. Having failed to have the matter heard, supporters of the hunger marchers began lobbying the Government. In addition around eighty hunger marchers entered Parliament in ones and twos, while around six hundred hunger marchers waited outside. With snow falling outside McGovern protested strongly that ill-dressed people were being kept waiting outside in terrible weather, and in frustration shouted, "Parliament is a farce". In response more protesters were allowed into the House of Commons but they were regularly ejected as they heckled MPs. It was the first time protesters had been allowed into the House of Commons and after the march benefits for the unemployed were raised slightly. The last hunger march on London happened in 1936 and involved ILP members. As in previous marches, ILP members and branches supported the marchers with donations, food and accommodation. On November 11th the hunger marchers laid wreaths at the Cenotaph in London honouring the almost nine hundred thousand dead from the war but asking, "What about the future for our youth?" ILP marchers who saw the war as an imperialist war were unhappy with this action and it was further condemned in the *New Leader*. As late as January 1937 the ILP were still issuing joint proclamations with the CPGB supporting the hunger marchers' demands:

- Abolition of the means test (a punitive measure whereby the unemployed could lose benefit if they owned anything of value - even a wedding ring - or if a member of the family was in work)
- Trade union scales of unemployment benefit
- Development of the distressed areas.[16]

The Labour Party rejected the manifesto and refused any unity pact with the CPGB and ILP.[17]

Within the ILP there was a group called the RPC or Revolutionary Policy Committee, who strongly supported the policies of the CPGB and had a long-term goal of creating one revolutionary party. The RPC was formed in 1930 by Dr Carl Cullen who wanted the ILP to move towards a revolutionary policy based on Marxist ideas. His views attracted many ILP members, including Jack Gaster, who became a leading member of the RPC. The RPC was particularly strong in the London Division of the ILP and looked to replace ILP gradualism with a revolutionary policy. During 1931-32 some members of the RPC actually joined the Communist Party. At the Bradford Conference on disaffiliation the RPC motion to define the break with the Labour Party as 'revolutionary' was defeated. It has been estimated they controlled around 50% of the delegates at the 1933 National Conference. At this conference the RPC won support for joining the Communist International (CI).[18] But by the time of the 1934 conference the Communist International's insistence that the ILP had to obey the policies of the CI meant that the ILP rejected its terms. It had also been discovered the two RPC men leading the 'Affiliation Committee', a committee pressing for the ILP to join the CI, were in fact secret members of the Communist Party. This affair totally discredited the RPC.

By 1935 the strength of the RPC was declining fast, so much so that, at the 1935 ILP conference, they were unable to stop criticism of the Soviet Union's foreign policy or to win support for their policy of assisting the 'League of Nations'[19] to become involved in the war in Abyssinia.[20] By October 1935 the RPC no longer had the strength to influence ILP policy and so they decided to close down their journal, *The Bulletin* and join the Communist Party en masse. Around sixty members, mostly in London, left the ILP. A small number of former RPC members stayed in the ILP as part of the 'Marxist Group' but they wielded little power.[21]

In 1932 when the ILP disaffiliated it decided to allow its numerically weak 'Guild of Youth' to be able to make its own policies. Like most youth wings its politics were to the left of the main party. It fully supported the new revolutionary policy of the ILP and in May 1934 sought sympathetic affiliation to the Communist Youth International (youth wing of the CI). By this time the 'Young Communist League' (the youth wing of the CPGB), especially its leaders, had infiltrated the ILP 'Guild of Youth'. The ILP responded by completely reorganising the youth section and replacing its leaders by those favourable to the main party. Around a quarter of the youth branches refused to accept the changes and several individuals joined the YCL. The 1938 ILP conference claimed that the youth section was flourishing with increased numbers, although it seems the membership and influence of the 'Guild of Youth' declined in the 1930's to an even greater degree than the parent party.[22]

Leon Trotsky[23] met with two leading ILPers in the 1930's, John Paton and C A Smith, and encouraged his followers to join the ILP but not to try to split the party or to win it over to Trotskyite[24] views. British Trotskyites had differing views about joining the ILP. A minority of the Trotskyite Communist League joined the ILP in 1934. Eventually the Trotskyites in the ILP comprised about seventy followers in London and there were smaller numbers across the country. In total they controlled six London ILP branches by 1935. At the 1935 ILP conference the 'Marxist Group', as they were known, were successful in winning a motion for 'workers sanctions' against Italy because of their invasion of Abyssinia. This decision was overruled at the insistence of the ILP leaders. Later the 'Marxist Group' split further; some staying in the ILP while others left to re-join or join Trotskyite groups. Attempts in 1934-35 for the ILP to join the Trotskyite Fourth International [25] were soundly defeated at conference.[26]

Not all members of the ILP supported the RPC's motion, won at conference, to work with the CPGB and implement the new revolutionary policies. A survey of ILP branches found there was widespread discontent at having links with the CPGB. In May 1934 Elijah Sandham, a member of the ILP NAC, left the ILP along with the bulk of the Lancashire branches and formed an Independent Socialist party. In addition Richard Wallhead, the ILP MP for Merthyr, and the Party's General Secretary, John Paton, left the party. The dissidents who left the party saw its policies in 1934 as fundamentally different from what the party had stood for when it disaffiliated only two years before. The new Independent Socialist Party saw its role as that of keeping alive the spirit of the old ILP.[27]

Having made a clean break with the Labour Party and the trade unions the ILP had to work out what its actual policy was. The so-called revolutionary policy of the ILP has been strongly condemned:

> "Subsequent commentators have been less kind, with Party policy described as 'revolutionary posturing' and 'quotation mongering' and the policy makers as 'cranks' and 'ideologues'." [28]

At the 1933 ILP conference a slim majority had approved the policy, proposed by the RPC, to set up Workers Councils inside the trade unions, trades councils and amongst the unemployed. In July 1933 the NAC decided that ILP members were to agitate to set up these councils. These were to be the focal point of working class control when the revolutionary crisis came. This policy was seen as a fresh start, an ILP policy as opposed to anything the CPGB or other parties were putting forward. Joint work with the CPGB was to take place. It was accepted that there was also a role for Parliamentary activity, and the ILP were to join the International of far-left Socialist parties.[29] The new policy saw less of a role for Parliament, closer working with the Communist Party and attempts to introduce a revolutionary policy on non-revolutionary bodies like the trade unions. All this achieved was to isolate the ILP further from the Labour movement and by 1935 only one ILP member was an elected delegate at the TUC. This was to be the ILP's lowest point; by 1939 it had members on the Executives of twelve trade unions.[30]

The ILP had adopted a very left wing anti-Parliamentarian stance at a time when it was mainly known for the activities of its MPs. But the defeat of the RPC meant the ILP policy became less revolutionary as the decade progressed. The ILP did not merge with the Communist Party or join the Communist International, and at the 1936 Conference, factions within the ILP were banned. Parliamentary ILP leaders were better able to control the policies of the party through the new Executive Committees. By 1937 the 'Unity Campaign' with the Communist Party had ended and the ILP were looking to re-join the Labour Party via its new 'Workers Front' policy. But the revolutionary policy in some form existed throughout the 1930's and disagreements about it were the reason for the RPC leaving the ILP and for the formation of the Independent Socialist Party.[31]

Membership of the ILP fell by 60% from 16,773 to 4,392 by 1935. One needs to treat membership numbers with some care since some activists were unemployed and did not pay fees and so would not be counted in the records. On the other hand, ILP branches, when asked for membership numbers, did tend to inflate them somewhat! Membership declined throughout the decade down to 2,441 in 1939. But continual membership decline throughout the decade is not the total picture. Many old members left the party and new young members joined. In some areas like Norwich the ILP branch grew in numbers throughout the period.[32] Financially the ILP was in a state of crisis and could no longer afford to support many paid officials. Its newspaper, the *New Leader*, was losing £20 a week and was over £5,000 in debt by 1933. Constant efforts to raise money to keep the newspaper afloat had only limited success and the *New Leader* had to change to a cheaper format twice during this period to cut costs.[33] The period 1932-1935 had been a disaster for the ILP as they had been cut off from the labour movement and forced more and more to ally with the CPGB. This alliance saw the ILP lose members and the CPGB gain members at the ILP's expense.

At the 1935 General Election the ILP put up seventeen candidates under slogans of 'Socialist and No More War candidates' and 'No war, No Rearmament, Workers' Rights and Socialism'.[34] The party polled 139,577 votes and won four seats, all in Glasgow: Reverend Stephen[35] won the Camlachie ward, John McGovern won the Shettleston ward, George Buchanan won the Gorbals ward and James Maxton, the ILP leader, won the Bridgeton ward.[36] In each seat won by the ILP the Labour Party candidate lost their deposit.

Elsewhere the ILP polled well although on a number of occasions a split Socialist vote between the ILP and Labour party candidates allowed the non-Socialist National candidate to win the seat.[37] The ILP had always seen local elections as its major strength and disaffiliation hit them very badly when most councillors left the Party in 1932. But in some areas the ILP were able to win council seats and to hold on to them, particularly in Glasgow, Bradford, Derby and Norwich. But if they could not make a deal on not opposing each other with the local Labour Party they were usually defeated, and once defeated it seems that council seats were lost for good.[38]

The most famous ILP Parliamentarian in the 1930's was James Maxton. He was born in 1885 in Glasgow and his parents were schoolteachers. Maxton himself gave up his studies at Glasgow University to become a teacher. He later returned to the University and graduated with an MA in 1910. At university he joined the Conservative club but after reading various classic Socialist texts and attending the university Socialist Study Circle he began to change his views. Contacts with the Marxist Social Democratic Federation and the renowned Marxist teacher John MacLean[39] led to Maxton becoming a committed life-long Socialist. In 1904 Maxton joined the ILP and held local and national offices and eventually became leader of the Scottish ILP from 1913-1919. During the First World War he was a pacifist and was jailed for a year for speaking in support of strikers on Clydeside. He failed to win the Glasgow Bridgeton seat at the 1918 General Election but was elected in 1922 and held the seat until his death in 1946. He campaigned strongly for better housing and campaigned on education issues both inside and outside Parliament. He was leader of the ILP between 1926-1931 and again from 1934 to 1939. Maxton was one of the strongest critics of the two Labour Governments when they failed to implement ILP policies.

Robert Skidelsky describes Maxton thus:

"with his long black hair, and his cadaverous features, was the conscience of the left, highly emotional, unbalanced, but universally loved."[40]

Maxton was recognised as an inspirational Socialist orator and a man of great personal integrity.[41]

During 1935 the ILP continued to criticise the Labour Party from a left wing perspective whereas the CPGB, acting on orders from the Communist International, were now seeking to affiliate to the Labour

3. L - R: James Carmichael, James Maxton and John McGovern. *(NL)*

Party and form an alliance with them. This was one of the reasons for the RPC leaving the ILP and joining the CPGB in December 1935. Surprisingly, in 1936 both parties agreed to a 'Unity Campaign' whose objective was to elect a Labour Government. The Labour Party refused to have anything to do with a campaign supported by the CPGB.

At the 1935 ILP national conference there was a serious disagreement of how to react to Mussolini's [42] Fascist Italian invasion of Abyssinia. The ILP conference voted in favour of working-class sanctions against Italy despite the wishes of the ILP leaders who believed both countries to be ruled by dictators, and wanted to remain aloof from the conflict. A threat by the ILP MPs to resign saw the policy reversed. Although this ILP policy decision was opposed by the CPGB, the 'Unity Campaign' continued and the Socialist League also became involved in 1937. This group was a left wing group inside the Labour Party, which contained many ex-ILP members. The CPGB, following instructions from the Communist International, wished to form a Popular Front [43] against Fascism that included any political party or individual who opposed Fascism. Internationally, Russia was seeking to ally with any country it could as a safeguard against the Fascist powers Germany and Italy. The ILP could not support this since it opposed British Imperialism and viewed any powerful international alliances as routes to war. Domestically it would have meant re-joining the Labour Party and losing its independence. Instead of a Popular Front the ILP desired a federation of working-class parties with similar goals and policies but with liberty to disagree.

During 1936 the Moscow 'Show Trials'[44] began. Many old Bolsheviks (Communists) and leading Party officials were accused of being Fascists and Trotskyite saboteurs. In its newspaper the *New Leader* the ILP denounced the trials. Fierce criticism and accusations from the CPGB led to relations within the 'Unity Campaign' becoming more and more strained. In March 1937 the Labour Party disaffiliated the Socialist League and later threatened to expel its members from the party. This led to its withdrawal from the 'Unity Campaign'. By the summer of 1937 the 'Unity Campaign' had collapsed; the ILP did not want a Popular Front and the CPGB did not want a federation of only left wing parties.

The break with the CPGB benefited the ILP because now the Labour Party was willing to talk to it again. In 1938 with the blessings of the Labour Party leader Clement Attlee, Stafford Cripps,[45] who had been leader of the Socialist League, approached the ILP leader James Maxton about the ILP re-joining the Labour Party. The ILP Parliamentary group were in favour of re-joining the Labour Party and this was put to the 1938 ILP conference. The conference agreed that the NAC should look into re-affiliation to the Labour Party but to explore whether ILP MPs would have to vote with the Labour Party on all matters. Not waiting for a reply, George Buchanan, an ILP MP, rejoined the Labour Party in May 1939. A special conference of the ILP was called for September 1939 to discuss re-joining the Labour Party but World War II broke out before the conference could take place. By the time World War II broke out the ILP as a national political force had virtually ceased to exist:

> "Having begun the decade a significant force, by the outbreak of war the ILP held a peripheral place in British politics."[46]

The ILP saw World War II as a war between imperial powers and opposed it. This opposition included: refusing to fight in the armed forces, propaganda against the war and putting up candidates in elections (the major parties had agreed a political truce of not putting up candidates against the party who currently held the seat). However many ILP members had been and remained committed anti-Fascists and joined the Armed Forces or served in other ways e.g. in Medical units.

After the war there was no more talk about re-affiliation because of the very different positions on World War II both parties had taken, with the Labour Party supporting the war and holding positions in the Coalition Government. At the General Election of 1945 the ILP won three Parliamentary seats, all in Glasgow, as the Labour Party won a landslide victory. In 1946 the charismatic ILP leader James Maxton died. The ILP held his seat in a by-election but during the next few years all the ILP MPs re-joined the Labour Party.[47] From 1947 onwards the ILP never elected another MP and its membership continued to decline in numbers. ILP members continued to be involved in the anti-nuclear movement particularly the Campaign for Nuclear Disarmanent (CND) and in the anti-colonial movement. ILP presence on Glasgow Council lasted right up until the ILP re-joined the Labour Party in 1975.[48] Finally in 1974 after many years of debate the ILP published a document called an 'Outline Perspective', which reaffirmed a Socialist commitment but proposed working inside the Labour Party. In 1975 the ILP became Independent Labour Publications and re-joined the Labour Party.[49]

From its inception the ILP was an internationalist party. It was passionately interested in world events and joined the Second International of Socialist Parties. In 1934 it voted to leave the Second International and join another International. It refused to join the Communist Third International because that would eventually have led to fusion with the CPGB, and it refused to join Leon Trotsky's Fourth International. Instead the ILP opted to join a group of dissident Marxist and Socialist groups called the International Bureau for Revolutionary Socialist Unity or as is was better known the 'London Bureau', which was its headquarters until 1939. Fenner Brockway was the Chairman of the 'London Bureau' for most of the 1930's. Groups who were affiliated to the 'London Bureau' were generally small dissident socialist or Marxist groupings with little national influence. These groups included the French Workers and Peasants Socialist Party (PSOP), the French Party of Proletarian Unity (PUP) the German Socialist Workers Party (SAP), the German Communist Right Group of Brandler and other similar groups including the Italian Maximalist Socialists, some Greeks associated with the journal *Archives of Marxism*, the Dutch Revolutionary Socialist Workers Party (RSAP), Hashomer Hatzair from Palestine and the Labour Party, the Polish Bund and Independent Labour Party, the Romanian Independent Socialist Party and the Swedish Socialist Party. They were joined also by a number of prestigious individuals with little influence amongst the masses such as the Frenchman Marcel Pivert,[50] the Germans Willi Brandt [51] and Heinrich Brandler [52] and the Spaniard Andreu Nin.[53] The one mass party was the Norwegian Labour Party, which had a membership of eighty thousand. Members of the 'London Bureau' were seen as sister parties of the ILP and were to be supported by the ILP in times of danger.

Significantly for the ILP the Spanish political party the 'Workers Party of Marxist Unification' or POUM were also members of the 'London Bureau'. When the Spanish Civil War broke out in July 1936 the ILP saw support for the POUM as more important than support for the Spanish Government and this dictated ILP policy during the course of the Spanish Civil War.[54]

Notes

[1] Hunger Marches occurred in the 1920's and 1930's and consisted of unemployed men (occasionally women were involved) marching from all areas of Britain to London to protest about unemployment and the low rates of relief.

[2] Major sources used for this chapter are:
Robert E. Dowse, *Left in the Centre: The Independent Labour Party 1893-1940* (London, Longmans, 1966), p185-202, Gidon Cohen, *The Failure of a Dream: The Independent Labour Party from Disaffiliation to World War II* (London, Tauris, 2007), Barry Winter, *The ILP Past and Present* (Leeds, Independent Labour Publications, 1993), p23-26

[3] Labour and Socialist International. This was the name given to the re-formed Second International after World War I.

[4] Cohen, op cit., p12

[5] Co-operative Movement. Formed in the mid nineteenth century it was a form of collective retailing and production, which brought together associations of members for trading purposes and the sharing of profits through dividends. In the 1930's Co-op shops were seen in virtually all cities and towns.

[6] Cohen, op cit., p33

[7] Ibid, p45-49

[8] Sir Oswald Mosley (1896-1980). At different times he was a Conservative MP, Independent MP, Labour Party MP and ILP member. In the second Labour Party Government as a Junior Cabinet Minster he proposed

large scale public spending to tackle the 'Depression', when this was rejected he formed the 'New Party' and then in 1932 the Fascist British Union of Fascists (BUF) which he led throughout the 1930's.
[9] Tony Kushner and Nadia Valman (editors), *Remembering Cable Street: Fascism and Anti-Fascism in British Society* (London, Vallentine Mitchell, 2000), p120
[10] Kushner and Valman, op cit., p119-120
[11] Jarrow Crusade 1936. This was the most famous hunger march of the 1930's. Unemployed workers from the North East shipbuilding town of Jarrow led by their left wing MP Ellen Wilkinson marched to London to highlight their plight.
[12] Workhouse. This was a place where the destitute could go and in return for work were fed and given accommodation. Conditions were deliberately harsh so only the truly desperate individuals or families would ask to be allowed to enter.
[13] George Buchanan. ILP MP for Glasgow Gorbals throughout the 1930's re-joined the Labour Party in May 1939.
[14] John McGovern. See following chapters.
[15] Clement Attlee (1883-1967). Labour Party leader and Prime Minster 1945-51. He visited the British Battalion of the International Brigades during the Spanish Civil War. The Number One Company being renamed the Major Attlee Company.
[16] Distressed Areas. These were areas of Britain with high long-term unemployment during the 1930's. These areas were those who were in particular reliant on heavy industry and exports like the South Wales mining communities and North-East England shipbuilding yards.
[17] Peter Kingsford, *The Hunger Marches in Britain 1920-1939* (London, Lawrence and Wishart, 1982), p 17, 119, 130, 147, 154, 156, 158-9, 167-8, 174-5, 186-7,193-5, 200, 216, 224
[18] Communist International. Also known as the Third International or Comintern. This was the Communist parties' International.
[19] League of Nations. The 1930's version of the United Nations an international body that attempted to use negotiation to avoid armed clashes. It proved to be a complete failure in this role in the 1930's.
[20] Invasion of Abyssinia. In 1935 Fascist Italy invaded the last independent African country and by 1936 had conquered Abyssinia.
[21] Cohen, op cit., p81-95
[22] Ibid, p143-149
[23] Leon Trotsky (1879-1940). Trotsky was second only to Lenin during the Russian Revolution of 1917. He founded and led the 'Red Army',

which enabled the Communists to win the Civil War against its enemies. But after Lenin's death in 1924 he was out-manoeuvred by Stalin and exiled from Russia in 1928. He was in exile throughout the 1930's where he had a small worldwide following who were organised through a Fourth International whose central belief was the idea of 'Permanent Revolution' as opposed to Stalin's belief in 'Socialism in One Country'.

[24] Trotskyism. This term refers to political parties or individuals who supported Trotsky and his views. But it could also mean any Socialist who opposed the views of Stalin the Russian Communist leader. Trotskyite and Fascist were used in official Communist language as one and the same thing.

[25] Fourth International. International founded by Trotsky to organise groups and parties who believed in 'Permanent Revolution'.

[26] Cohen, op cit., p102-108

[27] Ibid, p95-102

[28] Ibid, p110

[29] International for Left Socialist Parties. Better known as the 'London Bureau' an International of left wing Socialist parties who did not want to join either of the other Internationals.

[30] Cohen, op cit., p61

[31] Ibid, p110-122

[32] Ibid, p36-37

[33] Ibid, p51-53

[34] Ibid, p69

[35] Reverend Stephen. Full name Campbell Stephen he was ILP MP for Glasgow Camlachie throughout the 1930's re-joined the Labour Party in October 1947.

[36] F. W. S. Craig (compiler and editor), *Minor Parties at British Parliamentary Elections 1885-1974* (London, MacMillan, 1975) p41

[37] Cohen, op cit., p71-73

[38] Ibid, p73-80

[39] John McLean (1879-1923). He was a famous Scottish Marxist teacher. He was imprisoned several times during World War I for his revolutionary activity. He was appointed the First British Consul for the new Communist Russian regime.

[40] John Ramsden (editor), *The Oxford Companion to Twentieth-Century British Politics* (Oxford, Oxford Univ. Press, 2002), p428

[41] Ramsden, op cit., p428

[42] Benito Mussolini. He was the Fascist dictator of Italy throughout the 1930's. He sent large quantities of military supplies including hundreds

of airplanes to aid the Spanish Fascist rebel forces and also thousands of Italian soldiers.

[43] Popular Front. This was an alliance instigated by the Communist parties to unite all political parties against Fascism. In France and Spain the Popular Front won general elections and became the Government. In Spain it was a Popular Front Government that the right wing forces rebelled against.

[44] Moscow Show Trials. These were trials in the 1930's in which leading Communist figures from the Revolution period were charged with treason and condemned to death. The main reason for their death being the removal of any possible rivals to the Russian leader Stalin.

[45] Sir Stafford Cripps (1889-1952). During the 1930's leader of the left group within the Labour Party known as the 'Socialist League'. Later he was Chancellor of the Exchequer 1947-50 in the Labour Government of 1945-50.

[46] Cohen, op cit., p14

[47] Craig, op cit., p42

[48] Cohen, op cit., p226

[49] Winter, op cit., p26

[50] Marcel Pivert. Leader of the small French Socialist Party the PSOP.

[51] Willi Brandt (1913-1992). He was a member of a small German Socialist party, the SAP. This party had split away from the main German Socialist party in exile. In 1933 Hitler had crushed and banned all opposition political parties in Germany. Brandt was a member of the 'London Bureau' Youth Executive. He was in Spain during the Civil War where he was journalist in Barcelona. He fled Spain in 1937 after the suppression of the fellow 'London Bureau' political party the POUM. After the war he re-joined the SPD the German Social Democratic Party and became its leader from 1964-1987. He was Head of the German State (Chancellor) 1969-1974.

[52] Heinrich Brandler. He was originally a high-ranking member of the German Communist Party but thrown out for his right wing views. He led a small right wing German Communist party in exile.

[53] Andreu Nin. See following chapters.

[54] Cohen, op cit., p166-170, Victor Alba and Stephen Schwartz, *Spanish Marxism Versus Soviet Communism: A History of the P.O.U.M.* (Oxford, Transaction Books, 1988), p155-156

CHAPTER 3

The Spanish Republic and the Formation of the POUM 1931-36

EARLY TWENTIETH CENTURY SPAIN WAS seen as one of the most backward parts of Europe. Spain was a poor country and had more in common with North Africa than Europe. After a disastrous war with the Americans in 1898 Spain lost most of what was left of her empire, which left the Spanish Army no longer trusting Spain's politicians. From this time onwards, the Army believed it would be necessary to intervene in the running of the country if Spanish politicians should bring further dishonour to Spain, as they saw it. Spain began the twentieth century as a monarchy governed by two political parties: the Liberals and the Conservatives. These two parties voluntarily swapped as the Government of the day at each general election. The policies of the two parties were virtually the same, only the political parties and their leaders changed.

The two main left wing groupings in Spain expanded significantly during the early twentieth century, and by the time of the Spanish Republic in 1931 both organisations had over a million members each. The first left wing organisation was the Socialist Party (Partido Socialista Obrero de Espana [PSOE]) and its trade union, the Union General de Trabajadores (UGT). The second organisation was unique to Spain and was the Anarchist movement, dominated by its trade union, the Confederacion Nacional Trabajadores (CNT) and its militants' organisation the Federacion Anarquista Iberica (FAI).

In 1921 a military disaster in the last Spanish colony in Morocco led to attempts to investigate army corruption and incompetence. This resulted in a military coup by Primo de Rivera, who was supported by King Alfonso XIII. Primo de Rivera went on to rule Spain as a dictator from 1923-1930. By 1930 the Left, along with the Liberal Republicans, had formed the 'Pact of San Sebastian', which aimed to replace the monarchy by a Republic. By 1931 there was a new army dictator, Damaso Berenguer who was unpopular, and in the elections the Left and the Republicans defeated monarchist candidates in the towns and cities. In April 1931 the King abdicated and the new Spanish Republic was proclaimed with much popular rejoicing.[1]

The first Government of the new Republic was a coalition of Liberal Republican parties and the Socialist Party. During this period the Government introduced left-leaning policies such as the secularisation of education (which had been pretty much run by the Catholic Church for centuries); a reduction in the number of Army officers; improvements in employment rights for workers; and the beginnings of the re-distribution of land to the peasants. At the November 1933 elections the Republicans and Socialists were divided and fought the election as separate entities. They were defeated by a right wing coalition. This coalition undid many of the reforms of the previous Government and a huge strike by the Socialist Peasants' Union was defeated. In 1934, when it seemed that members of the semi-Fascist party the CEDA (Confederacion de Derechas Autonomas) were to enter the Government the Left attempted direct action to prevent it. Strikes broke out in several areas and the regional Government of Catalonia - the Generalitat - declared its independence from Spain. Most significantly, for two weeks in Asturias, a workers' alliance of Socialists, Anarchists and Communists set up a Workers' Government (or Soviet), until it was crushed by force. Alarmed by these actions even though they had failed, the Government imprisoned thousands of its political enemies. When elections for a new Government were held in February 1936 the Left (including the POUM) were united again as a Popular Front. At the elections the Left won a majority and became the new Government.

From February to July 1936 Spain was in a state of near anarchy. There were regular gun battles in the streets of the major cities between left wing militants and the rapidly expanding Fascist party, the Falange. There were constant strikes and many illegal land seizures by peasants in the countryside. The chaos on the streets in the cities, plans to grant some form of self-government to the Basques and the freeing of the political prisoners from the Asturias uprising led some in the Army to plot a coup to restore order. Starting on July 17th 1936 parts of the Spanish Army supported by right wing civilian sympathisers rebelled against the Republican Government and Civil War broke out.[2]

In 1935 the second-largest left wing force in Catalonia after the

Anarchists was a political party known as the Workers' and Peasants' Bloc (BOC). This party was originally the official Catalonian section of the Spanish Communist Party (Partido Communista Espana [PCE]) but it had broken away as a protest against the sectarian policies of the PCE. The BOC had around 7,000 members and controlled a significant number of sections (union branches) in the UGT and CNT. It had its own newspaper called *La Batalla*. The BOC strongly favoured a 'Workers' Alliance' of all left wing parties. This idea was rejected by the major left wing powers: the Socialists and Anarchists, and by the small Communist Party, although several minor Socialist, Syndicalist and Marxist groups did support the alliance. In 1935 the BOC attempted to persuade these minor parties to join a new independent Communist political party; however only one tiny party joined with them. This was the Left Communist Party of Andreu Nin, which probably numbered no more than a dozen individuals. These two parties joined to form the POUM in September 1935.[3]

The leader of the BOC was Joaquim Maurin (1893-1973). Maurin was a teacher in his early life and became involved in student political movements in 1918 in support of the Russian Revolution. His open support for the Russian Revolution meant he had to flee from the authorities. From 1919-1921 he served in the army as part of his national service and he attended the CNT congress in Madrid in 1919 in military uniform. On leaving the army he joined the CNT. In 1921 Maurin went to Moscow as part of a CNT delegation to a Congress of the Red International of Trade Unions (RILU).[4] When he returned to Spain Maurin failed to persuade the CNT to join the Third International but he still became the General Secretary (leader) of the CNT in 1922 and edited its newspaper. In 1925 Maurin was imprisoned, when the dictator Primo de Rivera forbade the Anarchist press. When he attempted to escape from prison he was shot in the leg. He hurt his leg again in another escape attempt, and was finally released in 1927, going into exile in Paris until 1930. In 1931 Maurin went to Moscow again, this time to argue against the ultra-left line of the Third International. This ultra-left line was called 'Class against Class' and denounced all other workers' parties as Fascists because they were out of line with the Communist viewpoint.

Maurin returned to Spain and made links with the CNT and PSOE, but eventually joined the BOC and became its General Secretary (leader) in 1933. Later Maurin wrote the political programme of the POUM together with Andreu Nin, when the POUM was formed in 1935.

Maurin was appointed the leader of the POUM and became its only deputy in the Spanish Parliament, the Cortez, when he was elected in February 1936. When the military rebellion broke out Maurin was in Galicia. This area fell to the Fascists and Maurin found that he was trapped. To try and protect him the POUM leadership announced that Maurin was dead. While trying to get back to Republican territory he was arrested in Jaca, but was not recognised. Maurin escaped from prison and tried to cross over to the Republican lines but he was captured. This time a former Barcelona policeman recognised him and he was imprisoned under threat of death. Maurin was formally sentenced to ten years imprisonment. Several attempts by his supporters to organise a prisoner exchange failed to obtain his release. Maurin was released in 1946 after over ten years imprisonment with his health broken by his experiences. He left for the USA in 1947 where he edited the newspaper *Free Spain*. He died in New York in 1973.[5]

The other leader of the newly formed POUM was Andreu Nin (1892-1937). Nin's working-class parents had made great sacrifices to enable them to send him to a teacher training college in Tarragona. After college Nin left for Barcelona and became a journalist for a Catalan Nationalist newspaper. He was briefly a member of the Socialist Party but, influenced by the events of the Russian Revolution, he joined the CNT. Nin attended the same CNT congress as Maurin, in Madrid in 1919, and spoke strongly in favour of the CNT joining the Communist Third International. During 1919-21 Nin became a leading CNT militant and was imprisoned several times as well as narrowly escaping assassination. In 1921 Nin went to Moscow in a delegation that included Maurin. On his return journey in 1922 Nin was imprisoned in Germany until January 1923 when he was released. He returned to Moscow where he lived until 1930. In Moscow Nin became a prolific writer for the Red Trade Union International (RILU). He travelled around Europe and appeared as a special delegate at a meeting of the Italian Communist Party. He married a Russian called Olga Kareva; he became a member of the Russian Communist Party, a deputy to the Moscow Soviet [6] and learnt to speak Russian fluently. Nin was even for a time the secretary of Leon Trotsky. This later meant he was dubbed a Trotskyite, although there is copious correspondence between the two men that shows they clearly disagreed on many aspects of the policy of the POUM.[7] Nin became involved in Russian politics and sided with the Opposition group [8] against Stalin. In 1930 he and his family were deported from Russia.

Back in Spain Nin disagreed with Maurin over the political direction of the BOC and decided not to join the BOC but to set up the tiny Left Communist Party which supported the views of the Left Opposition in Russia. In this period Nin also translated many Russian classics into Spanish. After eventually joining with the BOC to form the POUM, Nin wrote the political programme of the new party with Maurin. He was appointed to lead the trade union side of the new party. At the 1936 election Nin failed to be elected after being given the town of Teruel to fight. This town had few, if any, POUM supporters. When the Civil War broke out, with Maurin trapped in enemy territory, Nin became the new leader of the POUM. He became the Counsellor for Justice in the Catalan Generalitat (Government) in 1936, making Nin the only POUM member to hold high office during the Civil War. Throughout the Civil War Nin supported the Spanish Revolution [9] and opposed any attempts to crush it. Eventually this led to the suppression of the POUM and his own death at the hands of the Communist Secret Police in June 1937. In the hands of the Secret Police Nin showed great bravery in refusing to confess under torture to the false charges that the POUM were in league with the Fascists.[10]

At the formation of the POUM a commission was drawn up between the BOC and the Communist Left and it was agreed that Maurin would be General Secretary and Nin part of the Executive Committee and that the paper *La Batalla* was to continue with a print run of 10,000 with Maurin as editor. Nearly everyone who had been involved in founding Communism in Spain in the 1920's was in the new party. The POUM affiliated to the 'London Bureau' as the BOC before it had done. It was decided not to join the Communist Third International or Trotsky's Fourth International. Within six months POUM membership had risen to 9,000. Nin was to be in charge of trade union affairs and editor of the theoretical magazine *La Nueva Era*. After the first Executive meeting the POUM wrote to all working-class parties inviting them to meet to discuss the Italian invasion of Abyssinia and the coming world war. It also wrote to the workers' parties asking them to form an electoral 'Workers Front'. Both invitations were rejected.

Reluctantly the POUM joined the Popular Front in the General Election of February 1936. (The exiled Trotsky called Nin and Maurin traitors as a result of this decision.) Once again the POUM were rebuffed when they wanted to field candidates in Catalonia where they were strongest. Instead the Popular Front gave them only one seat in Catalonia, where Maurin was elected in Barcelona. During the election campaign POUM orators stressed the need for a 'Workers Front', declaring that a military coup was imminent and policies should be put in place to prevent it.

During the period of the Popular Front Government the POUM continued to gain members and it membership had increased to 10,000 by July 1936. In the Cortez Maurin spoke four times, twice to deliver a political speech and other times to query why left wing Army Officers involved in the uprisings in 1934 were being barred from returning to the Army and why reactionary panels were choosing new teachers. In his first Cortez speech Maurin hinted at the revolution to come:

> "To my mind, what is happening is that those working class parties that believe in the efficacy of the People's Front (and I do not believe in its efficacy) have formed with the Republicans a People's Front Government... And then the workers will go beyond the People's Front Government; to the formation of a workers' Government that will solve the problems of the Spanish Revolution.
> The choice is – I repeat - Fascism or Socialism; we Socialists naturally, pronounce ourselves for Socialism. Nothing more." [11]

The new Popular Front Government voted by a large majority to remove the President of the Spanish Republic, Alcala Zamora, and replace him with the Republican Azana. Maurin voted for a Socialist called Pena who had been one of the leaders of the Asturias uprising. Prophetically in his second political speech delivered in June 1936 in the Cortez, Maurin predicted a Fascist coup within two months; he was wrong by a month as it occurred one month after his speech.

In May 1936 Nin called a conference to bring together those union branches controlled by POUM militants. The POUM controlled unions in Lerida, Girona, Tarragona, some in Barcelona and some in other cities. It was agreed that Nin would head a new organisation called FOUS (Workers Federation for Trade Union Unity, Federacio Obrero d'Unificacio Sindical). Its goals were to recruit more workers to the new organisation over and above the 60,000 that they currently controlled. In addition, the FOUS would help to unify and give leadership to these disparate groups. A second conference was to be held in the autumn of 1936 where FOUS would work towards a unification of all trade unions including the CNT and UGT. Events were to overtake the FOUS, making its impact very limited. Also the POUM formed a youth wing that was called the Iberian Communist Youth, or Joventud

Communista Iberica (JCI) and introduced a second newspaper called *Avant*.

On Thursday July 16th 1936 the POUM Executive met because it expected a military coup at any moment. Maurin and Nin were sent to meet with Luis Companys, the head of the Catalan Government. He said that he had been unable to contact Madrid and had heard there were rumblings in the military barracks in Barcelona. Maurin left to go to Madrid and spoke to members of the Cortez including a personal friend of the President, who assured him it would be safe to visit Galicia. Maurin spoke to POUM activists in Santiago de Compostela on the 18th of July but by the 20th he was trapped in rebel-held Spain. Nin and the rest of the POUM executive had to react to a military rebellion in Barcelona on July 18th 1936. The Spanish Civil War had begun; the Spanish Revolution was soon to begin also and the POUM was to be amongst its strongest supporters.[12]

Notes

[1] Raymond Carr, *Spain 1808-1975* (Oxford, Clarendon Press, 1982), chps 11-14.
[2] Carr, op cit., chp 15, Stanley G. Payne, *Spain's First Democracy: The Second Republic 1931-1936* (London, Univ. of Wisconsin, 1993)
[3] Victor Alba and Stephen Schwartz, *Spanish Marxism Versus Soviet Communism: A History of the P.O.U.M.* (Oxford, Transaction Books, 1988), chp 2
[4] RILU (Red International of Trade Unions) Similar to the Third International but was the International for Revolutionary or Communist trade unions.
[5] Don Bateman, *Joaquim Maurin 1893-1973: Life and Death of a Spanish Revolutionary* (London, Independent Labour Party, 1974)
[6] Moscow Soviet. The equivalent of the city council of Moscow.
[7] Leon Trotsky, *The Spanish Revolution 1931-39* (London, Pathfinder Press, 1973). p211-221
[8] Left Opposition. A group that opposed the ruling Bolshevik party and sought the dismantling of its bureaucratic state system. Its leaders were expelled from the Communist Party in 1927 and many were killed in the 1930's.
[9] Spanish Revolution. See following chapter.
[10] Wilebaldo Solano, *The Spanish Revolution: The Life of Andres Nin* (London, Independent Labour Party, 1974)
[11] Alba and Schwartz, op cit., p102
[12] Ibid, p87-110

CHAPTER 4

The POUM and the Spanish Civil War 1936-37

IN JULY 1936 there was a right wing uprising throughout Spain and Spanish Morocco against the democratically elected Republican Government. The rebels comprised parts of the Army, including the elite professional 'Army of Africa' consisting of the Spanish Foreign Legion and Moroccan mercenaries, paramilitary police units and right wing civilian organisations, in particular the Fascist 'Falange' and the ultra-Catholic 'Carlists'. By the end of the month the rebels had conquered Spanish Morocco, the cities of Seville and Zaragoza, and much of Central Spain including the city of Burgos, which became the rebels' capital. But in most urban areas of Spain, especially in the large cities such as Madrid, Barcelona and Valencia, the rebels were defeated.

In many cases the success of the rebellion was determined by the loyalty of the police to the Republican Government, and by the decision of the local governor to arm the local workers' organisations. Where the local governor delayed giving arms to the people the rebels won the day, as happened in Seville and Zaragoza. In cities where the people were armed the rebels were defeated. The defeat of the uprising and the arming of the people led in some areas to a revolutionary situation; fired by their success the workers spontaneously took control. In Barcelona the biggest and strongest group of workers was the Anarchist dominated CNT-FAI, and this was where the revolution was at its strongest.

The POUM supported the revolution and saw its membership grow rapidly as it became involved in running many cities and towns in Catalonia. The POUM also became part of the 'Committee for Militias', the revolutionary Government of Catalonia for a time. The town of Lerida was completely controlled by the POUM. As the POUM's power grew, its leader, Andreu Nin, became a Minister in the Catalan

Regional Government. But by June 1937 Nin was dead and the POUM were declared an illegal party as the Spanish Government, supported by the Communists, crushed the revolution as part of regaining the reins of power.[1]

At the outbreak of the Spanish Civil War on July 18th 1936 the POUM executive met and decided that its militants needed to be armed and would form small shock units. In addition, a deputation met with the leader of the Catalan Regional Government and demanded arms. At first this demand was rejected. Two manifestos were written addressed to the soldiers in the barracks, telling them not to attack their proletarian brothers. This achieved little as the soldiers followed their officers into the streets of Barcelona in rebellion against the Spanish Republican Government in the early hours of July 19th. POUM groups fought throughout the city against the rebels alongside other workers and those police who had stayed loyal to the Government. The main POUM casualty in the fighting was Germinal Vidal the Head of the POUM Youth organisation, the JCI; he was replaced by Wilebaldo Solano. By midday the rebellion in Barcelona had been defeated. The POUM requisitioned several buildings including the Hotel Falcon on the Ramblas, which became its headquarters. Within two weeks of the defeat of the right wing military rising in Barcelona, POUM membership in Catalonia rose from around 10,000 to 30,000. The POUM was attracting new members who neither wanted the strict discipline of the official Communist movement or the indiscipline of the Anarchists,[2] although the number of genuine militants in Catalonia in July 1936 may have been as low as 3,000.[3]

The workers were in control in Barcelona and the Catalan Local Government existed in name only. On July 21st a Committee for Militias (Comite de Milicies) was formed to organise the armed workers into improvised armed militia units, each controlled by their own political party or trade union. For a time this committee became the Government of Catalonia and the POUM appointed Josep Rovira [4] to represent them on this committee. Its composition was as follows: [5]

- 3 members from the Esquerra (Main Catalan Nationalist party)
- 1 member from the Rabassaires (Group representing small farmers)
- 1 member from Accion Catalana (Small Catalan Nationalist party)
- 1 member from PSUC (Partido Socialista Unificado de Caluna, Communist Party in Catalonia)

- 3 members from the CNT (Anarchist trade union)
- 3 members from UGT (Socialist trade union)
- 2 members from the FAI (Anarchists)
- 1 member from the POUM

A variety of departments were linked to the Committee for Militias. The POUM ran the department for general education.[6] Like other parties the POUM set up free meals for the poor and for its members in restaurants and hotels. The POUM requisitioned houses and vehicles and plastered the walls in towns and cities with its posters and propaganda. Although the POUM Executive supported the revolution it often tried to stop its supporters' revolutionary excesses, such as the murder of some right wing opponents without trial. With Maurin stuck behind enemy lines Andreu Nin became the new leader (General Secretary) of the POUM. Throughout Catalonia POUM members were part of the new revolutionary local governments: the President and Chief Justice of Lerida were both POUM members and the new Lerida Government excluded all Liberal politicians.[7] Elsewhere in Spain the POUM was also part of the new revolutionary town councils. The POUM was even invited to be part of the Government in the Basque lands where no revolution had taken place.

From August onwards many foreign supporters of the POUM arrived at the Hotel Falcon many of whom had useful military experience.

The POUM's presses expanded greatly in the early months of the Civil War. In Catalonia the main newspaper was *La Batalla* now with a print run of 20,000. The POUM Youth published *Juventud Communista*, in Madrid the local POUM newspaper was *El Combatiente Rojo*, and in Lerida *Adelante*. In other towns the POUM published their own newspapers and news sheets, and *Alerta* was printed for the militia at the Front.

The POUM continued unsuccessfully to work for a 'Workers Alliance'. The Left Socialists seem to have had no particular political programme, the Anarchists saw the POUM as Marxist opponents and the official Communists in Catalonia, the PSUC, distrusted the POUM as dissident Communists.

The POUM's trade union organisation, the FOUS, was the major workers' organisation in Lerida and Girona, and had significant strength in Tarragona. On August 10th 1936 a law was passed that all workers had to be a member of a trade union; however this law only recognised the CNT and UGT. The POUM had no choice but to disband the FOUS, whose members then mostly joined the UGT and so came under PSUC control. Within two months of the beginning of the Civil War the POUM no longer had a base in any trade union. Similar events took place in the countryside where the POUM trade union members had formed an alliance with other non-CNT and UGT groupings but once again had to disband the grouping and join with the UGT.

In late August 1936 the 'Moscow Show Trials' began in Russia, where Stalin and his supporters condemned old Bolsheviks as traitors. In its newspaper the POUM condemned these trials and called them a "monstrous crime", going further than even the Anarchist press, who preferred not to condemn the 'Moscow Show Trials'. The POUM also expressed solidarity with the exiled Trotsky, whom Stalin had denounced as a traitor, and, while disagreeing with many of Trotsky's opinions, compared Trotsky favourably with Lenin. These views alienated the official Communist movement even further. To make matters worse, Nin proposed to the Catalan Generalitat that Trotsky be given asylum in Barcelona and his military experience put to use. The Catalan Generalitat rejected this proposal because the Russian Consul threatened to revoke all aid if Trotsky was allowed to come to Spain. Nin's action was political suicide for the POUM since it was now seen as an open supporter of Trotsky. Stalin, and hence the Spanish Communists, hated and feared Trotsky and so a Communist-led attack on the POUM could only be a matter of time.

At this point in history Stalin was looking for Western allies against the Fascist powers and did not want to be seen supporting a revolution which would alienate Britain and France in particular. So the Communist Party in Spain was ordered to support the Republican Government and to oppose the revolution. In the official Russian newspaper *Pravda* on December 17th 1936 the following appeared:

> 'In Catalonia the elimination of Trotskyists and Anarcho-Syndicalists has already begun; it will be carried out with the same energy as in the USSR.' [8]

This was written after Andreu Nin had been ejected from his role as Counsellor of Justice in Catalonia.

After the crushing of the right wing military rising in Barcelona the workers took control of the factories in the towns and cities and the land in the countryside. Government had broken down; no one was running the economy, so on August 11th the Economic Council was set up. Its importance was shown by the fact that Andreu Nin himself became the POUM representative. The Council's programme aimed for a Socialist transformation of society. Its proposals were as follows:[9]

- Control of production according to the needs of consumption.
- Monopoly of foreign trade.
- Collectivisation[10] of large agrarian estates, which would be developed by peasant unions and through compulsory syndicalisation of individual peasants.
- Partial devaluation of urban property by the imposition of taxes and reduction of leases.
- Collectivisation of major industries, public services, and local transport.
- Seizure and collectivisation of firms abandoned by their owners.
- Extension of the cooperative system in the distribution of goods.
- Workers control of banking operations and even nationalisation of banks.
- Workers syndical control over all firms that were still being privately developed.
- Rapid declassification of workers
- Rapid suppression of the various taxes in favour of a single tax.

Due to problems over currency and credit the Generalitat soon absorbed the Economic Council. By October the Catalan Local Government had been restored as the Government of Catalonia and the restored Government took over the running of the Economic Council and of the militias. The CNT-FAI and POUM protested about the dismantling of the Committee for Militias and the restoration of bourgeois Government but when all the other parties left the Committee they were forced to accept the inevitable and join the Generalitat. The new Generalitat Government consisted of:[11]

- 3 members from the Esquerra
- 3 members from the CNT
- 1 PSUC member
- 1 Rabassaires member
- 1 military advisor
- 1 POUM member

Nin was named Conselleria of Justice. In this role he widened the scope of the People's Tribunals to include military crimes. All crimes committed before July 19th were annulled so that any remaining revolutionary leaders could be released from prison. He purged the body of Magistrates because some of them had connived in the murders of right wing supporters in the early days of the revolution. He also re-structured the Peoples' Tribunals, giving each political party and trade union a Judge. The People's Tribunals were to include one magistrate, one prosecuting attorney and an eight strong jury with a member from each of the political groups and parties. Everyone was entitled to free legal defence or could defend him or herself instead.[12] Nin created a judicial body that reviewed death sentences. If appropriate the President of the Generalitat could review the sentences and commute them - a power previously held by the President of the Spanish Republic. Adulthood was legally set at eighteen and adoption laws were made easier so that war orphans could be adopted quickly. Women were given equal legal rights and a union official or a militia leader could legally perform marriage services.

The new Generalitat officially welcomed the Russian Consul to Catalonia at its first meeting. The Consul was Vladimir Antonov-Ovsyeyenko.[13] As the only fluent Russian speaker it was Nin who formally welcomed the Consul on behalf of the Generalitat! Nin and Antonov-Ovsyeyenko had known each other previously in Russia; however the Russian Consul pretended that they had never met.

The CNT and Nin proposed measures to set up a monopoly on foreign trade and to create a new bank for industry and credit; the non-revolutionary parties in the Generalitat rejected these measures. The PSUC followed the official Communist line to defend the democratically elected Republic and did all it could to weaken the revolution. The Generalitat dissolved the workers' control of the towns and cities and replaced them with new municipal councils. Each party got three members in the new administrations, based on the numbers each party had in the Generalitat. This meant that the POUM had three councillors in every city and town in Catalonia. This worked to its advantage in places where the POUM had few members but meant that the POUM lost control of areas it had once controlled completely. Nin had to visit Lerida with the President of the Generalitat, Luis Companys, to convince POUM members to accept the new law that put them in a minority in the new Lerida municipal council.[14] In Valencia the POUM and the CNT-FAI had controlled the city together through a revolutionary regime and had often blocked Government decisions. In November 1936 a new municipal council replaced this regime and control was lost.[15]

By October 1936 the membership of the POUM grew to 40,000, reaching a high watermark of 70,000 in December 1936. The POUM was busy: the party introduced classes on Marxism in Barcelona, and put the war wounded to work cataloguing books for a Museum to the Revolution. The Women's Section organised classes in nursing, childcare and even military drill, as some women fought in the militias. The POUM Red Aid (Socors Roig) set up an information service on the treatment of wounds and taught First Aid. It also set up a Tuberculosis Sanatorium in a castle at the Pyrenean town of Alp.[16] The POUM ran radio stations in Barcelona and Madrid and also ran a foreign language service. POUM members and the CNT organised and ran the new 'Free Expression' schools.[17] POUM members took over large areas of housing in Barcelona which had been abandoned by rebel-supporting owners and used these homes to house slum dwellers, and later refugees. In the early days of the revolution POUM member Josep Coll became General Secretary of the Commissariat of Public Order. This meant he was in charge of the workers' Control Patrols, which at first replaced the police forces and later worked alongside them, before the Patrols were finally abolished. But even in its stronghold of Lerida the POUM never fully controlled policing.

Economically the POUM had three main strands:

- Workers' control of government
- Workers' control of the economy
- Socialisation, where a new society would be based on the means of production.

When it came to agriculture the POUM favoured allowing individuals to keep their land, regardless of the size of the farm, but it also favoured farmers' co-operatives. The trade unions were to co-ordinate the various sized farms. This brought the POUM into conflict with the Spanish Republican Government and the Communists, who believed that governmental control was the way to win the Civil War, rather than revolutionary means. The POUM supported the CNT in pressurising the Generalitat to legalise the collectivisation of industry and the land. This became law on October 24th 1936 although they were forced to accept that shareholders should be compensated for any losses.[18]

From October 31st to November 2nd 1936 the 'London Bureau'

(an organisation of dissident Marxist and Socialist groups called the International Bureau for Revolutionary Socialist Unity, (to whom the ILP were affiliated) met in Brussels. The congress condemned the Moscow 'Show Trials' and pledged solidarity with the POUM. Julian Gorkin[19] represented the POUM at the congress. It was agreed the next meeting of the 'London Bureau' would be in Barcelona in the spring of 1937. Internationally the POUM was the only Spanish party that demanded Moroccan independence on moral and military grounds as the right wing rebels' best forces came from Morocco.

In November in *La Batalla* the POUM condemned the Russians for using military aid as a lever to crush the revolution. Nin had already angered the Spanish Communists by proposing asylum for Trotsky in Spain and this was the final straw. At Communist insistence Nin and the POUM were ejected from the Generalitat in December 1936.

The offensive by the Communists against the POUM had begun in Madrid. During the siege of Madrid, which began in November 1936, the Republican Government of Spain left for Valencia. In its absence the city was governed by a 'Defence Council', from which the POUM were excluded. Even POUM Executive members could not get the POUM represented.[20] The POUM's newspapers and journals were suppressed, its radio station and its Red Aid organisation were closed down and its military formations refused arms. (This was at a time when Jesus Blanco, the local POUM leader, was killed at the Front.) By the end of the year POUM militia in Madrid were instructed to join the CNT militia, and POUM militants were ordered to Barcelona for their own safety.

Although no longer part of the Catalan government the POUM continued to put forward proposals and policies. Regular Army formations replaced the militias in most parts of Spain so the POUM proposed the formation of a Revolutionary Red Army based on the Russian 1918-20 model in December 1936.[21] This army would include Commissars who would control army officers and would be run by Soldiers' Councils. Trotsky's *Red Army Handbook* was published and distributed by the POUM. All the other groups opposed these proposals and they came to nothing.

For several weeks *La Batalla* called fruitlessly for the POUM to be represented in the Generalitat. In April 1937 the POUM called for Soviets to replace the trade unions. The POUM youth movement, the JCI, called for the Spanish Parliament to be disbanded and replaced by a revolutionary government.[22] The POUM's attempts to work more closely with the Anarchist CNT-FAI had some success; the JCI formed a revolutionary 'Youth Front' with the Anarchist youth movement the 'Juventudes Libertarias'. This group included the feminist Anarchist group 'Mujeres Libre' or Grouping of Free Women. In its attempts to work more closely with the CNT the POUM publicised its differences with the official Trotskyite movement. The POUM included a small Trotskyite group Bolshevik-Leninist Section of Spain (SBL) who made attempts to win over the POUM rank and file members to a more revolutionary policy.

The attack on the POUM had begun in Madrid but was now in full flow everywhere outside Catalonia. By April 1937 the only POUM newspaper outside Catalonia that was still printing was *El Communista* in Valencia. In many large industrial undertakings POUM militants were expelled from the factory committees which were running these enterprises. Even in Catalonia, unrest between the Government and its Communist supporters and the revolutionaries of the POUM and CNT-FAI was reaching boiling point. The May Day parades in Barcelona were cancelled for fear of violence.

But violence did erupt on May 3rd 1937. Government police attempted to take over the Telefonica, the main telephone exchange in Barcelona in Placa Catalunya, which was at that time controlled by the CNT. The attack on the Telefonica led to a General Strike and to street fighting that lasted for six days. The revolutionaries only ended the fighting thanks to the pleading and intervention of the Anarchist Government Ministers.[23] There was fighting throughout Catalonia. The POUM and Anarchists joined together, often occupying Catalan Communist Party (PSUC) buildings and, in some cases, managing to disarm the local police. The POUM stronghold of Lerida was completely controlled by the revolutionaries.

Because the uprising had been spontaneous, Anarchist leaders were unsure what they should do, and rejected the POUM leaders' offer of an alliance against the Government and the Communists.[24] The Spanish Government, however, responded to the rebellion by taking charge of public order from May 6th. The following day Assault Guards (paramilitary police) arrived from Valencia to restore order in Barcelona. The POUM leadership had supported the Anarchists during the 'May Days' but they did not attempt to lead them and, in fact, warned the Anarchists against being provoked into fighting. But once the fighting broke out, the majority of POUM leaders felt they had to support the POUM membership and the Anarchists who wished to fight rather than give up the revolution. When, eventually, the Anarchists gave up the fight the POUM leaders ordered their members to do the same. Some local committees and the small group of Trotskyites of the SBL tried to continue the rebellion but they had to admit defeat when the local Anarchists would not help them.

During the 'May Days' events around five hundred people were killed, one and a half thousand were wounded and over two hundred people were arrested. By joining the Anarchists in the 'May Days' rebellion the POUM had been defending their core beliefs, that

"...the war could not be won without completing the revolution" [25]

and

"there was no place in Spain in 1936 for a democratic republic. The conflict was one between Fascism and Socialism." [26]

But by fighting for its principles the POUM had rebelled against the Government and could expect serious consequences. The POUM Executive instructed its members to prepare for underground work, yet they still set a date for its Congress on June 18th 1937 as if they were expecting only a minor punishment. The leader of the Spanish Communist Party, Jose Diaz accused the POUM of being agents of Franco.[27] Posters appeared around Barcelona with a mask and the hammer and sickle of the POUM. Behind the mask was an evil face with a swastika, suggesting that, behind their left wing masks, POUM members were secret Fascists. The Soviet Ambassador visited the Republican Prime Minster, Largo Caballero,[28] and demanded the suppression of the POUM. Caballero saw the POUM as a working class anti-Fascist organisation so he refused to crush it, but he said that he would bring them before the courts because of their act of rebellion. In a vote of 'No Confidence' Caballero lost the Premiership and was replaced by Negrin [29] who, unlike Caballero, had no sympathy for the revolution in Catalonia and believed that the POUM and other revolutionaries were damaging the war effort.[30] With Negrin now in charge the revolutionaries in Catalonia lost control of public order, the militias were replaced by a Regular Army and the Catalan Government was now centrally controlled.

For a few weeks after the 'May Days' nothing but verbal threats had been aimed at the POUM. Membership was still high at around

40,000, possibly as high as 60,000, and many POUM members believed they might just be able to continue as before.[31] Communist propaganda continued to condemn the POUM as both a Fascist and a Trotskyite party. Nin's links with Trotsky allowed them conveniently to ignore the fact that Trotsky had consistently condemned the POUM's policies. In fact Trotsky had stated that the POUM were no better than Communist and Socialist traitors.

On May 28th *La Batalla* was suppressed and Julian Gorkin indicted for an editorial in which he called on the workers to be waiting with arms 'at the ready'.[32] On June 16th 1937 the suppression of the POUM began suddenly and without warning, when armed police arrested Nin at the POUM headquarters in broad daylight. In the evening many other members of the POUM Executive had also been arrested. By July nearly a thousand POUM militants had been held.

The CNT helped to save many POUM members by allowing them to join CNT military units and trade union groups. The POUM were also accused of insulting a friendly country, i.e. Russia.[33] POUM leaders were charged with being Fascist spies; a faked map of Madrid, known as 'Map N', was produced as evidence of this. The map was discovered on the person of a known Fascist called Golfin; the 'N' was supposed to be Nin. Golfin was arrested, as were POUM leaders. At the trial of the POUM leaders in October 1938 the charge of spying was dropped.

The Government announced to the public that it had discovered a major enemy espionage network. Of the thousand or so POUM members arrested, around fifty were killed. Foreign supporters of the POUM were subject to the most severe treatment. Among those foreigners killed was the prominent Austrian Marxist, Kurt Landau.

No one knew what had happened to the POUM leader, Andreu Nin. Graffiti appeared on walls, asking where Nin was. It is believed that Nin was taken to a secret Communist 'cheka' (secret prison) where he was tortured in an attempt to make him to confess to being in league with the Fascists. When Nin refused to confess he was murdered. In August 1937 a foreign correspondent said that Nin had been murdered and was found dead in the suburbs of Madrid.[34]

The POUM was now illegal and all its Executive members had been arrested. (A second Executive was later also arrested.) Young, inexperienced militants were now running the party. Individual POUM members continued to serve in the armed forces and to work in the war industries. A few brave militants kept the memory of Nin alive and propagated the POUM message at great personal danger. The POUM's main newspaper, *La Batalla*, reappeared again in July 1937, lasting for 35 more issues. In September 1937 it was discovered that Maurin, the former POUM leader, was still alive in enemy territory. Attempts by foreign supporters of the POUM to get Maurin exchanged for right wing prisoners held by the Republicans came to nothing. Maurin was imprisoned by the Nationalist authorities and was not released until 1946. Most supporters of the Republican Government supported the suppression of the POUM, even some of the Anarchists.[35] To the Communists, POUM members were dissident traitors; to the more bourgeois Republican Government they were revolutionaries who resisted its efforts to centralise the war effort. Many Anarchists saw the plight of the POUM as merely a Communist dispute which did not concern them.

Between October 11th and 22nd 1938 the imprisoned leaders of the POUM were put on trial in Barcelona and accused of being traitors. An ex-minister and ex Prime Minster spoke in their defence and a Trotskyite, Munis,[36] gave evidence that the POUM was in no way a Trotskyite organisation. The POUM prisoners were judged to be true Socialists, and were cleared of espionage and treason.[37] In the end the POUM leaders were found guilty of only one offence: that of rebelling against the Government. An extract from the court findings states:

> 'On the contrary, it may be deduced from the foregoing that the accused all enjoy a great and long-established anti-Fascist reputation, that by their efforts they have made their contribution to the fight against the military uprising and that the stance they espouse is designed solely to remove the democratic republic in order to install a regime consonant with their own social outlook. These facts we declare proved.'[38]

The POUM and JCI were both legally dissolved. Four POUM leaders were sentenced to imprisonment for fifteen years, one to eleven years and two were acquitted. The imprisoned POUM leaders asked to be released to fight at the Front because Republican forces in Catalonia were collapsing against the Nationalist attacks, but this request was refused. POUM members were still being imprisoned as the right wing rebels converged on Barcelona. The POUM underground organisation worked its hardest to try and release their comrades before the Fascists captured Barcelona. In January 1939 the fall of Barcelona was imminent and prison staff began fleeing the city. In the chaos most of the POUM prisoners escaped - often aided by fellow POUM members who had been in hiding and fled to France. The imprisoned POUM Executive members took the Prison Warden hostage and used him as security to get to the French border. On reaching France many POUM members found themselves in concentration camps, still being persecuted by the Communists.

After they had crossed the French border the POUM Executive met in Paris. During World War II many POUM members fought in the French Resistance - the 'Maquis' - against the Nazi occupiers. Numerous POUM supporters died in Nazi German concentration camps, while the official Communist movement continued to persecute other POUMistas. After the war the POUM organised underground groups in Spain during General Franco's dictatorship [39] by continuing to propagate their message to the people and by supporting the guerrillas fighting the Francoist Spanish Government. When Franco died in 1975 and democracy began to be restored in Spain, the POUM voted to dissolve itself and to join the PSOE (the Spanish Socialist Party) in 1976.[40]

Notes

[1] The major source for this chapter is Victor Alba and Stephen Schwartz, *Spanish Marxism Versus Soviet Communism: A History of the P.O.U.M* (Oxford, Transaction Books, 1988). For the outbreak of the Spanish Civil War I have used, Hugh Thomas, *The Spanish Civil War*. 3rd edition (London, Penguin Books, 1986).

[2] Thomas, op cit., p301-2

[3] Pierre Broue and Emile Temime, *The Revolution and the Civil War in Spain* (London, Faber and Faber, 1972) p71-72

[4] Josep Rovira. See following chapters.

[5] Broue and Temime, op cit., p131, Thomas, op cit., p249-250

[6] Broue and Temime, ibid, p133

[7] Ibid, p128

[8] Ibid, p235

[9] Ibid, p168

[10] Collectivisation was the name given to Workers' control of industries and agriculture, and was inspired and encouraged by Anarchist militants. In its most extreme form in the countryside all farmers worked

communally and all equipment was pooled for the collective's use. On occasions even money was abolished and the collective members ate free from a communal store.
[11] Broue and Temime, op cit., p202-5
[12] Ibid, p216-7
[13] Antonov-Ovsyeyenko or Ovseenko, Vladimir Alexandrovich (1884-1939). He was a major military leader in the Russian Civil War. He lost influence as he had supported Trotsky and was sent abroad as ambassador to several countries. His last job was in Spain. On his recall to Russia he was executed.
[14] Broue and Temime, op cit., p205
[15] Ibid, p215
[16] Alba and Schwartz, op cit., p141
[17] Free Expression Schools. These were schools where children were allowed to study and learn as they wished rather than follow a set curriculum.
[18] Broue and Temime, op cit., p224
[19] Julian Gorkin (1901-?). Founded the Communist Party in Valencia, later joined the POUM. He was one of the leading militants in the POUM and Executive Committee member.
[20] Broue and Temime, op cit., p239-40
[21] Alba and Schwartz, op cit., p172
[22] Broue and Temime, op cit., p276-7, Thomas, op cit., p302
[23] Anarchist Government Ministers. In November 1936 four members of the CNT-FAI joined the Republican Government until May 1937.
[24] Broue and Temime, op cit., p283, Thomas, op cit., p657
[25] Alba and Schwartz, op cit., p203
[26] Broue and Temime, op cit., p198
[27] Alba and Schwartz, op cit., p205
[28] Largo Caballero (1869-1946). He was leader of the PSOE and UGT and Prime Minster of the Republic September 1936- May 1937.
[29] Juan Negrin (1889-1956). He was a right wing member of the PSOE and Republican Prime Minster May 1937 to the end of the Spanish Civil War in March 1939.
[30] Thomas, op cit., p706-7
[31] Ibid, p523
[32] Broue and Temime, op cit., p300
[33] Ibid, p300-1
[34] Ibid, p303
[35] Thomas, op cit., p708
[36] Grandizo Munis. Spanish Trotskyite and leader of the tiny SBL (Bolshevik-Leninist Section of Spain).

[37] Thomas, op cit., p866
[38] Jose Peirats Valls, *The CNT in the Spanish Revolution: Volume 3* (Hastings, Christie Books, 2006) p193
[39] Francisco Franco y Bahamonde (1892-1975) was leader of the Spanish Fascist rebellion against the Republican Government and Dictator of Spain after the Civil War until his death in 1975. He was sometimes known as 'El Caudillo'.
[40] Alba and Schwartz, op cit., p275-276

4. Lance Rogers, ILP Merthyr Activist and
International Brigader *(IBMT)*

CHAPTER 5

The ILP and the Spanish Civil War

WHEN THE CIVIL WAR BROKE OUT IN SPAIN in July 1936, the ILP and other members of the 'London Bureau' looked to help their sister party in Spain, the POUM. This support for the POUM meant that the ILP also supported the revolution instead of the Republican Spanish Government. Despite being a small party the ILP threw itself wholeheartedly into anti-Fascist activities to support the POUM. From the earliest days it raised money to help the POUM. John McNair headed a political office in Barcelona which was used to channel international aid to the POUM. The ILP raised funds to buy medical supplies and to equip an ambulance, which was driven to Spain and handed over to the POUM. Members of the ILP fought in Spain, both in their own contingent in the POUM militia, and in the International Brigades. In 1937 the ILP raised money to equip a food ship for Spain and organised accommodation for Basque refugee children. After the suppression of the POUM the ILP was involved in three delegations to Spain to try and release anti-Fascist revolutionary prisoners, gaining some successes. The ILP also tried unsuccessfully to organise a prisoner exchange to free Maurin, the POUM leader held in Nationalist Spain. The ILP in Britain also took part in some joint 'Spanish Aid' activities with the CPGB and other groups.

At the start of the Civil War the ILP had less than five thousand members, was in debt and had no financial reserves. The 1936 ILP Summer School decided to send John McNair, a successful businessman and good linguist, to Spain so that he could report on the situation he found there. In Britain the ILP ran several public meetings at which the main speakers were the Parliamentarians James Maxton, John McGovern and Campbell Stephen, and other high-ranking party officials such as Bob Edwards and Fenner Brockway. They also asked for contributions through their newspaper, the *New Leader*. Local ILP branches also organised fund raising activities like fetes, raffles, flag days and collections.[1] The Glasgow ILP was the biggest of the ILP branches and raised £250 during one flag day event.[2] Other fund raising activities included a 'self-denial' week in which members gave up a luxury for a week and donated the money they had saved to Spain. Women members were encouraged to knit socks and sweaters for Spain.[3]

In a short time the ILP had raised £500, which was given to McNair to take to Spain. McNair first travelled to Paris and met Marceau Pivert, an old friend and a member of the French Government. Pivert helped McNair to reach the French border city of Perpignan and put him in contact with the Franco-Spanish Committee. At an agreed meeting-place – a bar – McNair was met by two Spanish militiamen who took him by car to Barcelona. In Barcelona he was taken to meet the POUM Executive. McNair spoke to them in French and handed over the £500 in banknotes. When McNair enquired what further aid the POUM needed, they replied they were short of medical supplies. He met with a doctor who gave him a list of the supplies that were needed. McNair returned to Britain in September 1936 and spoke to the ILP leaders about the POUM's request. To raise the money the ILP organised an extensive series of meetings, addressed by leading ILP figures. At these meetings McNair spoke of his experiences in Spain. Within ten days a large amount of money was raised, and medical supplies were purchased and sent by air to Paris and then on to Barcelona.[4]

Having collected over £1,000 the ILP were able to provide more help for the POUM. A fully equipped ambulance was bought for £250 and named after the (presumed dead) POUM leader, Joaquin Maurin. On

5. Ambulance drivers. *(NL)*

September 27th 1936 the ambulance set off from Clapham, driven by William Martin of the ILP and John Gordon.[5] Another source says that the other driver was the ILP National Committee member, Bob Edwards, and not Gordon.[6]

Two nurses who belonged to the separate Spanish Medical Aid Committee[7] also travelled in the ambulance and left the ambulance once in Spain. Gordon returned home soon after entering Spain, but William Martin, the other driver, joined the POUM militia after he had delivered the ambulance.[8] The ambulance was used at the Huesca Front by the POUM and staffed by a Doctor Morros and a German nurse.[9]

6. Maurin Ambulance. (NL)

During October 1936 the POUM requested that McNair return to Barcelona and set up an office in Barcelona to (1) organise international support and (2) arrange for one of their MPs to visit Spain. McNair returned to Spain with the ILP MP John McGovern. The Catalan Government made McGovern their guest and he spoke at a large rally in which the other speakers were POUM Executive members Julian Gorkin and Andreu Nin. From Barcelona McGovern travelled to the frontlines in Madrid, then returned home after his short propaganda visit. The ILP office was run by John McNair; its staff included Bob Smillie, Ted Fletcher, and Sybil Wingate, who became McNair's secretary. She was the daughter of Brigadier Orde Wingate, who became a famous Second World War British leader in Burma. Later Eileen Blair, wife of the writer George Orwell (Eric Blair) worked in the office.[10]

7. John McNair. *(ILP archive)*

8. John McNair with POUM members in Barcelona, 1936 to 1937.
(Photo courtesy A. Potts)

John McNair was born in Boston, Lincolnshire, in 1887 and died on Tyneside in 1968. McNair came from a poor family background and was sent away aged three to live with his grandparents in Scotland. He later rejoined his family in Tyneside. After leaving school at thirteen McNair worked as an errand boy and later as a clerk for a shipping company. During his teens he read various Socialist classics like *Merrie England* and joined the ILP when he was nineteen. On joining the ILP he rode around the pit villages of the North East spreading the Socialist message. In 1910 he helped in the election campaign of the independent Socialist MP Victor Grayson in the Colne Valley in Lancashire and was billed as the 'boy-orator from the North'. One evening McNair addressed a mass meeting single-handed because Grayson was drunk and incapable of addressing the rally. Grayson went on to lose the election and McNair continued to be a part-time ILP propagandist. In 1911 McNair went to work in France. He claimed later, that in 1914 he was so close to where the French Socialist leader Jaures was assassinated in Paris that he heard the shot. During World War I McNair was in Paris, having failed a medical examination for the armed forces.

By 1923 McNair had become a successful businessman and had savings of £3,000. When he returned to England he offered to be an unpaid ILP propagandist. The ILP readily accepted his offer. Soon McNair was offered a paid job as Organising Secretary at the ILP Head Office in London. During the 1924 General Election McNair worked prodigiously and became ill. His doctor ordered him back to France for the good of his health and he stayed there for the next twelve years, returning to England in 1936. During the Spanish Civil War he was Head of the ILP office in Barcelona, where he smuggled money into Spain, helped in fund raising activities, wrote a pamphlet about the Spanish Revolution called *In Spain Now!* and was forced to flee along with other ILP Contingent members after the POUM had been suppressed. After Spain he became General Secretary of the ILP, and an ILP parliamentary candidate. In retirement, aged seventy-one, he obtained a degree, following this with a master's degree when he was seventy-three.[11]

The other major figure in the ILP office in Barcelona was Edward Joseph Fletcher. Ted Fletcher, as he was known in Spain, was born in 1911. He was educated at Fircroft College in Birmingham and he later became a trade union official. At the 1943 ILP conference his motion to reject the ILP leadership's planned alliance with the new Commonwealth Party won enough support to defeat the leadership.

He became a councillor in Newcastle from 1952 onwards and was the Labour Party MP for Darlington from 1964 until 1983 when he died.[12]

The main focus of ILP involvement in Spain so far had been in Catalonia where its sister party, the POUM, was strongest. In the spring of 1937 the ILP looked to help in another area of Spain, the Basque country. The right wing rebel forces had launched a major offensive on the independent Basque lands, overrunning most of the Basque country and blockading the Basque capital, Bilbao, by land and sea. The campaign by the Nationalists against the Basques was made notorious by the aerial bombing of the unarmed towns of Durango and Guernica, resulting in a large number of civilian casualties. In spring 1937 the ILP decided to raise money to send a food ship to Bilbao to help feed the beleaguered inhabitants. The ILP plan was to hire a ship, staff it with volunteers, fill it with food and sail it to Bilbao to feed the starving Basques. It planned to borrow £40,000 and the profits from the trip would help to pay back this money. The writer Ethel Mannin agreed to lend most of the money. In one week the ILP raised £6,000 - enough to fill the ship with food. This was a major achievement for a small party acting alone. But at the last minute the Spanish Government turned down the ILP's offer. Some of the money was used to send food to Bilbao on another ship and the rest was used to support the Basque refugees after they had come to Britain.[13]

9. Food ship for Bilbao cartoon. *(NL)*

Besides trying to send food into Bilbao the ILP were involved in the movement to help evacuate Basque children from Bilbao for humanitarian reasons. In all, around four thousand Basque refugee children were housed in Britain in dwellings dotted throughout the British Isles. The ILP housed and paid for the upkeep of around forty Basque children of Anarchist parents in Street in Somerset. The Clarks, a Quaker family and famous shoe manufacturers, provided the house for the children.[14] The children travelled by bus from a camp at Stoneham to the Street house on June 7th 1937. The house they lived in was called 'The Grange' and included a big kitchen, washhouse and a boiler that could supply hot water. There was a large lawn for the children to play on and two large rooms for recreation or lessons. There were desks and a blackboard available so the Basque children could receive schooling. A committee headed by Mrs Clark was formed to deal with any problems and to distribute gifts of clothing, furniture, bedding, crockery and foodstuffs. A housekeeper was employed to manage the house. The Bristol ILP was the nearest major branch, and it organised collections to help finance the running costs of looking after the children. The house had been empty for ten years and was repaired and re-decorated by the Clark family. The sleeping arrangements were designed so the Basque teachers could sleep with the children and help the children, especially the younger ones, to settle. A local doctor agreed to treat the Basque children free of charge.[15]

10. House in Street, Somerset for Basque refugee children. *(NL)*

11. Basque refugee children. *(NL)*

ILP leaders visited 'The Grange' to see the Basque children and described some of the typical activities at the Street house. They saw boys and older girls playing football; they dropped in on a school lesson; they saw the children eating scrambled egg; they listened to the children singing and watched a girl dancing. Two Basque women looked after the welfare needs of the children, along with a matron called Miss Becker. A German refugee, Hans Rhee, acted as a teacher. The Basque children also played the local school at football. Fenner Brockway commented he would have liked to get the boys a football strip in the Anarchist CNT colours of red and black! The trade union at the local Clarks boot factory agreed to a monthly collection to help with the upkeep of the house. In one week they raised £6 10s.[16] The Basque children stayed in the house for two years until June 1939. At the end of the Civil War most of the Basque children returned to Spain, but those with no parents stayed in Britain and were adopted by friends of the colony and ILP members.[17]

At the outbreak of the Civil War Joaquin Maurin, the leader of the POUM, was visiting a new POUM branch in Northern Spain. The area in Northern Spain was captured by rebel troops and Maurin found himself cut off behind enemy lines. He was reported captured and executed by rebel forces in the *Times* newspaper of September 17th 1936.[18] In the ILP newspaper, the *New Leader*, leading ILP figure Fenner Brockway wrote a tribute to Maurin, whom he called the "Lenin of Catalonia".[19] The ILP ambulance was named after Maurin in his honour. However, rumours began to reach the ILP that Maurin was still alive, but at first they were dismissed. In August 1937 Maurin's wife Jeanne was lecturing at the ILP Summer School. She showed Brockway a letter addressed to her under her maiden name with handwriting that was definitely Maurin's. She received monthly letters from her husband until he was finally recognised and put under strict confinement. Jeanne contacted a cousin who was a Bishop General in the Nationalist forces; it is possible that his appeal to the Fascist junta was what saved Maurin's life. John McNair claims that James Maxton also played a major role in saving Maurin's life.[20] When ILP MP John McGovern went to Spain as part of a foreign delegation, he presented the Republican Minster of Justice with a list of prominent right wing prisoners held by the Republic, including a Cortez deputy, whom he suggested they use in a prisoner exchange for Maurin. Attempts to get Maurin exchanged for a Fascist prisoner came to nothing and he was sentenced to ten years imprisonment by a Francoist court.

In early 1937 three leading POUM comrades, including Maurin's brother and Julian Gorkin, had flown to Britain to help in a campaign to promote the views of the ILP and the POUM on the war in Spain. But on their arrival at Croydon Airport the British authorities arrested them. Before he was deported Gorkin dictated his speech to Brockway who had it reproduced in a pamphlet.[21]

After the suppression of the POUM the ILP were involved in three foreign delegations that attempted to free the imprisoned POUM leaders and revolutionary anti-Fascists. The first international delegation to Spain to try and gain the release of POUM prisoners was led by the ILP's Fenner Brockway.

Archibald Fenner Brockway was born in 1888 and first came to prominence in the 'No Conscription Fellowship' during World War I. He was imprisoned four times for refusing to fight in Britain's armed forces, serving over two years in jail in total. For a third of that time Brockway was held in solitary confinement. During the 1920's he was part of the left wing of the ILP and supported the 'Socialism in our Time' policy. He was elected MP for Leyton in 1929 and was one of the 1929-31 Labour Government's fiercest critics. Because of this, he was not selected to fight the seat in 1931. When the ILP left the Labour Party in 1932 Fenner Brockway was its leader, or Chairman. During the 1930's he attempted to develop a Socialism which was somewhere between that of the Labour and Communist Parties. The Spanish Civil War and World War II tested his pacifist views and after the war he rejoined the Labour Party. He became Labour MP for Eton and

12. Fenner Brockway *(ILP archive)*.

Slough from 1950-64 and became a major figure in the colonial freedom movement and the break-up of the British Empire. He also became a major figure in CND. His long support for colonial independence led him to be known as the 'Member for Africa'. He accepted a peerage in 1964 and continued to be involved in radical causes up to his death in 1988.[22]

Brockway travelled alone from Britain and travelled through France and Spain by train, finally reaching Barcelona in July 1937. Once there, he made contact with a journalist friend and then went to the local CNT headquarters. He was advised by the CNT to avoid Communist-controlled Madrid and to go to Valencia where the Republican Government resided. The CNT would provide transport. Brockway was joined by a French delegation before he set out for Valencia. It was decided that the French should visit the Catalan Government Ministers and Brockway should travel on to Valencia. In Valencia Brockway met with Vasquez, the leader of the CNT, who was sympathetic to Brockway's attempts to free the POUM prisoners. On advice from the CNT's lawyer Brockway made contact with the British Embassy in Valencia and was given written introductions to meet with Spanish Ministers. The next day Brockway and the French delegation met with Largo Caballero, the former Prime Minster of the Republic and leader of the Socialist trade union, the UGT. Largo Caballero claimed that he could do little to help, thanks to Communist influence in the UGT. Two days later Brockway met with the Liberal Republican Foreign Minster Jose Giral [23] who stated that the Republic had no intention of charging the POUM with being a pro-Fascist organisation. By telegram from Madrid the Home Secretary told Brockway that all the POUM leaders were alive, and that a public trial would take place shortly. While he was in Spain Brockway also visited collectivised farms and industries, and spoke with foreign POUM supporters in hiding and with the wives of leading POUM figures. During or after Brockway's visit no POUM prisoners were released, and shortly after Brockway left Spain, Andreu Nin was murdered. However, no more POUM leaders were murdered after this, and the imprisoned POUM leaders believed that Brockway's visit had at least made this possible. While in Spain Brockway also helped to gain the release of Scottish Anarchist Ethel MacDonald who had been imprisoned by the authorities for her pro-revolutionary views.[24]

The second ILP delegation, led by the Parliamentary leader of the ILP, James Maxton, visited Spain in August 1937. The delegation included members of the French Socialist Party, the French League for Human Rights, the French Peasants Party and Sneevliet from the Dutch Socialist Party. This delegation headed by Maxton and Sneevliet managed to gain the release of several minor POUM prisoners and a promise that the POUM leaders would be put on trial shortly. This did not happen.[25] The delegation visited Barcelona and Valencia where its visit enabled Irujo, the Justice Minster,[26] to transfer the POUM leaders to a prison in Valencia where they were safer from possible Communist attack.[27]

The third delegation to Spain arrived in November 1937 and was led by the ILP MP John McGovern and the French human rights campaigner Professor Felicien Challaye. John McGovern was born in 1887 and was an ILP MP for Glasgow Shettleston from 1930 to 1947 and a Labour MP from 1947 to 1959. McGovern had an interesting and controversial political life. He was one of the signatories to the 'Mosley Memorandum' where Mosley, then a Labour MP, proposed radical economic solutions to the growing unemployment problems. McGovern withdrew his support when Mosley decided to form the 'New Party', which became the British Union of Fascists. During the 1930's McGovern attempted to challenge the Communists' leadership of the hunger marches and the organised unemployed. He was leader of one Hunger March and tried to represent and lead the unemployed in the House of Commons. In his controversial political career McGovern briefly supported Guy Aldred's Glasgow Anarchist movement, was arrested and fined over his support for free speech, was suspended several times from Parliament and was expelled from the Labour Party over an election scandal. Later in his political career he became less radical and very anti-Communist, and his Roman Catholicism became a more important factor in his life. He died in 1968 after retiring as an MP in 1959.[28]

During the Spanish Civil War McGovern visited Spain twice; first on a propaganda trip and second to try and free POUM prisoners. After his return from his first trip to Spain he produced a pamphlet *Why Bishops back Franco*, denouncing the Catholic's church support for Franco even though he himself was a Catholic. This pamphlet sold 28,000 copies and McGovern took part in high profile public debates with leading Catholic figures defending his views on Spain.[29] Catholic support for the ILP fell in Glasgow because of ILP support for the Spanish Republic, leading to a reduction in the ILP vote in the local elections. A leading ILP member even lost his safe council seat and because of this, he defected to the Labour Party.[30] During McGovern's second trip to Spain he claimed that the Communists were out to kill him.

The delegation's role in Spain was to:

- Interview members of the Spanish Government.
- Press for a quick trial for the imprisoned POUM leaders.
- Request an amnesty for imprisoned anti-Fascists.
- Investigate prison conditions.

The delegation went to Barcelona where the Spanish Government was now situated. They met with the Republican Minster of Justice, the Basque Irujo. He offered to try and free the anti-Fascist prisoners and gave the delegation permits to visit the Model Prison in Barcelona, where many anti-Fascist prisoners were being held. In the prison were around five hundred prisoners including many foreign anti-Fascists. Several prisoners spoke of having been tortured in secret Communist chekas.[31] The delegation also visited the Women's Prison, where they talked with foreign women who had been members of the POUM. After the visits to the prisons the delegation met with the Republican Home Secretary, who again promised to speed up amnesties for anti-Fascist prisoners. The delegation's attempt to gain entry to a known Communist cheka was refused even though they had official Government passes, and even when the Minster of Justice personally requested they be allowed to enter.[32] After the delegation left Spain they published a detailed report of their findings. Around a dozen minor prisoners were released, but overall the main aims of the delegation were left unfulfilled.[33]

The leader of the ILP 'Guild of Youth', Bob Smillie, had served with the ILP Contingent and was arrested while trying to leave Spain without the proper papers. He was taken to Valencia and imprisoned. While in prison he fell ill and died in June 1937. During his imprisonment and after his death an ILP businessman called David Murray, who spoke good Spanish, volunteered to try and find out why he had been arrested, how he was being treated in prison and later why he died. In Britain James Maxton approached the Spanish Ambassador to try and get Smillie released and many Labour MPs and trade unionists wrote to the Spanish Embassy requesting his release. Smillie fell ill on June 4th and was given medical attention on the 8th. On June 9th he was taken into the prison hospital where he was diagnosed with appendicitis; however it was not possible to operate because of ward congestion. He was belatedly transferred from the prison hospital to the local hospital where unattended he fell into a coma. When he was finally examined at the local hospital it was decided by the medical staff that because of congestion in his lower abdomen it was not possible to operate. On June 11th Bob Smillie died in the Valencia Provincial Hospital. He was buried the next day. On June 12th Murray was told Smillie was dead and was allowed to visit his grave. Murray received no information about Smillie's condition for three days, and when he was finally told something, Smillie had been dead for 24 hours. During Smillie's illness the British Embassy, his lawyer, Murray and his family had received no news from the prison authorities about his illness. The ILP report into his death concluded:

> 'We consider that Bob Smillie's death was due to great carelessness on the part of the responsible authorities, which amounted to criminal negligence.' [34]

Considering that the ILP knew of the suppression of the POUM, the imprisonment of its leaders, the murder of Nin and secret Communist chekas, this was a rather generous statement. Various sources agree with the ILP view that Smillie's death was a result of criminal negligence rather than a political murder, although it could be argued that his poor treatment was politically motivated.[35] At the time, many people believed Smillie's death was a political assassination or at least politically motivated; a view supported by some modern sources.[36] Other writers find it difficult to decide how Smillie actually died.[37] Author Tom Buchanan, using the personal papers of David Murray, believes that the real facts of the case may never be fully uncovered. Buchanan criticises Murray for not making enough use of British Embassy officials to try to gain Smillie's release. Buchanan also believes that the ILP's public announcement about the cause of Smillie's death was constrained by the ILP's desire not to harm its continuing support of the Spanish Republic.[38]

Although the ILP raised its own military unit to fight alongside the POUM forces, some ILP members volunteered to fight in the Communist-organised International Brigades. The International Brigades was a multi-national volunteer force that fought in nearly all the battles of the Civil War. Around 40,000 men and women served in the International Brigades and over 2,000 in the British Battalion of the International Brigades. As shock troops and frontline soldiers, its losses were very high: over five hundred members of the British Battalion were killed and most of the rest were wounded. Over half of the British Battalion belonged either to the Communist Party or Young Communist League (YCL). The others belonged either to other parties or to no party at all. In Spain each International Brigader had a passbook with the entry for 'Political Party' stating 'Anti-Fascist'. The great majority of the volunteers were working class men and few in the British Battalion had had any previous military training.[39]

Richard Baxell in his study of the British Battalion of the International Brigades, the number of known volunteers who were members of the Independent Labour Party is put at fifteen.[40] This is the figure for known ILP members who served in the International Brigades the actual figure is likely to be much higher.[41] A few volunteers who served in the ILP Contingent also served in the International Brigades.[42] Some members of the ILP Contingent and John McNair met the British Battalion Commissar called Wally Tapsell [43] in Barcelona both before and after the 'May Days' in Barcelona to discuss the possibility of them joining the British Battalion. McNair feared that the ILP volunteers' involvement in the 'May Days' events and their link with POUM might lead to poor treatment in the British Battalion, in addition the very hostile reports about the POUM and the 'May Days' events in the Communist newspaper the *Daily Worker* alienated the ILP volunteers and so the talks broke down and this led to only one member of the ILP Contingent joining the British Battalion of the International Brigades at this time.[44]

Two senior members of the ILP Merthyr branch, Evan Peters and Lance Rogers, joined the International Brigades as individuals. While in Spain Lance Rogers condemned the policy of the POUM, denounced the 'May Days' events and joined the Communist Party. But on his return to Britain he rejoined the ILP and became a conscientious objector during World War II.[45] Another ILP member who joined the International Brigades was John Mileno Smith, a Canadian born in Scotland and living in London. He joined the International Brigades in March 1938; he was seen as politically suspect because of his ILP connection and what happened to him during the Civil War is not known. A second known Scottish ILP volunteer who served in the International Brigades was Archie McBride from Ayr.[46] At least two ILP members were killed fighting in the International Brigades firstly there was Walter Sproston from the Swinton ILP Branch in Salford (near Manchester). By profession Sproston was an engineer. He was killed in March 1938 at Calaceite. Secondly from Liverpool was a carpenter called James W Stewart who was killed in February 1937 at the Battle of Jarama.[47] Other ILP members from Merseyside who served in the International Brigades included George Wilding a painter, George Wilfred Hardy a horse dealer and Thomas Fagan a seaman and a member of the National Union of Seamen.[48] The leader of the ILP MPs, James Maxton, was keen to volunteer for the International Brigades but knew no doctor would give him a clean bill of health.[49]

David Murray the ILP businessman also helped relatives to find out the whereabouts of missing sons and husbands in the International Brigades. In particular while he was in Spain he assisted imprisoned (usually for desertion or ill-discipline) Scottish International Brigaders with supplies such as cigarettes, clothing, underwear and money. The families of such men were not told what had happened to them so the ILP had an important role in passing on news about these men to their families.[50] This humane role performed by the ILP was not something that would have improved relations with the British Communist Party who wanted to keep secret any disciplinary problems in the British Battalion of the International Brigades.

Throughout the Spanish Civil War the ILP stayed a principled anti-Fascist political party. Up to the suppression of the POUM in June 1937 the ILP supported both its sister party and the Spanish Revolution. After the suppression of the POUM the ILP did all it could to help to release POUM and anti-Fascist prisoners but the ILP also continued to work where possible with the Communist Party at home supporting the Spanish Republic. In Newport, South Wales, the Secretary of the local 'Spanish Relief Committee' was an ILP member. He reports that the two parties worked well together throughout the War, linking up with the Spanish Consul to send medical and food supplies to Spain and supporting financially the Basque children's home at Caerleon.[51] In another part of South Wales, Merthyr, the ILP and the CPGB were on friendly terms, working together for Spanish Aid at least as late as September 1937.[52] In Aberdeen the two parties at first worked together for 'Spanish Aid' but after the suppression of the POUM the local Communist Party refused to work with the local ILP,[53] whereas in Norwich the ILP branch worked together with the local Trotskyites in defence of the POUM.[54]

For a party as small as the ILP its members raised large amounts of money, which was used to support the POUM, Aid for Spain initiatives and the Basque children's home at Street. Some members fought in its own military Contingent, some in the International Brigades and others in different military forces of the Spanish Republic.

The ILP's massive efforts during the Spanish Civil War led to the loss of many members for a variety of reasons. Some members left because they believed that the party was pursuing foreign affairs at the expense of national and local issues. Other members disliked the revolutionary rhetoric of the ILP's support for the POUM and the Spanish Revolution, and also left. Many Catholic supporters in the ILP stronghold of Glasgow left the party in protest at ILP attacks on the Catholic Church's support of the Fascists. Some members were incensed at the increased links with the Communist Party at home (even though the Communists had supported the crushing of the POUM and had denounced the ILP's links with the POUM) and refused to work with the CPGB any longer. Many pacifists left the party when the ILP abandoned its pacifism and openly supported the anti-Fascist side in the Spanish Civil War.

Tom Buchanan states:

"The fault of the ILP in the Spanish Civil War lay not so much in dogmatism, but rather in the unwillingness of a once-great party to accept its decline into irrelevance, and a fatal naivety in dealing with international Communism in its most murderous phase."[55]

Its support for the Spanish Revolution further weakened the ILP in its relations with other parties of the Left in Britain:

"The Spanish Civil War saw the party increasingly ostracised within the British 'Left' and unable to effectively pursue its aims of supporting revolutionary elements within the Republican forces."[56]

While ILP efforts during the Spanish Civil War in no way compare with the efforts of the Communist Party, the ILP supported the anti-Fascist cause to the maximum of its ability. The Spanish Republican Government and the Communist Party condemned the support of the ILP's sister party, the POUM, for the Spanish Revolution, judging it as undermining the war effort. The POUM's refusal to abandon the revolution led to it being crushed. As a result of the ILP's support of the POUM in the Spanish Civil War it has been strongly criticised and its role in the Civil War being largely ignored. This chapter and the resulting chapters aim to show that the ILP and the members of the ILP Contingent were committed anti-Fascists.

Notes

[1] Peter Thwaites, The Independent Labour Party Contingent in the Spanish Civil War, *Imperial War Museum Review*, 1987, p51
[2] Thwaites, op cit., p59
[3] Gidon Cohen, *The Failure of a Dream: The Independent Labour Party from Disaffiliation to World War II* (London, Tauris, 2007) p179
[4] John McNair, *Spanish Diary* (Stockport, Independent Labour Publications, ND) p5-9
[5] Jim Fyrth, *The Signal was Spain: The Spanish Aid Movement in Britain 1936-39* (London, Lawrence and Wishart, 1986) p80
[6] Thwaites, op cit., p52
[7] Spanish Medical Aid and Aid Spain Movement. Included up to two hundred men and women who served in Spain in the medical services and helped with relief work, while thousands in Britain helped to raise money for food-ships, medical supplies and looking after refugees both in Spain and in Britain.
[8] Fyrth, op cit., p81

[9] *New Leader* 13.11.36
[10] McNair, Spanish Diary, op cit., p9-13
[11] Ibid, p1-4
[12] Don Watson and John Corcoran, *'An Inspiring Example': The North East of England and the Spanish Civil War 1936-1939* (Newcastle, McGuffin Press, 1996) p49
[13] Fyrth, op cit., p249-50
[14] Ibid, p230
[15] *New Leader* 04.06.37
[16] *New Leader* 24.09.37
[17] John McNair, *James Maxton: The Beloved Rebel* (London, George Allen and Unwin, 1955) p259, Cohen, op cit., p190
[18] Don Bateman, *Joaquim Maurin 1893-1973: Life and Death of a Spanish Revolutionary* (Leeds, Independent Labour Party, 1974), p10
[19] *New Leader* 25.09.36
[20] McNair, *Beloved Rebel*, op cit., p259
[21] Fenner Brockway, *Inside the Left: Thirty Years of Platform, Press, Prison and Parliament* (London, George Allen and Unwin, 1942) p299-300
[22] John Ramsden (editor), *The Oxford Companion to Twentieth-Century British Politics* (Oxford, Oxford Univ. Press, 2002) p75-76
[23] Jose Giral (1880-1962). He was a Liberal Republican politician and Prime Minster of Spain May-August 1936
[24] Brockway, op cit., p306-317, Daniel Gray, *Homage to Caledonia: Scotland and the Spanish Civil War* (Edinburgh, Luath Press, 2008) p173. Ethel MacDonald (1909-1960) was a supporter of Glasgow Anarchist Guy Aldred all her life. In Spain she worked for the Anarchist radio station and sent regular information about the revolution back to Scotland. She was nicknamed the 'Spanish Pimpernel' while in Spain she was imprisoned on two occasions by the Republican authorities for her revolutionary views. On her return to Scotland in November 1937 she denounced the Communists role in suppressing the revolution in Spain.
[25] McNair, *Beloved Rebel*, op cit., p259, William Knox, *James Maxton* (Manchester, Manchester Univ. Press, 1987) p129
[26] Manuel Irujo. He was a Basque Nationalist member of the Spanish Republican Government and Minster for Justice May 1937- January 1938.
[27] Victor Alba and Stephen Schwartz, *Spanish Marxism Versus Soviet Comm-unism: A History of the P.O.U.M.* (Oxford, Transaction Books, 1988) p238
[28] Ramsden, op cit., p410-11
[29] Cohen, op cit, p177, Tom Buchanan, *Britain and the Spanish Civil War* (Cambridge, Cambridge Univ. Press, 1997) p184

[30] Knox, op cit., p129, Cohen, ibid., p 76, 177
[31] Chekas. Secret or openly Russian controlled prisons.
[32] John McGovern, *Terror in Spain* (London, ILP, 1937) p7-13, John McGovern, *Neither Fear Nor Favour* (London, Blandford Press, 1960) p104-111
[33] Alba and Schwartz, op cit., p239
[34] *New Leader* 11.03.38
[35] McNair, Spanish Diary, op cit., p21, Tom Buchanan, *The Impact of the Spanish Civil War on Britain: War, Loss and Memory* (Brighton, Sussex Academic Press, 2007) p232
[36] McNair, *Spanish Diary*, ibid., p21, George Orwell, *Homage to Catalonia: and Looking back on the Spanish War* (London, Penguin, 1988) p205, John Newsinger, The Death of Bob Smillie, *The Historical Journal*, 41, 2, 1998 p575-8
[37] Michael Shelden, *Orwell Authorised Biography* (London, Politicos, 2006) p295, Bernard Crick, *George Orwell: A Life* (London, Secker and Warburg, 1981) p224
[38] For in depth accounts of Bob Smillie's arrest and controversial imprisonment and death see Buchanan, Impact of the Spanish Civil War, op cit., p106-121, Cohen, op cit., p188-9, Gray, op cit., p155-166
[39] Richard Baxell, *British Volunteers in the Spanish Civil War: The British Battalion in the International Brigades, 1936-1939* (London, Routledge, 2004 and Warren & Pell, Abersychan, 2007), Bill Alexander, *British Volunteers for Liberty: Spain 1936-39* (London, Lawrence and Wishart, 1982), Ken Bradley, *International Brigades in Spain 1936-39* (London, Osprey, 1994)
[40] Baxell, op cit., p15
[41] Gray, op cit., p142. Gray believes as many as 100 ILP members from Scotland served in the International Brigades or the ILP Contingent.
[42] Men who fought in the ILP Contingent and also the International Brigades included John Donovan, Thomas Farrell, David Wickes, Jock Connor and William Clarke. See chapters 7-9 for more details.
[43] Commissar and Walter Tapsell. Commissars were officers in the Republican Army and in the International Brigades whose role was to check on the loyalty of the other officers, look after the needs of the men and to discipline any troublemakers. Most Commissars tended to be Communists and supported the Party line and openly expressed this to the men. Walter Tapsell was Commissar of the British Battalion November 1937 until he was killed at Calaceite in March 1938.
[44] Alexander, op cit., p108., Thwaites., op cit., p57. Marx Memorial Library, International Brigade Archive, Box 13/7a 'Report on the English Section

of the POUM' and Box 13/10 'Report on the position with regard to the ILP Group'. Richard Baxell, *Unlikely Warriors: The British in the Spanish Civil War and the Struggle against Fascism* (London, Aurum Press, 2012)

[45] Hywel Francis, *Miners Against Fascism: Wales and the Spanish Civil War* (London, Lawrence and Wishart, 1984) p211, 252

[46] Correspondence with Jim Carmody. Chief Researcher, International Brigade Memorial Trust.

[47] www.wcml.org.uk for details about Sproston this source claims he was killed at Belchite not Calaceite. Alexander, op cit., p274 and in the most recent roll of honour of those Britons killed fighting in the International Brigades compiled by Richard Baxell and Jim Carmody they agree with Alexander, www.international-brigades.org.uk/british_volunteers/roll_of_honour.htm The names of the Merseyside ILP volunteers who served in the International Brigades is from an exhibition held at 'Peoples Centre' in Liverpool on 03.09.08, *The Northwest and the International Brigades* by Simon Hawkesworth and Dan Payne.

[48] Hawkesworth and Payne, op cit.

[49] Knox, op cit., p125

[50] Gray, op cit., p119, 196-197

[51] Letter 1930's ILP activist Sidney Robinson to author, 11.07.2007

[52] Francis, op cit., p136

[53] Cohen, op cit., p40

[54] Ibid, p108

[55] Buchanan, *Britain and the Spanish Civil War*, op cit., p78

[56] Cohen, op cit., p198

CHAPTER 6

The Revolutionary Militias and the POUM

AFTER THE DEFEAT OF THE RIGHT WING MILITARY UPRISING in the major cities of Spain, the people no longer trusted the old army and so the various left wing political parties and trade unions armed and raised their own formations. An estimated one hundred and fifty thousand people volunteered to fight in the militias. These militia formations were poorly armed, poorly trained, poorly disciplined and often badly led; but in the early days of the Civil War they comprised the majority of the anti-Fascist forces. By the end of 1936, the central zone of the Spanish Republic was replacing militia forces with new regular Popular Army formations. In the northern zone, however, the militia forces were never really regularised. In Catalonia and Aragon the revolutionary parties (including the POUM) resisted the militarisation of the militias until the summer of 1937. The militias alone could never have won the War but they gave the Spanish Republic a breathing space to train its new Regular Army. The militias were often defeated by smaller rebel forces and were incapable of launching large-scale attacks. They did virtually nothing on the Aragon Front for months against a numerically weaker enemy. Yet they played a key role in saving Madrid and launched the most successful Republican offensive of the war, capturing much of Aragon. The ILP volunteers ended up being part of these militia forces and experienced the high and lows of this type of military force.[1]

It was common for militia volunteers to receive little or no military training and at best they were given fairly pointless drill (marching up and down) instruction. Useful training, such as: use of weapons (especially machine guns); taking cover; throwing grenades; or building trenches, often only occurred when the volunteers reached the Front. The militia columns were organised in an ad hoc way. A militia column could be any size, often a few thousand strong, and was usually recruited from one political party only. Frequently a renowned militant like the Anarchist Durutti would lead a column.[2] Unfortunately the Regular Army advisor, who accompanied the leader, was often viewed with suspicion by the members of the column and so his advice was regularly ignored. The smallest group in a militia unit usually consisted of ten men; this group was part of a Century of one hundred men, which was part of a group of five hundred men. At each level the men chose a delegate. These delegates discussed with the men any orders that were issued and passed on the men's decisions to the War Committee. The War Committee consisted of the militia column leader, the military advisor and delegates of the five hundreds. Unpopular orders could be rejected, and then the leaders would have to argue their case with the men to get them to obey such orders. Each column usually had a well-armed group of shock troops, a machine gun section and medical support, which was often very basic.[3]

13. Milicianos fortify a position in the Sierra de Alcubierre, 1936 to 1937.
(Fototeca, Diputación de Huesca)

The biggest criticism of the militias was levelled at their poor discipline. Clearly, if a leader had to persuade his soldiers to obey an order, this could take up valuable time and might lead to fatal delays. In the early days of the Civil War many militia members would go home to eat and sleep if their militia were fighting near to home. Dirty or unpleasant jobs were often not carried out. Anarchist sectors of the Front were often easily identifiable by the lack of latrines and hence their awful smell. Guard duty was made shorter to persuade the militia to do it, although it was common for the militiamen on duty to fall asleep, or simply to refuse to do guard duty in the first place. The Anarchists had a policy of releasing men from prisons in the areas they had liberated, and many ex-prisoners fought in their militias. One column known as the 'Iron Column' was made up entirely of ex-prisoners. Many of these ex-prisoners were genuine anti-Fascists; however some continued with their criminal activities under the cover of the militias. Some columns included prostitutes and in one famous case they were executed on the orders of Durutti. At one stage his column had more losses from venereal disease than in battle.

There were some desertions in the militias but not to any significant level. Militia columns would generally only fight together with members of another column if they were of the same political persuasion, so, for example, Anarchist and Communists rarely, if ever, joined together. This weakened the effectiveness of the militias as a fighting force. The militia forces' greatest act of discipline was to man the Aragon Front for long periods of time until the Regular Army was ready to replace them.[4]

The morale of the militias in the early days of the Civil War was very high because most of the young militants from each political party or trade union were fighting in them. The downside of this was that these troops were often reckless in attack and would refuse to take cover if shot at. This led to unnecessary losses from the militias. In most militia columns the leader was a trusted and admired militant. The delegates in the column were all elected by the men and were therefore also trusted. The high morale in the militia columns stemmed from the respect in which the leadership in most columns was held. Most of the militants had been working towards the revolution all their lives and they were willing to defend it to the death. In the open, attacked by modern weapons like planes and artillery, the militia often fled but when they were defending their own areas and cities they fought courageously. In the battle for Madrid in November 1936 the militias played a central role in repelling the Fascist attack. Morale fell on the Aragon Front when little new weaponry arrived at the Front and it became obvious they would not capture Zaragoza and Huesca quickly. The death of many of the best militants in the early clashes of the war, coupled with the arrival of new volunteers who joined the militias only because of the high pay further reduced the morale of the militia formations.[5]

In the first days of the Civil War militias wore civilian clothes decorated with the insignia of their political party. Socialists and Communists wore red scarves around their necks and the Anarchists wore red and black scarves. The initials of the political party or trade union were often stitched onto a hat or on clothing. This could be PCE or PSUC or JSU (Young Communist and Socialist Group) for the Communists; PSOE and UGT for the Socialists; and CNT, FAI and FIJL for the Anarchists. Some militia, particularly those in Northern Spain, had 'UHP' stitched on their clothes or hats. This stood for 'Unite Proletarian Brothers', a hope that all Parties of the Left would unite together. Within a few weeks the most common militia uniform became a type of blue dungaree known as a 'mono'. Headgear was varied ranging from a sombrero to the more common beret, or a side cap known as 'gorillo'. Badges like a red star, or a hammer and sickle for Socialists and Communists, were often pinned to the hats. Anarchist side caps were often half red and half black. Footwear ranged from straw scandals called 'alpargatas' to army boots. Militia members wore ex-Army straps and belts, as well as civilian and home made ones, to hold grenades, ammunition and food. Some militia looked like Mexican bandits with two belts of ammunition across their body. Later some khaki tunics were issued and also some metal helmets, from abroad and from the Spanish army. It is fair to say a militia column often looked very irregular, with no two-militia men dressed the same. The militias carried their own flags; these were usually red for the Socialists and Communists, and red and black for the Anarchists. The name of the column, or the initials of the party or trade union would appear on the flags; sometimes there would also be a revolutionary slogan. The Communists nearly always displayed the hammer and sickle on their flags.[6]

The biggest weakness of the militias was their lack of arms. Many left wing militants had revolvers for street fighting, and gun shops had been looted when the military rebellion broke out; but most of the weapons at the Front were old Army issue. The main rifle used by the militias was the German Mauser dating from 1896. In militia columns there was usually a variety of rifles and ammunition, which made supply and logistics very difficult. Militia soldiers frequently did not know how to clean or repair a rifle properly, which exacerbated the lack of useable armaments. On occasions individual militiamen would

14. POUM miliciano in the Sierra de Alcubierre, 1936 to 1937.
(Fototeca, Diputación de Huesca)

customise their rifle by removing the sights and shortening the barrel; this further reduced the weapon's effectiveness. When militiamen went on leave they often left their rifles behind so the relieving force could use them.

15. POUM position in the Sierra de Alcubierre, 1936 to 1937
(Fototeca, Diputación de Huesca)

Grenades were often home-made. The most notorious grenade was the 'FAI bomb', which sometimes blew up the thrower if not thrown rapidly. At the Front revolutionary weapons were still being used. These included dynamite and Molotov Cocktails (petrol bombs). Machine guns were rare amongst the militia and tended to be World War I or even pre-World War I vintage. Artillery was old, if it was available at all. Militias used the megaphone to good effect, persuading enemy troops to desert to the Republican side. Later in 1937 the Spanish Government released better weapons to the militias, but only in small quantities. The occasional Soviet artillery piece and plane appeared on the Aragon Front. Since they lacked tanks, the revolutionary groups, particularly the Anarchists, attempted to make their own. These were often lorries which had been armour plated and then armed with machine guns and rifles. They were quite effective in the streets of cities and towns, but virtually useless in the open as they could only travel on roads. They were slow and unwieldy, and sitting ducks from an air attack. They proved to be of little military use.[7]

An estimated five thousand foreign volunteers served in the militias. The first foreign volunteers were in Barcelona for the anti-Fascist Olympics (an alternative left wing Olympics in protest against the Berlin Olympics of 1936) and some of these athletes took part in the street fighting. German anti-Fascist volunteers came to Catalonia and fought in the Thaelmann Centuria named after the jailed German Communist leader. This force served on the Aragon Front until August 1936 when they left to join the International Brigades. Several hundred Italian exiles, led by the Italian Social Democrat, Carlo Roselli, fought on the Aragon Front. Other Italian volunteers fought at Irun in the Basque lands and in an Anarchist column at Madrid; however, like the Germans, the majority of the foreign volunteers left to join the International Brigades in late 1936. The largest contingent of foreign volunteers in the militias was the French. They were involved in the fighting at Irun, on the Aragon Front, in the disastrous militia attack on Majorca and at Madrid. Again the majority of the French volunteers eventually joined the International Brigades. Most foreign volunteers who did not join the International Brigades tended to be Anarchist volunteers and the 'Durutti Column' had an international section. When the militias were being regularised many Anarchist foreign volunteers either went home or refused to fight.[8]

British and Irish involvement in the militias was small in scale.[9] At the early stages of the Civil War these volunteers arrived in ones and twos, and fought in the militias because there was nothing else organised at that time. Seven Britons were involved in the disastrous attack on Majorca, where one of them was wounded. A British Communist, Nat Cohen, showed such good leadership qualities during the Majorca campaign that he was asked to stay in the PSUC militia. He eventually commanded three hundred men until he was wounded and invalided home in April 1937. Other Britons fought in the 'Thaelmann Centuria' and in Anarchist columns. Many British and Irish volunteers were horrified by the chaos of the militias and left them to join the International Brigades. The Communist artist, Felicia Browne, was one of only two British women to fight in the militias. She was killed on the Aragon Front in August 1936, trying to help a wounded comrade.[10] Another known British fatality fighting in the militias was Emmanuel Julius who had originally gone to Spain as a quartermaster with the Spanish Medical Aid group.[11]

One unique aspect of the revolutionary militias was the presence of a small number of female miliciana. Spain was a traditional country where a woman would be chaperoned on a date with a man. A woman's place was in the home and her major role was the rearing of children. When the revolution broke out the left wing parties liked to publicise the new liberation of women, and were especially proud of those women who were fighting in the militias. However the Fascists preferred to portray militia women as no better than she-devils and prostitutes, and even the Republicans would sometimes try to portray them as women of ill repute. Some prostitutes did pretend to be militia women and gave the miliciana a bad name.

Women in the militias wore the same clothing and were armed in the same way as the men. They usually cut their hair short to reduce the chances of lice. At the Front many women served in traditional roles: washing, cooking and in the medical services. But some women served as militia soldiers and fought with the men. Anarchist posters portrayed them as the embodiment of the revolution.

In action there could be problems: militiamen would sometimes act recklessly to try to impress the miliciana, causing unnecessary injuries. If a militia woman was injured, then several men would try to rescue her, increasing the number of potential casualties. Any militia woman knew she faced rape and death if captured by the Fascists. The Fascist leader, Franco, had ordered all captured militia women to be executed. Several militia women became known for their bravery: women such as Lina Odina who blew up herself and the enemy rather than surrender; Aida de la Fuente, who was killed in Asturias, and Rosario Sanchez who was nicknamed 'Rosie the Dynamiter'. A women's unit took part in the defence of Madrid. But by 1937 the role of women was again reverting back to the more traditional role.[12]

The end of the militias began during the siege of Madrid in October 1936 when the Republican Government introduced the Mixed Brigades by merging militia and loyal Regular troops together. By December 1936 several thousand ex-Army officers were brought back to be officers in the new Regular Army. Training schools were set up for new officers and political officers, known as Commissars. In January 1937 the elite Communist 5th Regiment was broken up and divided up amongst the new Mixed Brigades to give each Brigade a professional core. Women were banned from fighting in the Front line. On the Aragon Front the militias were renamed as Regular Army units and the militants and delegates received military ranks, but in reality little had changed. From June 1937 a regular officer took over command of the Aragon Front and Communist Commissars were introduced into the non-Communist units. If these units opposed this move they were starved of new armaments. By the end of the summer of 1937 the revolutionary militias in Spain had ceased to exist and had been incorporated into the new Communist-dominated Regular Army.[13]

The ILP's sister party, the POUM, was one of the major supporters of the revolutionary militias, controlling several thousand militiamen. The POUM militia had many similarities with the militias of the other revolutionary groups. Military training was short - often only two weeks - and took place in the Lenin Barracks in Barcelona. Many volunteers did not get to fire a rifle until they reached the Front.[14] Like other militia units, the POUM was organised along decimal lines with a section of around thirty men, then a century of a hundred men. It was then further organised into groups of five hundred, and a thousand, and finally the column itself. Well-known militants commanded the militia columns controlled by the POUM; men such as Joseph Rovira, Arquer and Grossi.[15] The leading members of the column were usually party militants. In POUM militia columns, the militiamen and women chose the political delegates. They scorned Regular Army practices such as saluting and addressing leaders by formal titles. Unlike the Anarchist militias, the POUM had Commissars whose job it was to maintain morale, look after the welfare of the troops, propagate the party line, root out any traitors, countersign any military orders and keep a check on the loyalty of the Army Officers.[16] The POUM had its own shock troops who were better armed and equipped than the rest of the column. The most well armed troops and holders of senior positions in the POUM militia were Party members. Early in the war the POUM militia were predominantly Party members or members of the youth movement, the JCI, but by the summer of 1937 possibly as many as 80% of the POUM militia were non-party members.[17]

The POUM had its own doctors and hospitals, situated behind the Front. They used existing medical facilities in major towns and cities. At the Front medical support was more basic and often included no more than First Aid men and stretcher-bearers, with the wounded being driven out to the hospitals from the Front line. In Barcelona the POUM had the 'Sanatorium Maurin' where it sent its injured militia to recuperate.[18]

The POUM militia columns were originally named after major revolutionary figures such as Lenin and Maurin (presumed dead at this time), but by April 1937 the POUM columns on the Aragon were re-named the 29th Division as part of the process of militarising the militias.[19] The various section leaders and political delegates received military ranks such as Cabo (Corporal), Sargento (Sergeant), Teniente (Lieutenant). Column leaders like Rovira were made Majors but were not allowed to rise above that rank until they had been to officer training school.[20]

The POUM militia lacked discipline, as did the other revolutionary militias. Militiamen defecated in the trenches, which increased the risk of disease and death. Orders were often challenged and leaders had to argue with the militia to get the orders obeyed.[21] There were some desertions from the POUM militia, caused by inaction on the Aragon Front and the time spent in the trenches; but most militia stoically manned the trenches for long periods of time with little or no relief.[22] Morale in the POUM militia was generally high, often leading to reckless behaviour. On one occasion a machine gun crew caught in the open under fire refused to take cover when their gun jammed.[23] A failed attack by the POUM on the town of Perdiguera was judged by the British Communist John Cornford to have been caused by lack of planning, leadership and training and not because of cowardice.[24] Morale in all the militias fell as non-political volunteers joined the militias for the good pay of ten pesetas a day. In some cases parents were actually taking teenagers to enlist because of the high pay in the militias, rather than out of any political commitment.[25]

16. Milicianos of the Lenin Column and Macias Company Column resting after a meal. 1936 to 1937. *(Fototeca, Diputación de Huesca)*

Such uniform as was worn by the POUM militia looked more like civilian clothes than military uniform and was similar that of to the other militias. It also included corduroy trousers and zipped woollen or leather jackets. Headgear varied greatly, but always had attached a red star or hammer and sickle badge and/or the initials 'POUM' stitched onto the cap. These badges and initials were also worn on the clothes or on an armband.[26] Later in the Civil War the POUM, like other militia columns, received better weapons and metal helmets.[27] The POUM had their own red flags with a hammer and sickle in the corner, and the name of the column and the initials 'POUM' embroidered in white.[28]

The POUM's main weapon was the Mauser 1896 rifle, as it was for the other militias. These were often of poor quality and the barrel was liable to split when fired. Ammunition was of different calibres and quality, causing rifles to jam or even explode. Orwell writes that the first five POUM casualties at the Front were caused by the poor quality of their own side's weapons.[29] The POUM militia also used single shot Winchester rifles.[30] POUM militia were so short of rifles that, when they went on leave, militiamen would leave their rifles at the Front for their replacements to use.[31] Machine guns in POUM units were in short supply and could number as few as one per fifty men. Like the rifles, they were prone to jamming and lacked the correct ammunition.[32] The POUM had its own antiquated artillery unit commanded by ILP member W. B. Martin.[33] Early in the Civil War the POUM militia lacked equipment such as maps, charts, range-finding instruments, telescopes or binoculars, torches, flares, wire-cutters, field telephones and ramrods to clean rifles. Later the POUM received wire-cutters and field telephones.[34]

17. Milicianos of the Lenin Column and Macias Company Column in the Sierra de Alcubierre, 1936 to 1937 *(Fototeca, Diputación de Huesca)*

The POUM militia, like the Anarchist militias, included foreign volunteers from fourteen different countries. Most of the foreign volunteers came from Germany and France. The several hundred German volunteers, many of whom had previous military experience, were organised in a special shock unit known as the 'Batallon de Choque'. They wore green uniforms and were armed with the best weapons.[35] The German volunteers took part in a trench raid, and in assaults on a Fascist-held former lunatic asylum called Manicomio.[36] The POUM also had an international column led by Russo, an Italian with Regular Army experience. Members of this column dressed in khaki and wore a red kerchief around the neck. When they left for the Front they were given metal helmets.[37] The international column was involved in the POUM's last action on the Huesca Front, where they captured several enemy trenches but had to retreat due to lack of support.[38] Many of the 'rank and file' of the POUM international volunteers were working class, and some, but not all, of them had had previous military experience. Politically, all the foreign volunteers classed themselves as anti-Fascists. This broad grouping included Socialists, some Communists who stayed with the POUM because of their support for the revolution, and a tiny group of Trotskyites.[39]

One of the most famous Britons to serve in the POUM who had no link with the ILP or its contingent of volunteers was John Cornford, a Communist. Cornford fitted, in many ways, the (far from accurate) stereotype of the British volunteer: that of the 'intellectual poet' who went to fight in Spain. He had attended a private school and then gone on to study at Cambridge University, joining the Communist Party in 1933. Cornford served with a POUM unit on the Aragon Front in August 1936, but, horrified by the chaos of the militias, he returned home. Later he joined the International Brigades and was killed at Lopera in December 1936.[40] An Irishman called Patrick Trench served with the POUM militia during the autumn of 1936 before being invalided home suffering from tuberculosis. By profession an artist, Patrick Trench had earlier been a correspondent in Spain for the *New Leader*. He arrived in Spain a Communist, but on his return to Ireland he became a Trotskyite. He was the brother of Chalmers Trench, who served in the International Brigades.[41] Other British and Irish volunteers who may have served in the POUM militia include Cook, Bill Peel, Sidney Silvert and John Smith.[42]

The only known British woman to fight in the POUM was the rather exotic Greville Texidor. She was a peripatetic writer, married to a Catalan and living in Catalonia when the Civil War broke out. She divorced her husband and went to the Front with her new partner. She fought firstly in the POUM militia and later transferred to the Anarchist forces. She eventually emigrated to New Zealand.[43]

After the suppression of the POUM many foreign volunteers were imprisoned. Others fled the country; some also joined the International Brigades.[44]

The POUM included women in their militia forces.[45] In the autumn of 1936 Louise Gomez, the wife of the POUM militant Julian Gorkin, raised a women's regiment. They wore blue uniforms with split skirts, like culottes. They were drilled by male officers in the Lenin Barracks in Barcelona and received instruction in the firing of a rifle and a machine gun, and their dismantling and re-assembly. The force numbered around five hundred. No mention is made of this force fighting at the Front so it is possible that it took part in security patrols in Barcelona instead.[46] Some foreign women served in the POUM as soldiers and as nurses. In the most famous case Mika Etchebehere commanded a POUM column on the Madrid Front.[47]

In the first campaign in Aragon in July 1936 the POUM supplied a column of 2,800-3,000 volunteers led by Jordi Arquer and Manuel Grossi.[48] This column was larger than any group other than the Anarchists; however only 1,200 column members were armed, and the column had no machine guns. A second POUM column of 1,500 volunteers was raised in the same month.[49] By June 1937 the major POUM unit on the Aragon, the 29th Division, had grown to 6,000 men at the Front with 2,000 in reserve. Orwell estimated that the POUM-controlled forces at the Front numbered 8,000-10,000 men.[50] Durgan estimates that over all Fronts the POUM controlled 9,000-10,000 in its militias in the period 1936-37;[51] however others put the total POUM militia forces at 5,000 by September 1936, with 3,000 serving on the Aragon Front.[52]

From July 1936 onwards the main military efforts of the POUM militia were on the Aragon Front. It was part of several militia columns from various political parties and groupings that set out to re-capture Zaragoza. The POUM militia advanced as far as Lecinena before it was ordered to halt and dig in on August 5th 1936. On the way to Lecinena the POUM captured Monzon, Barbastro, Barbagal, Sarinena, Granen, Robres and Alcubierre.[53] The POUM Column had the Anarchist Ascaso Column to the north of them on the Front line and the Communist PSUC Column to the south. In September 1936 the Fascists attacked Lecinena, and were repulsed but the POUM were angered that their requests for more ammunition were ignored. In the same month a POUM attack on Perdiguera failed with the loss of several militants. A second Fascist attack on Lecinena, spearheaded by Moroccan troops [54] and tanks,[55] was successful. By October 1936 Rovira was in charge of the POUM forces on the Aragon and a force of international volunteers had joined them.[56]

The POUM re-published Trotsky's Red Army manual and suggested this was the best way to organise the Republican forces: as a revolutionary Red Army consisting of workers only.[57] It was to be a workers' revolutionary army controlled by the workers' organisations. The POUM proposed the conscription of men aged 18-30 and the formation of non-party units, consisting only of workers and excluding any middle-class elements. Only those officers seen to be loyal in July 1936 would be given commands. Instead, thanks to its lack of political power, the POUM had to accept the formation of the new Republican Peoples' Army.[58] The POUM hierarchy instructed its militants to form soldiers' committees to attempt to retain control of the officers and commissars.[59]

By October 1936 the POUM had more arms than before, including a few machine guns, and were buying arms abroad using money confiscated from known Fascists.[60] In November POUM shock troops launched an unsuccessful attempt to capture the Manicomio, the former lunatic asylum on the outskirts of Huesca.[61] In January 1937, fighting alongside Anarchist troops, they secured a ridge above the villages of Apies and Lierta.[62] On January 23rd 1937 the POUM shock troops, supported again by Anarchist troops, failed in an attack in the direction of Vivel del Rio, when the PSUC Division refused to support them.[63] In March 1937 there was another unsuccessful attack on the Manicomio, possibly sabotaged by treachery from a pro-Fascist officer and a lack of promised air support.[64] Another attack by the POUM shock battalion against the Loma Verde ridge to the north of Huesca was repulsed.[65] There were some successful actions involving POUM forces. In April 1937 POUM forces advanced their frontlines one kilometre while under fire and in the same month they successfully took part in a trench raid at Ermita Salas where they captured useful military supplies.[66]

Some Anarchist and POUM troops temporarily left the Front during the 'May Days' events to help their comrades in Barcelona. However the majority of these were persuaded to return to the Front, thus preventing it being unmanned.[67] The POUM Commander, Rovira, took an escort of shock troops who were in reserve and together with Anarchist military commanders went to negotiate with Communist commanders. It was agreed that if the POUM and Anarchist headquarters were no longer surrounded then POUM members and Anarchists would return to the Front.[68] After the 'May Days' events the 29th Division (the main POUM force) remained on the Aragon Front and took part in an unsuccessful attack near Huesca in July. This was a diversionary attack to support a major attack by the Anarchists to cut off the Jaca road. The POUM forces captured a position called Loma de los Martires and held it for two days before being forced to retreat. The POUM were blamed for the failure of the attack, but they pointed to the lack of support from the Communists. After this the POUM 29th Division was disbanded, with the soldiers being mainly transferred to non-Communist units.[69] At the trial of the POUM in October 1938 the Communists accused the 29th Division of having a non-aggression pact with the Fascists and of leaving the Front during the 'May Days' events. The court dismissed these charges.[70]

The Aragon Front remained predominantly static from August 1936 to the end of the militias in June 1937. Although the enemy were outnumbered, they were entrenched and better armed and trained. Trenches on the Aragon Front were often hundreds of yards apart and could sometimes consist of only isolated strong points and fortified villages. On the other hand, trench systems could also be like First World War trenches and include barbed wire, trip wires to warn of surprise attacks, sand bagged positions with loop holes to fire through and bomb-proof shelters. Near Huesca the Nationalists even had concrete defences made by German engineers.

18. Front line in the Sierra de Alcubierre, 1936 to 1937.
(Fototeca, Diputación de Huesca)

As the campaign on the Aragon became a stalemate, conditions for the militia got worse. Food supplies consisted mainly of beans or arrived cold, and supplies of cigarettes ran short. Changes of clothing were rare; in winter this meant they stayed wet and damp, and in summer lice got into every part of the clothing and hence the body. Clothing turned to rags, boots rotted and rifles became dirty and useless. Hygiene was poor, with men defecating and relieving themselves in the trenches and there was little water to wash with. Men slept in the trenches and there was often a shortage of blankets under which to sleep and to keep out the cold.[71] When the POUM moved to the Alcubierre section of the Aragon Front they slept in caves lighted by home made oil lamps.[72]

Both Cornford and Orwell commented on the lack of military action. John Cornford's poem 'A Letter from Aragon' starts with the line:

"This is a quiet sector of a quiet front"

This line is repeated at intervals throughout the poem.[73] George Orwell wrote in February 1937:

"...nothing happened, nothing ever happened."[74]

19. Miliciano serving wine in a shelter in the
Sierra de Alcubierre, 1936 to 1937.
(Fototeca, Diputación de Huesca)

What activity there was on the Aragon Front involved small-scale actions aimed at taking an enemy village or a strongpoint, or a raid to gain information or supplies. On the Aragon Front the Fascists were unable to launch an offensive because they lacked manpower, whereas the militias were incapable of launching a successful offensive, because they were too disorganised and lacking in unity, training and arms. Instead the militias opted to defend the revolution behind the Frontline.[75]

20. Milicianos of the POUM and Macia Companys Column in the Sierra de Alcubierre, 1936 to 1937
(*Fototeca, Diputación de Huesca*)

21. Miliciano in the Sierra de Alcubierre, 1936 to 1937
(*Fototeca, Diputación de Huesca*)

22. Milicianos by the entrance to a shelter at a position in the Sierra de Alcubierre, 1936 to 1937.
(*Fototeca, Diputación de Huesca*)

There were POUM militia forces on other Fronts, as well as on the Aragon. On the Madrid Front the POUM had a motorised militia column commanded by the Argentine Trotskyite, Hipolito Etchebehere. After his death in combat his wife Mika commanded this unit. She led a POUM column that held Siguenza for a week against superior Fascist forces before it was forced to retreat.[76] The POUM column that took part in the defence of Madrid during the Nationalist assault in November 1936 was well supplied with arms; however, once the danger was over it was starved of arms and its political leaders were persecuted. The column was disbanded and its members joined an Anarchist militia column.[77] The POUM militia fought several actions on the Madrid Front on the Pozuelo sector, and at Pinar de Humera and at Cerro de Aguila. By February 1937 less than a hundred of the original POUM column in the Madrid area had survived.[78]

The POUM also had militia columns from the cities of Valencia and Castellon fighting around Teruel.[79] A POUM militia column of three hundred took part in the failed attack on Majorca in August to September 1936.[80] In the campaigns in the north of Spain, POUM militants fought in Anarchist units. A POUM member, Doctor Luis Jose Arenillas, was Head of the Medical Services of the Northern Republican forces and tried to continue resistance in Santander to the end, but was captured and hanged by the Fascist forces.[81]

As many as ten thousand men and women fought in the POUM militia on many Fronts, in particular on the Aragon Front. Several hundred foreign volunteers served in the POUM; many as part of an elite 'Shock Unit' which spearheaded most engagements in which the POUM were involved. Throughout this period the POUM lacked the arms and the training to launch any major offensive. The actions in which the POUM did take part were small, fairly insignificant events aimed at capturing a specific position or capturing enemy supplies. In the early days the POUM militia were highly motivated and most of its members were militants. Later, as its forces grew, politically motivated members became a minority and overall morale fell. Reports suggest that only a small number of POUM troops left the trenches during the 'May Days' events, so they did not endanger the Front. The impact of the POUM militia on the whole of the Civil War was minor, but by helping to hold the Aragon Front for a year it allowed the Republican Government and its Communist allies to build, arm and train a Regular Army, and to concentrate its strength around Madrid and repulse all efforts to conquer the capital.

Notes

[1] The main sources for this chapter are: George Orwell, *Homage to Catalonia: and Looking Back on the Spanish War* (London, Penguin, 1988), Christopher Hall, *Revolutionary Warfare: Spain 1936-37* (Pontefract, Gosling Press, 1996)

[2] Buenaventura Durruti (1896-1936). Leading Anarchist militant throughout the 1930's. In the Civil War he commanded the 'Durutti Column' of Anarchist militia men and women and was killed during the siege of Madrid in November 1936.

[3] Hall, op cit., p9-10, 16-18

[4] Ibid, p18-19

[5] Ibid, p19-21

[6] Ibid, p10-12

[7] Ibid, p12-15

[8] Ibid, p32-35

[9] Correspondence with Jim Carmody. Jim Carmody has done extensive research on British and Irish volunteers who served in Spain in the International Brigades and in the militias. The following are a list of volunteers he sent to me, along with some I have mentioned in this chapter. To go into details about these volunteers is out of the scope of this book, but would make an excellent companion volume to this work. The following British and Irish volunteers served in the militias:

Majorca campaign: Nat Cohen, Mike Milton or Wilton, Bill Peel, Lee Bradley, Richard Kisch, Tony Willis and Paul Boyle. Kisch was wounded in the campaign.

Those serving in other militia units included Edward Guerin (Anarchist Durutti Column), James Johns and James Ricketts (Basques). James Albrighton, Albert Bentley, Patrick Hill, William Hudson, Lloyd Jones, George Middleton (Anarchist, 'Muerte es Maestra' Column) and Samuel Rees (Anarchist, Iron Column). Frederick Walker claimed he served in the Communist 5th Regiment at Madrid. George Tioli in the 'Tom Mann' (named after a famous British Trade Unionist) Centuria in Barcelona. A person called Chambers was repatriated from Valencia in April 1937.

Richard Baxell, *British Volunteers in the Spanish Civil War: The British Battalion in the International Brigades, 1936-1939* (London, Routledge, 2004 and Warren & Pell, Abersychan, 2007), p49-52 (W & P p55-61) describes the actions of the 'Muerte es Maestra' Column and gives a fuller list of names of British and Irish Volunteers, these include the following not mentioned by Jim Carmody: John Beale, Bruce Campbell, Frank Garland,

Michael Harris, John Henderson, David McKenzie, Sidney Morton, Frank O'Connor, Patrick O'Malley and Benitzelos Zanettou. Of these men Lloyd Jones was killed in fighting around Madrid in October 1936 and Middleton and Bentley were killed in the defence of Madrid in November 1936. He also gives a full list of the actions and members of the 'Tom Mann' Centuria. These included: Sid Avner, Jack Barry, Lorimer Birch, Nat Cohen, Ray Cox, John Donovan (not the John Donovan who served in the ILP Contingent), Phil Gillan, Richard Kisch, David Marshall, Sam Masters, Bill Scott, Alex Sheller, Keith Watson, Tom Wintringham.

Ciaran Crossey, *No Pasaran: "We intend to show the World"* (Belfast, Belfast and District Trades Union Council, 2007), p14. States two Irish volunteers who served in Anarchist units, Jim Campbell and Jack White.

[10] Hall op cit., p35-36, 38
[11] Tom Buchanan, *The Impact of the Spanish Civil War on Britain: War, Loss and Memory* (Brighton, Sussex Academic Press, 2007) p47
[12] Hall op cit., p38-41
[13] Ibid, p42-45
[14] Orwell, op cit., p7-17, Christopher Hall, *'Disciplina Camaradas': Four English Volunteers in Spain 1936-39* (Pontefract, Gosling Press, 1994) p33-34
[15] Josep Rovira, Jordi Arquer and Manuel Grossi. See later chapters for details of the life of Rovira. Arquer was a member of the POUM Executive Committee, militia column leader and was sentenced to 11 years imprisonment in 1938. Before the Civil War Grossi had been condemned to death for his part in the Asturias miners armed uprising against the right wing government in 1934. He was a POUM militia commander during the Civil War.
[16] *Revolutionary History, The Spanish Civil War: the View from the Left* (London, Socialist Platform, 1992) p291, Andy Durgan, International Volunteers in the POUM Militias.
http://libcom.org/history/international-volunteers-poum-militias p2.
[17] *Revolutionary History*, op cit., p288, Durgan, op cit., p3
[18] Orwell, op cit., p190-191
[19] Durgan, op cit., p9, Pierre Broue and Emile Temime, *The Revolution and the Civil War in Spain* (London, Faber and Faber, 1970) p140
[20] Hall, *Revolutionary Warfare*, op cit., p42-43
[21] Ibid, p16, Orwell, op cit., p30
[22] Hall, Ibid, p46, Orwell, Ibid, p105
[23] Hall, Ibid, p19, Orwell, Ibid, p44
[24] Hall, Ibid, p20, Peter Stansky and William Abrahams, *Journey to the Frontier: Two Roads to the Spanish Civil War* (London, Constable, 1966) p339

[25] Orwell, op cit., p15
[26] Hall, *Revolutionary Warfare*, op cit., p10, Hall, *Disciplina Camaradas*, op cit., p34
[27] Hall, *Revolutionary Warfare*, Ibid, p14, Orwell, op cit., p73
[28] Bernard Crick, *George Orwell: a Life* (London, Secker and Warburg, 1981) fifth photograph between p130-131
[29] Orwell, op cit., p37, Hall, *Revolutionary Warfare*, op cit., p12
[30] Hall, *Revolutionary Warfare*, Ibid, p12, Hall, *Disciplina Camaradas*, op cit., p34
[31] Hall, *Revolutionary Warfare*, Ibid, p12, Hall, *Disciplina Camaradas*, Ibid, p71
[32] Orwell, op cit., p35, Hall, *Revolutionary Warfare*, Ibid, p13, *Revolutionary History*, op cit., p287
[33] Durgan, op cit., p2
[34] Orwell, op cit., p82, 87
[35] Durgan, op cit., p7
[36] Hall, *Revolutionary Warfare*, op cit., p34, Orwell, op cit., p74, 84-99
[37] Hall, *Revolutionary Warfare*, Ibid, p35, Mary Low and Juan Brea, *Red Spanish Notebook: the First Six Months of the Revolution and the Civil War* (San Francisco, City Lights Books, 1979) p69
[38] *Revolutionary History*, op cit., p296-297, Victor Alba and Stephen Schwartz, *Spanish Marxism Versus Soviet Communism: a History of the P.O.U.M.* (Oxford, Transaction Books, 1988) p242
[39] Alba and Schwartz, op cit., p124
[40] Stansky and Abrahams, op cit., p313-390
[41] Chalmers (Terry) Trench, *Nearly Ninety: Reminiscences* (Ballivor, Ireland, Hannon Press, 1996), p126-130
[42] Durgan, op cit., p19 (Cook). Antonio Diez, *Brigadas Internacionales. Cartas desde España* (Brenes, Muñoz Moya Editores, 2005), p69 cites a Manchester volunteer, Sidney Silvert who served with the POUM militias on the Aragon front from early 1937 and later in Catalonia near Tortosa. He transferred to the International Brigades in April 1937. Correspondence with Jim Carmody,(Peel), Peel was later killed in World War II at Dunkirk 1940, (John Smith, alias of Gopal Hudder) National Archives, Cat no. Kv/5/12 MI5 List of British Individuals who travelled to and from Spain 1936-39.
[43] Correspondence with Andy Durgan.
[44] Durgan, op cit., p12
[45] Orwell, op cit., p11
[46] Low and Brea, op cit., p186-190
[47] Durgan, op cit., p7, Alba and Schwartz, op cit., p285
[48] Alba and Schwartz, Ibid, p115, 150

[49] Ibid, p122
[50] Orwell, op cit., p63, 165
[51] Durgan, op cit., p2
[52] Broue and Temime, op cit., p141
[53] Alba and Schwartz, op cit., p151
[54] Moroccan Troops. Fierce native mercenary troops from the Spanish colony of Morocco. Elite troops in the Fascist Army and feared by Republican soldiers.
[55] Alba and Schwartz, op cit., p152-153
[56] Durgan, op cit., p6
[57] Alba and Schwartz, op cit., p154, Broue and Temime, op cit., p219
[58] Peoples Popular Army. New Republican Regular Army brought about by mixing up remnants of the old Regular Army with the militias and new conscripts. Based on the Russian Red Army.
[59] Durgan, op cit., p3
[60] Alba and Schwartz, op cit., p154
[61] Durgan, op cit., p6
[62] Ibid, p9
[63] Ibid, p9, Alba and Schwartz, op cit., p184
[64] Durgan, Ibid, p9, Orwell, op cit., p74
[65] Durgan, Ibid, p9
[66] Durgan, Ibid, p9, Orwell, op cit., p80, 84-99
[67] Alba and Schwartz, op cit., p197, Broue and Temime, op cit., p284
[68] Durgan, op cit., p10
[69] Ibid, p11, Alba and Schwartz, op cit., p242-243
[70] Alba and Schwartz, Ibid, p270-272
[71] Hall, *Revolutionary Warfare*, op cit., p28-30, Orwell, op cit., p18-104, 172-178, *Revolutionary History*, op cit., p285-286, 294
[72] Hall, *Disciplina Camaradas*, op cit., p47
[73] Stansky and Abrahams, op cit., p352
[74] Orwell, op cit., p71
[75] Hall, *Revolutionary Warfare*, op cit., p30
[76] Alba and Schwartz, op cit., p285
[77] Ibid, p162, Broue and Temime, op cit., p253-254
[78] Durgan, op cit., p7
[79] Ibid, p2
[80] Alba and Schwartz, op cit., p153
[81] Broue and Temime, op cit., p412

CHAPTER 7

The ILP Contingent

RIGHT FROM THE OUTBREAK of the Spanish Civil War in July 1936 the ILP was firmly committed to supporting the anti-Fascist Spanish Republican Government. Unlike other political groups in Britain the ILP channelled its support to its sister party in Spain, the revolutionary POUM. The ILP had always been a pacifist political party and had opposed both the Boer War and World War I, during which many of its members were imprisoned for their pacifist beliefs. The Parliamentary ILP leader, James Maxton, and the Head of the ILP, Fenner Brockway, were both imprisoned during World War I for opposing the war.

Support for the POUM included raising money, organising medical supplies and buying an ambulance; all of which could be seen as non-military assistance. But younger members of the ILP began to argue that pacifist views were no longer sufficient when faced with Fascism, and that, by supporting the Spanish Revolution and fighting with the POUM, they would be fighting a revolutionary war, rather than an imperialist one. Once the ILP National Administrative Council (NAC) had become convinced that sending a military unit would help the POUM the go-ahead was given to raise a volunteer unit. The ILP unit served on the Aragon Front from January to April 1937. After the 'May Days' events a reduced ILP Contingent served on the Aragon Front again until the end of May 1937, with the odd individual staying at the front until the POUM military forces were forcibly disbanded in July 1937.

I have used the ILP newspaper the *New Leader* as a major source of information about the Contingent and its time in Spain. It should be borne in mind that this newspaper was clearly partisan and at times exaggerated the role of the volunteers. The other major source I have used for information about the ILP Contingent is an article by Peter Thwaites.[1]

In November 1936 Bob Edwards, who had been in Spain with the 'Maurin' ambulance, put before the NAC his proposals to raise a military unit to fight in Spain with the POUM. After some discussion the NAC was in agreement with him and so he was told to organise the raising of volunteers to fight in this unit. A lead article in the *New Leader* on December 4th 1936 stated that it was the duty of workers around the world to defend the Spanish Revolution and it called for the raising of a military unit, appealing for volunteers. In late December and early January advertisements for volunteers appeared in the *New Leader*.

The first advertisement was headed 'Volunteers for Spain'. It said that Bob Edwards, the ILP Lancashire representative on the NAC, was organising the raising of a Contingent for Spain. Volunteers were to send full particulars to the ILP at 35 St Bride Street, London.[2] The second advertisement, entitled 'Off to Spain', stated that an ILP Contingent was ready to leave for Spain in a few days. Volunteers could still apply to join the Contingent but were asked to give the following details to the ILP Head Office in London: their experience, age, health, dependents etc and to supply political references.[3] In the final advertisement, 'Away to Spain', potential volunteers were told that the Contingent was leaving that week but that new volunteers could join the Contingent in Spain. They were asked to send their details as before. Those volunteers who could afford it were even expected to contribute towards the cost of getting themselves to Spain.[4]

23. ILP volunteers leaving London. *(NL)*

24. ILP contingent at Victoria Station enroute to Spain.
(Courtesy of A. Potts)

The ILP Contingent left for Spain from Newhaven on January 10th 1937, not without a little theatrics from the police. It was suspected that a CID officer kept Bob Edwards, the leader of the ILP Contingent, under constant surveillance all the way down from Lancashire to London. Plainclothes policemen regularly walked past the ILP Head Office, scrutinising faces, while Special Branch watched the ILP Head Office from a building across the road. It was alleged that members of Special Branch regularly visited the ILP bookshop and bought its literature and even tried to join the 'Left Book Club'[5] at 10.30pm. (This was against the law since shops were not allowed to be open in the evening.) Fenner Brockway even rang the Head of the Political Department of Scotland Yard to ask if he could invite the detectives for tea. The police chief claimed to have no idea that his men were there, but if they were he had no problems with them having tea. The invitation was then put to the detectives, who referred it to their Superior. Half an hour later they disappeared.

A mystery caller told Brockway and Edwards that the border between France and Spain was closed. They checked this 'information' with comrades in France and found it to be false. The passport authorities used minor technicalities to try and delay the Contingent's departure from Britain. Three detectives even tried to join the ILP Contingent to get information but were spotted and ejected from the

Contingent. Brockway received a call from a Scottish 'volunteer' whom he recognised as a detective, asking when the volunteers were leaving the country. Brockway lied to him, saying the Contingent was leaving on the Sunday night boat train. It was then decided that they would leave on Sunday morning. This was so sudden that one Scottish volunteer only just managed to board the train in the nick of time as it was leaving Victoria Station.

The first group of approximately twenty five volunteers were to be the vanguard of a larger force; but the day before they left the country, the British Government made it illegal to volunteer to fight in a foreign war by enforcing the 'Foreign Enlistment Act' of 1870. Since it was now illegal to fight in Spain the ILP suspended its recruiting. The Contingent reached Paris here they were supported by French Socialists of the 'London Bureau', who arranged train travel to Perpignan. There the Contingent met representatives of the POUM who gave them their papers and took them by road to Figueras and on to Barcelona, where they arrived on Tuesday January 12th 1937.[6]

Once in Barcelona the ILP Contingent were welcomed by the POUM and then taken to the Lenin Barracks, a former cavalry regiment barracks, to begin their military training. This training proved to be very basic and involved mainly 'square bashing' - marching up and down. This proved to be of little use when they actually reached the front line. The ILP Contingent chose three of its members as trainers. One taught marching, another lectured on the use of rifles, machine guns and Lewis Guns (a type of machine gun) and the third taught how to handle and aim a rifle. The training lasted less than two weeks before the Contingent left Barcelona on January 20th 1937. A POUM band played revolutionary songs and crowds cheered as the Contingent marched to the station where a slow train took them to Lerida. At Lerida they were fed and given another rousing send-off by a cheering crowd. They travelled by train to Barbastro and then by motor coach to the Front at Alcubierre.[7]

The first volunteers were mostly ILP members and single men, as the party had stipulated that only unmarried men could volunteer. However this was not strictly enforced – Bob Edwards was himself married and some volunteers simply lied. Some volunteers were viewed as too politically unreliable to join the International Brigades and had been rejected by the Communists and so joined the ILP Contingent. Some had applied for both and found that the ILP had processed their request quicker. Even some non-political types joined the Contingent, including an army deserter.[8]

Bob Edwards, the Contingent leader, describes the Contingent in the *New Leader* as:

> "...twenty five good fighting men; with one or two exceptions... have exceptionally good qualifications."[9]

It is unclear whether he meant 'qualifications' in the military or political sense; one suspects he meant the latter.

The volunteers came from all over Britain: Glasgow, London, Bristol, Manchester, Portsmouth, Aberdeen, Llanelli and many other places.[10] There were miners from South Wales, volunteers from Lancashire and even a Scotsman who was an ex-amateur boxing champion of Scotland and stood over six feet tall. Most of the Contingent were members of the ILP, although there were a few Communist and Labour Party members and one or two volunteers had no political links to any party.[11] A small number had fought in World War I or served in the British Army in peace time or with the Irish Free State Army, and there were some ex-grammar or public school boys with OTC (Officer Training Corps) experience. Many of the volunteers were young and several held anti-military or pacifist convictions, so it is likely the majority of the Contingent had no —military experience at all.[12]

A photograph in the *New Leader* of February 5th 1937 shows the ILP Contingent on parade at the Lenin Barracks before leaving for the Front. It shows they had no formal uniform and wore similar clothes to the other militia members, but with the addition of leather boots, which promptly fell apart during their stay at the Front (see page108).

Some of the volunteers would later swap their boots for militia footwear such as the alpargatas (a type of canvas shoe). The volunteers are shown wearing woollen hats, some with a POUM badge or hammer and sickle, some without, and red scarves. Some wore a zipped jacket of wool or leather, others a checked jacket or thick cotton shirt, worn with corduroy trousers or 'granaderos' which looked similar to riding breeches. The 'uniform' was finished with puttees (strapping worn around the lower leg) and ex-Spanish Army belts, straps and pouches.[13] Once the ILP Contingent had arrived at the Front there were no reserve supplies of clothing and equipment, and so they became a fairly ragged-looking unit in a short time. Any replacement equipment came from home, or was got at the Front from the enemy or other units, or was bought in Barcelona when volunteers were on leave.[14]

25. ILP Contingent in Lenin Barracks. *(NL)*

Decent weapons suitable for trench warfare were in short supply. The ILP volunteers had few, if any pistols; no wire cutters, torches, field glasses or anything similar, nor did they possess tin helmets. Rifles were only given out when the volunteers reached the Front, and most of these were old and of doubtful use. The most common rifle was the 1896 Mauser; other rifles included Winchesters and Mauser cavalry carbines. Each man was issued with 50 rounds of poor quality ammunition which they were expected to use sparingly, and a few home made grenades, often more dangerous to the thrower than to the enemy. One hostile eye-witness states that they were told on their first night in the

26. Part of the ILP Contingent *(left)* and the ILP Soldiers' Committee *(right)*. *(NL)*

trenches to stop firing at the enemy in case they 'provoked them'. This eye-witness believes that this was because there was a non-aggression agreement between the two sides, but it could also equally be explained by having a limited supply of ammunition. There was no gun oil and few ramrods to keep rifles in good condition.[15]

From March 1937 the Contingent's weapons improved slightly and included a metal helmet, bayonet, more bombs and one hundred and fifty rounds of ammunition. Officers seem to have had access to a field telephone.[16] Small quantities of Russian equipment seem to have reached the Front, including Russian 75mm guns. The occasional Russian aeroplane was seen raiding enemy lines.[17] When the Contingent went on leave in April 1937 they left their rifles at the Front for their replacements to use, which suggests that these replacement troops had no rifles themselves.[18]

The POUM had its own hospitals near the Front and a sanatorium in Barcelona with its own nurses and doctors. These included foreign volunteers. An American doctor called Louis Levin accompanied the ILP Contingent when they left Britain on January 10th 1937.[19] Two members of the ILP Contingent acted as stretcher-bearers-cum-First-Aiders with enough basic knowledge and skills to treat wounds, and another volunteer worked with Doctor Levin.[20] Another Contingent volunteer talks about the Red Cross tending the wounded in 'No Man's Land' during a ceasefire, although whether this was the actual Red Cross or medical staff/First Aiders from both sides wearing Red Cross armbands to retrieve the wounded is unknown.[21]

When the ILP Contingent reached the Aragon Front the situation was one of stalemate. During the training in the Lenin Barracks the Contingent had been reinforced by three Britons who were already in Spain, a Spaniard and two Americans. At the Lenin Barracks the POUM agreed with the wishes of the ILP leadership that they form a separate unit. Bob Edwards, the ILP Contingent's leader, explained the advantages of this:

> "It is much better...that our boys should train and fight together. As a homogeneous body of English-speaking comrades, they will be able to pull their weight, whereas, if they are disseminated among our Spanish comrades, they will not be anything like so effective."[22]

The ILP Contingent, now numbering approximately thirty men, formed a Section in a Centuria of a hundred men commanded by the

Belgian volunteer Georges Kopp. A dozen Spanish machine gunners armed with a Hotchkiss heavy machine gun were attached to the Centuria. At times on the Aragon Front the ILP volunteers went into action with other units and later had Spanish men in their section, but mostly they formed their own self-contained unit. During its time in Spain the ILP unit was reinforced by individual British and Irish volunteers; in all, around forty men served in the ILP Contingent (see full list of volunteers further on in the chapter for details).

On February 3rd 1937 they took up position in a mountainous region near Zaragoza called Mount Oscuro. Here there were no continuous trench systems but strong points dug into the mountains at around three thousand feet. The ILP occupied three positions about one hundred yards apart connected by communication trenches, and around two to four hundreds yards from the enemy. The enemy were above them and dug in. Life for the ILP volunteers consisted of strengthening their own positions and scavenging for food and fuel. They suffered constantly from lice and rats, and the cold weather. What military action there was consisted of sniping, odd patrols and shouting propaganda at the enemy in the hope that it would encourage them to desert to the Republican side.[23] At nights the Contingent slept in nearby caves using oil lamps made out of old sardine tins and a wick.[24]

On one occasion the Contingent was subjected to artillery fire, bombing and machine gun fire for two hours in darkness and in appalling weather conditions. The Spanish machine gunners replied to the enemy firing while the Contingent stood in the trenches with rifles at the ready. After two hours the enemy firing stopped and patrols showed no enemy troops had advanced. Only one of the Contingent was injured, breaking an ankle. It was apparent that during the attack the Contingent did not panic and held its nerve.[25]

Within four days of the Contingent's taking up their positions on Mount Oscuro (called 'Black Mountain' by the local people) sixteen enemy soldiers deserted to the Contingent and a young Spanish militia boy was killed by enemy shelling. According to a partisan source, as many as a hundred Spanish enemy troops deserted to the ILP/ POUM forces in their sector; however, a hostile eye-witness source claims he never saw any enemy troops desert to the ILP force. The Contingent were involved in four activities: holding the line, building a road, creating a large dug-out so the Contingent could debate and talk in safety and training for an advance. The leader of the Contingent, Bob Edwards, requested that *New Leader* readers write letters to the volunteers and send woolly clothing to help combat the cold. He also called for more volunteers, while the editor asked for funds for medical supplies.[26] On a cold front the POUM militia and the ILP Contingent lacked blankets for sleeping and greatcoats to keep warm, although one Contingent member mentions a waterproof garment worn like a poncho, which kept him warm.[27]

The Contingent was organised along militia lines rather than that of a regular military unit. Leaders carried no outward sign of rank and were not saluted. Pay was the same, regardless of rank, although it seems the Contingent were rarely, if at all, paid. Eileen Blair, Orwell's then wife working in the Barcelona ILP office, ended up buying things that the Contingent members needed.[28] Military orders were discussed and, in theory, could be disobeyed. From contemporary accounts it seems discipline was generally good in the Contingent, although when they first arrived in Barcelona there was some acts of drunkenness and maybe some volunteers visited brothels and on at least one occasion volunteers took unauthorised leave from the Front. A hostile eye-witness source claims that one volunteer disobeyed an order, was disarmed and then deserted from the ILP Contingent and joined another unit.[29] But in general insubordination or disobeying of orders seems to have occurred rarely if at all, possibly because they were discussed first.[30]

Bob Edwards was the leader of the Contingent and was given the rank of Captain by the POUM although he had no military experience at all. One hostile eye-witness account claims the first leader of the ILP Contingent was W. B. Martin, who had earlier driven an ambulance to Spain and had stayed in Spain to command a militia artillery unit, because of his World War I military experience (see chapter 5). He was removed from his command, allegedly for being drunk on the way to the Front, and replaced by Bob Edwards. Possibly because of Edwards's lack of military experience the NCOs were chosen more for their military experience than political convictions. One NCO proved not to be suited to the task and was voted out of his rank by the other Contingent members. The Contingent also had an elected Commissar who seems to have been chosen more on his ability to communicate with the Catalans in the Centuria and Battalion than for any other reason. Although on arrival in Barcelona the ILP Contingent were assigned an English-speaking POUM member to help with communications, it seems he did not go to the Front with them. It seems the role of Commissar in the ILP Contingent was more of a liaison role than a political role, as it was in the International Brigades. There was also an elected five man political committee whose job was to "regulate the affairs of the Contingent".[31] The Soldiers' Council was first set up when the Contingent arrived in Barcelona and a new Soldiers' Committee was formed after Bob Edwards, who was a member, returned to Britain for an ILP conference in March 1937.[32] Major decisions were taken by the entire Contingent in council, although it seems that only the Contingent leader and the NCOs made the more mundane, day-to-day decisions.[33]

Two members of the Contingent, Stafford Cottman and Bob Smillie, describe in a *New Leader* article the organisation of the ILP Contingent as they saw it:

> "In the ILP British Section fighting on the Aragon front with the POUM militia we have a military leader, a political leader, four officers and a political committee, all elected by ourselves, responsible to us and in constant contact with the Military Committee of the sector. This co-ordination between what are known in the British Army as 'officers' and men is of great value to the morale and welfare of the militia. Operations are carried out efficiently and thoroughly without any officiousness or domineering, the orders being given quickly, and the common knowledge and acceptance of discipline aiding the spirit of all. Officers have no particular uniform."[34]

(The 'officers' mentioned here by the two authors are likely to be NCOs.)

Due to the quiet nature of this particular Front the inexperience of the volunteers and lack of formal military training did not prove a severe handicap. The Contingent seems to have reacted well when under fire and artillery bombardment, and took part willingly in patrols and sniping at the enemy.[35] They got on well with their assigned Spanish machine gunners and morale was generally good. Food rations were not well liked and included a thin soup, artichokes, rice and sardines and stale bread, although the coffee was better received.[36] With plenty of time on their hands the Contingent members often spoke about politics. Although there were political differences between the volunteers there seem not to have been any major disagreements. Generally the Contingent seems to have been a well-motivated and cohesive unit, although there were some tensions.[37]

Some members found Eric Blair, better known as George Orwell, a snob and thought he despised the working classes. Orwell himself states he use to laugh at the political arguments, which would not have endeared him to some of the other volunteers.[38] Many members were becoming frustrated with the quiet of the Aragon front and some wished to join the International Brigades around Madrid. The lack of action at the Front was affecting the morale of the Contingent. John McNair, the ILP representative in Barcelona, commented in April 1937:

"...I noticed the boys were getting restless at the inactivity and I did what I could to calm them."[39]

Orwell more ironically comments:

"Meanwhile nothing happened, nothing ever happened. The English had got into the habit of saying that this wasn't war, it was a bloody pantomime."[40]

This led to political arguments. Many of the Contingent believed in the POUM philosophy of winning the war by defending the revolution. They saw the desire to join the International Brigades as support of the Communist attitude of winning the war first and then thinking about the revolution.[41] Walter Tapsell the British Battalion Commissar (hardly an un-biased source) in his meetings with some of the ILP Contingent members lists five complaints of the volunteers:

- Lack of activity in their section of the Front.
- Poor quality and always the same food.
- The lack of tobacco.
- Rigid censorship of any letters home and few parcels from home ever reached the Front.
- The only British newspaper available to read was the ILP *New Leader.*

These complaints are hardly mutinous, the first three complaints are almost certainly the same for any soldiers involved in boring trench warfare. The last two were mirrored in the International Brigades letters home were censored, parcels from home often did not arrive and the *Daily Worker* was the main newspaper supplied to the British Battalion. Tapsell's list of complaints as aired by members of the ILP Contingent hardly shows a force in open revolt. In addition he listed those ILP volunteers who wished to leave the POUM militia, those in hospital, those who supported the revolution and those who had left the unit.[42]

In mid February 1937 the ILP Contingent was moved to another part of the Front near a farmhouse a mile and a half from the enemy held town of Huesca. The terrain here was flatter but there was more military action.[43] The Contingent were in positions about five hundred yards from the enemy positions guarding the Huesca to Zaragosa road. Above their sandbagged position flew a flag which read 'ILP Seccion Inglesa, POUM' ('ILP English Section, POUM') with a hammer and sickle in the corner. No colours are mentioned but it is likely that the flag was red with the lettering and hammer and sickle in white. Each day at 12.00am the enemy fired high explosive shells at the Contingent's position. Whether deliberately or by chance, the shelling was aimed at the area where the midday meals were cooked. In reply the Republican artillery fire caused little damage.[44]

While the Contingent was fighting on this Front, Bob Edwards left for Britain to attend the ILP conference and Eric Blair took over as Contingent leader.[45]

Having had only one man injured while in the mountains the Contingent suffered more casualties on this Front. An enemy sniper wounded one man and enemy shelling injured another.[46] During their time on the Huesca front the Contingent were bombed by Italian aeroplanes coming over from their base on Majorca.[47] In April the Contingent took part in an advance that pushed the line a thousand yards further forward in support of an Anarchist attack on the Jaca Road. The Front line was successfully moved forward a thousand yards but one member of the Contingent was wounded as a result.[48] On April 13th 1937 the ILP supplied fifteen volunteers for a night attack on the enemy trenches at Ermita Salas. For a time the Contingent volunteers and a similar number of Spanish volunteers captured and held a section of enemy trenches before they were forced to retire, but they returned with some valuable military equipment. The Contingent fought bravely and a further four volunteers were wounded in this action. In late April the Contingent was pulled out of the Lines and were sent on leave to rest in Barcelona.[49]

The night attack by the ILP Contingent was its major military action in Spain and is described in detail in the *New Leader* and by George Orwell in *Homage to Catalonia*. At 1.45am the fifteen ILP volunteers were given grenades and ordered to move quietly into 'No Man's Land'. The weather was poor: it was raining heavily and blowing a gale. The plan was for the Contingent, together with an equal number of Spanish volunteers, to attack an enemy position that dominated their lines. They advanced in single file in poor visibility and proceeded to cut the enemy barbed wire entanglements. They were spotted at thirty yards, shot at and responded by throwing their grenades. All hell broke loose, including machine gun fire, rifle fire and exploding grenades, but when the ILP Contingent and allies charged the enemy abandoned their position, leaving behind two dead. The Contingent then fortified the position they had captured and exchanged fire with the enemy, who were advancing in strength. The ground over which they had advanced was waterlogged and as a result almost a third of their rifles were clogged with mud and could not be used. They had also run out of grenades. The Contingent shouted, 'POUM' loudly to make it seem there were more men than there really were, and to attract help. They were reinforced by POUM 'shock troops' comprising three Germans and one Spaniard. But they were now being shot at on all sides by the enemy. After an hour they were forced to retreat to their own lines, taking two thousand rounds of ammunition and some enemy grenades, but unfortunately leaving behind a telescope, which would have been a useful addition to their meagre military equipment.[50]

After this action the weather at the Front got hotter and two Contingent members caught sunstroke having worked stripped to the waist moving sandbags.[51] Having spent a hundred days at the Front the Contingent members were given leave in Barcelona where they were hoping for a few days rest. However they became embroiled in the 'May Days' events.[52] Members of the Contingent were armed and took part in guarding several buildings held by the POUM for a few days. Only one ILP volunteer claimed to have been involved in any armed clashes during the fighting.[53] Before the 'May Days' some of the ILP volunteers had been interested in joining the British Battalion of the International Brigades or other Republican units. After the 'May Days' events and the accusations made that the POUM were Fascist traitors only one member of the Contingent volunteers joined the International Brigades at this time.[54] In the *New Leader* of April 2nd 1937 it was claimed that the ILP Contingent volunteered to go to the Madrid Front on its arrival in Spain but were instead sent to the Aragon Front.[55]

But the 'May Days' signalled the beginning of the end of the ILP Contingent. Some of the volunteers went home, having only signed on for three months. Some volunteers joined non-POUM units and the rest returned to the Front where the gaps in the Contingent were filled with Spaniards. The remaining Contingent members returned to the Front on May 10th just outside Huesca. Thanks to losses, men returning home and joining other units the Contingent was down to about half its original strength. Within ten days of returning to the Front the Contingent leader was wounded and joined two Contingent members still recovering from wounds and another volunteer who was in hospital with suspected tuberculosis.[56]

On June 16th 1937 the Spanish Government declared the POUM illegal, putting members of the ILP Contingent in great danger. One member was imprisoned at the border trying to return home for a propaganda trip and later died in prison. The remaining members of the Contingent and the office staff in Barcelona left Spain in secret and most of those who managed to escape imprisonment were home by August 1937. Most of the others returned home over the next six months, although some volunteers did not return until the last months of the civil war and another volunteer was killed fighting in an Anarchist unit. After the 'May Days' events and then the suppression of the POUM several volunteers left the ILP Contingent to join other Republican units and the International Brigades. While serving in these units many of the volunteers were wounded or taken ill and one man became a prisoner of war.[57] The ILP NAC made "considerable efforts" to get its volunteers home and allocated £150 in June 1937 to fund these efforts.[58] On returning home the volunteers were given a small amount of money until they could find work. At the ILP 1937 Summer School some of the volunteers were guests of honour. Back in Britain there was controversy when one member of the Contingent claimed there was fraternisation between the POUM and the Fascist soldiers. This was strongly refuted by fifteen of his comrades.[59]

There is no definitive list of volunteers who served in the ILP Contingent and not all members of the Contingent are known by name.

The following are known members of the ILP Contingent. Those with no reference by their name were those volunteers remembered by volunteer Stafford Cottman and related to Peter Thwaites:[60]

Commander in Chief POUM 29th Division
(the ILP Contingent were part of this Division)
Josep Rovira (Spanish)[61]

Battalion Commander
(the ILP Contingent were part of this Battalion; a Battalion is around 500-750)
Gregorio Jorge (Spanish) [62]

Centuria/Company Commander
(the ILP Contingent formed a section of this unit)
Georges Kopp (Belgian) [63]

Second in Command of the Centuria/Company
Benjamin Levinski (Polish) [64]

Commander of ILP Contingent
Bob Edwards

Commissar and an NCO
Eric Blair (George Orwell)

NCOs
Bill Chambers
John 'Paddy' Donovan
Buck Parker

British and Irish ILP militia men
John Agnew
Lewis Ernest Avory [65]
William Bennett [66]
John Braithwaite
Archie Buttonshaw (American)/ (Harvey Buttonshaw, Australian) (Probably British) [67]
Les Castle [68]
William Clarke [69]
Arthur Clinton
Tom Coles
Jock Connor [70]
Stafford Cottman
Charles Doran
Evans [71]
James Farrell [72]
Frank Frankford

George Gross
Reg Hiddlestone
Philip Hunter
Uriah Jones
Julius [73]
Charles Justesen
Robert MacDonald [74]
Hugh McNeil
Douglas Moyle
Patrick O'Hara (First Aid) [75]
John Ritchie
Bob Smillie
John Milnes Alan Smith [76]
'Tanky' (James Arthur Cope) [77]
Harry P. Thomas [78]
Douglas Thompson
Harry Webb (First Aid/stretcher bearer) [79]
David Wickes (Medical Assistant) [80]
Bob Williams
Mike Wilton

Foreign Volunteers in the ILP Contingent and Medical Personnel
Louis Levin (Doctor) [81]
Martin W.B. [82]
Harry Milton (American)/ (Wolf Kupinsky) [83]
Ramon (Spanish) [84]
Douglas Clark Stearns [85]
Sybil Wingate [86]

The volunteers who served in the ILP Contingent have been criticised politically for supporting the POUM and undermining the Republican war effort, and militarily for serving on a quiet Front and achieving little. If compared to the experiences of those who served in the British Battalion of the International Brigades, the role of the ILP Contingent was indeed minor. But are there any similarities between the two forces? Approximately 2,300 British, Irish and Commonwealth volunteers served in the International Brigades, who numbered between 35,000 and 60,000 men.[87] British, Irish and Commonwealth volunteers comprised approximately 4%-7% of the total International

Brigades forces. The ILP British and Irish volunteers numbered around forty men out of a POUM force on the Aragon of around 5,000 men, less than 1% of the total.

Most of the members of the British Battalion belonged to the Communist Party or YCL (Young Communist League);[88] similarly most members of the ILP Contingent belonged to the Independent Labour Party or supported the Spanish Revolution.

Most members of the British Battalion were under thirty years of age with the most common age being twenty-two [89] similarly, with its insistence on unmarried men, most ILP Contingent volunteers were also under thirty years of age. The majority of volunteers for the British Battalion came from large cities;[90] this was also the case with the ILP volunteers. In the British Battalion most volunteers were working-class recruits with manual or semi-skilled jobs and were trade unionists;[91] this was true of the ILP Contingent.

Those with previous military experience were in the minority in the British Battalion. Out of six hundred known records of British and Irish volunteers who fought in the British Battalion less than half recorded stated they had previous military experience.[92] Similarly ten ILP men had previous military experience, forming around a quarter of the Contingent.[93] Those who fought in the International Brigades fought in nearly every major battle of the Spanish Civil War suffering heavy losses in the process: in the British Battalion most volunteers were wounded and over 20% were killed.[94] Of the forty or so British and Irish ILP volunteers, two men were killed and up to fifteen were wounded or hospitalised while in Spain [95] This equates to over a third of the Contingent dying, being wounded or hospitalised while in Spain. The contribution of the ILP volunteers is recognised in the most recent work on the ILP in the 1930's:

> "Thus, despite the limited military role of the Contingent, a number of its members were injured during the Spanish Civil War. This effort signified for many the attitude of complete and unqualified commitment of the ILP towards the war during its early phase." [96]

Around forty volunteers organised by the ILP served in Spain from January 1937. They served on the Aragon Front until late April 1937, a period of over a hundred days without relief. They were poorly trained, armed and clothed. Most volunteers at the Front suffered from lice infestation, cold, bland food and poor conditions of trench warfare. In action and under fire the Contingent seem to have performed adequately and its general morale and discipline seems to have been high, although morale was lowered by boredom caused by inaction. After the 'May Days' events some members went home, others joined non-POUM units, while others returned to the Front; but after the POUM was declared illegal all Contingent members in the 29th Division left for home to avoid imprisonment. Around a third of the ILP Contingent members were killed or wounded in Spain, showing the commitment of the ILP volunteers to the Anti-Fascist cause and refuting the argument that they did nothing during their time in Spain.

Notes

[1] Peter Thwaites, The Independent Labour Party Contingent in the Spanish Civil War, *Imperial War Museum Review*, 1987, p50-61
[2] NL 25.12.36
[3] NL 01.01.37
[4] NL 08.01.37, Thwaites, op cit., p52-53
[5] Left Book Club. Began in May 1936 and lasted until 1948. At its height in 1939 it had 57,000 members. Each month members received a left wing book and a journal. Hundreds of thousands of working-class men and women were able though the LBC to read left wing books written by leading politicians and theorists of the day. Several titles were written about the Spanish Civil War.National Archives, KV/5/12 MI5 records of individual's from Britain going and returning from Spain 1936-39, Spanish Revolution, Vol 2, No 2, February 3rd 1937, http://contendm.warwick.ac.uk/cdm/compoundobject/collection/scw/id/7116/rec/2
[6] NL 15.01.37, Thwaites, op cit., p53-54, Fenner Brockway, *Inside the Left: Thirty Years of Platform, Press, Prison and Parliament* (London, George Allen and Unwin, 1942) p298. Richard Baxell, *British Volunteers in the Spanish Civil War: The British Battalion in the International Brigades, 1936-1939* (London, Routledge, 2004, p5, National Archives, op cit, Spanish Revolution, op cit.
[7] NL 22.01.37, NL 29.01.37, Thwaites, Ibid, p54, Christopher Hall, *'Disciplina Camaradas': Four English Volunteers in Spain 1936-39* (Pontefract, Gosling Press, 1994) p33-34
[8] Hall, op cit., p28,75 , Bernard Crick, *George Orwell: A Life* (London, Secker and Warburg, 1981) p208, Spanish Revolution, op cit.
[9] NL 15.01.37

[10] NL 15.01.37
[11] Hall, op cit., p75, George Orwell, *Homage to Catalonia: And Looking Back on the Spanish War* (London, Penguin, 1988) p57. ILP volunteer Stafford Cottman in his interview for the Imperial War Museum describes the different volunteers as 'a mixed bunch' some: 'booksy', 'political activists' (of all left wing persuasions), some'discontented individuals', 'some workers', 'some intellectuals' some 'a little off-beat'. Stafford Cottman IWM 9278/7, Spanish Revolution, op cit.
[12] NL 15.01.37, Thwaites, op cit., p53-54, Hall, Ibid, p75, Sonia Orwell and Ian Angus (editors), *The Collected Essays and Letters of George Orwell: Volume 1: An Age Like This 1920-1940* (London, Penguin, 1970) p362, Marx Memorial Library, International Brigade Archive, Box C 13/12, John Donovan letter 27.05.37
[13] NL 05.02.37
[14] Thwaites, op cit., p54, Orwell op cit., p12, Hall, op cit., p81
[15] Thwaites, Ibid, p54, Orwell, Ibid, p20, 35-36, Hall, Ibid, p34, 71. Marx Memorial Library, International Brigade Achive, Box c 13/12 H.P. Thomas letter
[16] Orwell, Ibid, p73, 82
[17] Ibid, p83
[18] Ibid, p104
[19] Ibid, p117, John McNair, *Spanish Diary* (Stockport, Independent Labour Publications, ND) p16-17. Spanish Revolution, op cit.
[20] Orwell, op cit., p178. Author correspondence with Richard Baxell
[21] Hall, op cit., p99
[22] Thwaites, op cit., p54, 60. Thwaites guesses the two Americans were Milton and Buttonshaw. Milton was American, Buttonshaw may have been Australian but more probably he was British and joined the ILP Contingent in London (see chapter 9). Other American volunteers who served in the ILP Contingent included Stearns, and possibly Justesen, correspondence with Jim Carmody. Spanish Revolution, op cit.
[23] Ibid, p55, NL 12.02.37, Orwell, op cit., p38-39, 42-43, 74-75, Hall, op cit., p47
[24] Hall, Ibid, p47
[25] NL 26.02.37, Orwell, op cit., p43-44
[26] NL 19.02.37. Thomas letter, op cit., We Carry on: Our Tribute to Bob Smillie. http://contentdm.warwick.ac.uk/cdm/compoundobject/collection/scw/id/12169/rec/1
[27] Orwell, op cit., p12, 31, Hall, op cit., p34
[28] Peter Davison (editor), *Orwell in Spain: The Full Text of Homage to Catalonia with Associated Articles, Reviews and Letters from The Complete Works of George Orwell* (London, Penguin, 2001) p10

[29] Daniel Gray, *Homage to Caledonia: Scotland and the Spanish Civil War* (Luath Press, Edinburgh, 2008) p78, Imperial War Museum, interview with Frank Frankford IWM 9308/5, M.M.L. Thomas letter, op cit.
[30] Hall, op cit., p81
[31] Thwaites, op cit., p55, Orwell, op cit., p29. Spanish Revolution,op cit., MML Thomas letter, op cit., most likely it was Chambers who was the NCO removed from office.
[32] NL 23.04.37
[33] Hall, op cit., p74, Thwaites, op cit., p55
[34] NL 25.06.37
[35] NL 19.02.37
[36] Hall, op cit., p47
[37] NL 05.03.37, Thwaites, op cit., p55-56
[38] Orwell, op cit., p66
[39] McNair, op cit., p22
[40] Orwell, op cit., p71
[41] Thwaites, op cit., p55-56, Orwell, Ibid, p66, 70
[42] Marx Memorial Library, International Brigade Archive, Box C 13/7a 'Report on the English Section of the POUM'.
[43] Thwaites, op cit., p56, Orwell, op cit., p45
[44] NL 05.03.37
[45] Thwaites, op cit., p56
[46] Orwell, op cit., p71
[47] Hall, op cit., p47
[48] Orwell, op cit., p80-81
[49] Thwaites, op cit., p56, NL 26.03.37, NL 23.04.37, Orwell, Ibid, p104
[50] NL 30.04.37, Orwell, Ibid, p84-99
[51] Orwell, Ibid, p100
[52] Ibid, p116-143
[53] Gidon Cohen, *The Failure of a Dream: The Independent Labour Party from Disaffiliation to World War II* (London, Tauris, 2007) p183. Although a volunteer called Buttonshaw claims he shot at the Communists during the 'May Days' events, see chapter 9 for details.
[54] Richard Baxell, *The Unlikely Warriors: The British in the Spanish Civil War and the struggle against Fascism* (London, Aurum Press, 2012), p191, Thwaites, op cit., p57; NL11.06.37; South Wales Coalfield Collection, Urias Jones interview, (09.10.74), AUD/177, Swansea University;
Marx Memorial Library, International Brigade Archive, Box 13/7a and Box 13/10, 'Report on the position with regard to the ILP Group'. Those volunteers listed as desiring to leave the POUM militia included the

following: Blair (Orwell), Wilton, Stearns, Donovan, Ritchie, Jones, Moyle, Julius and Williams. Coles, Evans, Jones and Williams tried to join the International Brigades but Tapsell had left Barcelona so they joined the Communist PSUC unit instead.

[55] NL 02.04.37

[56] Thwaites, op cit., p57, Orwell, op cit., p172, 177, 190

[57] South Wales Coalfield collection, Urias Jones interview, op cit. After the 'May Days' possibly up to 11 ILP Contingent men joined other Republican units. Coles, Evans, Jones and Williams joined the Communist PSUC, Hiddlestone joined an unknown Republican unit possibly Catalan. Donovan, Chambers and Stearns joined Anarchist units, and possibly Buttonshaw did too. Correspondence with Jim Carmody, Baxell, (unlikely warriors) op cit., p191, List of British and International Brigaders with annotated notes presented to author by Local History Society, author unknown; Farrell and Wilkes and also possibly Connor and Donovan joined the International Brigades, with Farrell becoming a POW.

[58] Cohen, op cit., p185, 239

[59] Thwaites, op cit., p57-58, NL 18.06.37, NL 06.08.37, NL 13.08.37, NL 24.09.37. One other volunteer agreed with this view. MML Thomas letter, op cit., while many volunteers by May 1937 wished to join other Republican units see chapters 8 and 9.

[60] Thwaites, Ibid, p60

[61] Victor Alba and Stephen Schwartz, *Spanish Marxism Versus Soviet Communism: A History of the P.O.U.M.* (Oxford, Transaction Books, 1988). There are many references to Rovira as a POUM military leader contained within this work.

[62] Josep Pane, Gregorio Jorge: l'heroi desconegut
http://www.funanin.org/pane.htm
This work briefly covers the life of Gregorio Jorge.

[63] Orwell op cit, Andy Durgan, *International Volunteers in the POUM Militias* http://libcom.org/history/international-volunteers-poum-militias , *Revolutionary History, The Spanish Civil War: The View from the Left* (London, Socialist Platform, 1992) p242-252. Durgan and in particular Orwell make many references to Kopp.

[64] Orwell, Ibid, Durgan, op cit. Both these works make several references to Levinski.

[65] Correspondence with Jim Carmody.

[66] Thwaites, op cit., p55. Bennett is portrayed in a photograph with other volunteers.

[67] Durgan, op cit., p19 states Buttonshaw's first name was Harvey and he

was Australian not American. Also. Amirah Inglis, *Australians in the Spanish Civil War* (London, Allen & Unwin, 1987), p219. Most probably Buttonshaw was British see chapter 9.

[68] South Wales Coalfield collection, Urias Jones interview, op cit.
[69] Jack Coward, *Back From the Dead* (Liverpool, Merseyside Writers, ND), p12
[70] Correspondence with Jim Carmody.
[71] South Wales Coalfield collection, Urias Jones interview, op cit.
[72] Correspondence with Jim Carmody.
[73] Marx Memorial Library, International Brigade Archive, Box C 13/7a 1937. Tapsell Report 30.05.37
[74] [74] Correspondence with Jim Carmody.
[75] Orwell, op cit., p91. States O'Hara was a First Aid man.
[76] National Archives, op cit., Marx Memorial Library, International Brigade Archive, Box C 13/7a Tapsell Report, 30.05.37.
[77] Correspondence with Jim Carmody and Robert Stradling, Wales and the Spanish Civil War: The Dragon's Dearest Cause? (Cardiff, Univ. of Wales, 2004), p186
[78] MML Thomas letter, op cit.
[79] Orwell, op cit., p178. States Webb was a First Aider and Stretcher Bearer.
[80] Baxell (unlikely warriors), op cit., p191
[81] Durgan, op cit., p22
[82] Ibid, p22
[83] Ibid., p21. States Harry Milton's real name was Wolf Kupinsky.
[84] Orwell, op cit, p39
[85] Ibid
[86] McNair, op cit., p16-17
[87] Richard Baxell, *British Volunteers in the Spanish Civil War: The British Battalion in the International Brigades, 1936-1939* (London, Routledge, 2004 and Warren & Pell, Abersychan, 2007) p8-9 (W & P p17-18)
[88] Baxell, op cit., p15 (W & P p22)
[89] Ibid, p16-17 (W & P p23-24)
[90] Ibid, p19 (W & P p26)
[91] Ibid, p21-23 (W & P p29)
[92] Ibid, p14 (W & P p21)
[93] Hall, op cit., p75, Thwaites, op cit., p55, Orwell, op cit., p13. ILP Contingent with previous military experience included Orwell, Donovan, Chambers, Jones, Parker, Clarke, Doran, Farrell, Tanky and H. Thomas see next chapters 8 and 9 for more details.
[94] Baxell, op cit., p147 (W & P p139)

[95] Thwaites, op cit., p60, South Wales Coalfield Collection, Urias Jones interview, op cit. Tapsell Report, op cit., Thomas letter, Baxell, (unlikely Warriors) op cit., p191, National archives, op cit., Chambers and Smillie were killed. Coles, Clinton, Evans Hunter, Parker, H. Thomas, Thompson, Hiddlestone, Orwell, Smillie, Tanky (James Arthur Cope), Wickes and Williams were wounded some more than once and Cottman, Williams and two other volunteers who got sunstroke were hospitalised.

[96] Cohen, op cit., p183

CHAPTER 8

Leaders of the ILP Contingent

Josep Rovira (1902-1968)

Josep Rovira, a Catalan POUM militant, was Commander of all the POUM forces on the Aragon Front and ultimately the overall commander of the ILP Contingent. Rovira was born in Barcelona in Catalonia in 1902.[1] His parents were both working class and Josep started work at thirteen as a bricklayer's assistant. Later he was called up for the Army to take part in the North African campaign against the Moroccan Riff rebels who wanted independence from Spain. Rovira, though, deserted from the Army and fled to France, where he met the future President of Catalonia, Francesc Macia. While he was still in France in 1926 Rovira became involved with the radical Catalanists, Estat Catala, who wanted an independent Catalonia. Rovira helped to organise the "Plot of Prats de Mollo" which was an attempt to organise armed guerrilla action against the Spanish monarchy.

When he returned to Catalonia Rovira had developed revolutionary Socialist views. He was still linked to Estat Catala, the extreme Catalan separatist party, although he did belong to its left wing, the 'Partit Proletari'. In January 1933 Rovira joined the BOC, the independent Marxist party led by Joaquin Maurin. Rovira rose rapidly in the BOC, and became a political organiser. In April 1934 he became a member of the Executive Committee [2] and in addition to this he was editor of the BOC Catalan magazine *L'Hora*.[3] In October that year Rovira played a leading role as leader of the BOC's 'Groups of Action' during the general strike in Barcelona. These groups were the forerunners of the militias and consisted of BOC militants who ensured that strikebreakers did not enter the factories, and responded in kind to any violent actions by employers or police forces.

As a member of the Executive Committee, Rovira was involved in the recruitment and training of young activists, and in the cultural aspects of BOC activities. It was through his cultural work that he met Maria Manonelles, one of the young female actors in the party, who became his partner or 'companera' in 1936. In time she would go to the Front with Rovira and into exile with him.

When the POUM was formed in 1935, Rovira was part of the BOC militants who negotiated the merger with Nin's Communist Left.[4] As a former leading BOC militant Rovira was appointed to the Executive Committee of the new POUM.[5] When the Army revolted in Barcelona on July 18-19th 1936 Rovira was the POUM's military leader, organising groups of armed POUM militants to help the suppression of the military uprising. At the formation of the Anti-Fascist Militia Committee - effectively the new revolutionary government of Catalonia - Rovira was chosen as the POUM representative.[6] The POUM sent Rovira to the Aragon Front in August 1936 to take command of all POUM forces. He commanded all the POUM's forces on the Aragon Front until July 1937 when the POUM 29th Division was disbanded, rising to the rank of Major, which was the maximum rank allowed to militia leaders.[7] When the POUM leaders were seized and imprisoned on June 16th 1937 Rovira escaped because he was at the Front. In July 1937 Rovira's forces took part in an unsuccessful offensive near Huesca. The Army Command sent Rovira two messages: the first congratulated him on the behaviour and bravery of his troops and the second ordered him to report to Headquarters.

When Rovira arrived at the Headquarters of the Army of the East in Barcelona he was arrested,[8] but thanks to appeals by Anarchist Commanders of the 28th and 25th Divisions and the Minster of Defence he was released after twenty days.[9] After his release Rovira set up an office in Barcelona to organise the disbandment of the 29th Division. He managed to get most of the POUM militants transferred to non-Communist units where they would be safe from persecution.[10] After the suppression of the POUM and the disbandment of its 29th Division, Rovira was chosen as a member of the clandestine POUM Executive.[11] Rovira was jailed again in October 1938 and was charged with ordering his troops to leave the Front during the 'May Days' events of 1937. This charge was dropped through lack of evidence.[12] In January 1939 Rovira was still in jail when Franco's troops were closing in on Barcelona. Along with the other POUMistas in the jail, Rovira was rescued by armed POUM militants and escaped across the border into France.

When the Second World War broke out Rovira was at first involved in getting aid to imprisoned POUMistas. Later in the war he became involved in the French Resistance and helped Jews to escape capture by the Pro-German Vichy Government forces. In November 1944 POUM militants gathered in Toulouse to discuss the future. As a result of a strong disagreement over the direction that the POUM should take, Rovira left the POUM to set up a new movement called the Socialist Movement of Catalonia (MSC). Although he had left the POUM Rovira took part in the 30th anniversary celebrations of the founding of POUM in 1965. Josep Rovira died in Paris in 1968.[13]

Gregorio Jorge (? -1938)

Gregorio Jorge was a Catalan POUM militant who was a Battalion Commander in the 29th Division, which contained the ILP Contingent. Orwell mentions Jorge as the commander of the combined Spanish/British force in his account of the night assault at Ermita Salas, although Orwell wrongly calls him Jorge Roca.[1] Jorge led the mixed nationality force in the dark across 'No Man's Land'. When they got to within a hundred or a hundred and fifty yards of the enemy position, Jorge halted the men until the stragglers caught up. Leading the way, Jorge cut the enemy's outer barbed wire with wire cutters at around fifty yards from their position and then cut the second wire entanglements at about twenty yards from the enemy strongpoint. As the POUM/ILP force crawled through the wire they were discovered and shot at. Immediately Jorge knelt on one knee and threw a grenade into the enemy strongpoint. The Fascists had spotted the Republican troops and around twenty rifles blazed back from the enemy position, wounding Jorge. He took no more part in the action and was rescued by the First Aid team and taken to a dressing station where it was discovered he had a light shoulder wound.[2] Jorge based his planning of this attack on evidence he had gained from patrols in 'No Man's Land'.[3]

A small, thin man who was originally a farmer from Castile, Jorge rather surprisingly left the farm to become a policeman, a member of the hated 'Guardia Civil' who were used ruthlessly to crush any peasant discontent. He joined the POUM and stood as one of their candidates in the General Election of February 1936. Jorge was one of the first POUM militants to go to the Front and once there he never left the Front line. He was married with children so comrades in Lerida looked after his family in his absence. As a leading POUM militia leader it was Jorge's role to make sure supplies reached the militia on the Aragon Front. He neither smoked or drank and gave away his pay to charities and relief organisations.

Although the Front was very quiet Jorge was a meticulous soldier and had the militia strengthen their defences regularly. He himself went on patrols so he knew the enemy's defences well, enabling him to plan possible ambushes. He liked to patrol around dinnertime, reasoning that the enemy soldiers would be distracted by eating and therefore less likely to spot him. Jorge would make detailed drawings of the enemy positions including where the barbed wire was thickest, where the machine guns were situated, etc. In fact he got so close to the Fascist positions he used to listen to their conversations to try and overhear what the enemy was planning. He taught his men the rudiments of war based on his military experience and dealt strongly with any problems of indiscipline. He used smugglers to find out about the enemy defences and to gain information about their rear areas.

He was not like his subordinate Georges Kopp, who liked to wear decorative uniform to show off his rank; he wore a plain uniform and carried a long-nosed pistol that reached nearly to his knee. Like Kopp he was rather short but while Jorge was slender, Kopp was a little fat and together they looked like 'Laurel and Hardy'. Jorge was against the regularisation of the POUM forces into part of the Popular Army. He had the total loyalty of his men and only needed to raise his arm to get them to obey his orders.[4]

Besides the night attack Orwell also talks about an operation commanded by Jorge, in which the POUM militia advanced the line forward up to a kilometre:

> "The whole move was beautifully planned. In seven hours six hundred men constructed twelve hundred metres of trench and parapet, at distances of from a hundred and fifty to three hundred yards from the Fascist lines, and all so silently that the Fascists heard nothing..."[5]

After this action an assault was planned on the Fascist lines but was called off at the last moment. Orwell makes a brief comment that some youngsters from the POUM youth (the JCI) were not told of the withdrawal back to their own lines and were pinned down with little cover. Of the twelve youngsters trapped, seven were killed. Orwell merely says that the rest escaped at night.[6] One or two who were uninjured or slightly wounded did escape back to their own lines, but Jorge planned and implemented the rescue of the bodies and the seriously wounded. Under Jorge's command the POUM forces fired everything they could at the enemy lines to try to stop them firing at the JCI youngsters during the day. At night Jorge and a small group of volunteers crawled to where the JCI group were and carried and dragged the wounded back to the waiting stretcher bearers and medical staff. Jorge himself carried a rather chubby wounded youngster back to his own lines. They brought back some of the dead and Jorge was to be present at their funerals, taking them back to their own villages and speaking emotionally on behalf of the POUM. He was a noted POUM orator who could deliver moving and political speeches.[7]

After the 'May Days' Jorge was involved in the failed attack on Huesca. When the 29th Division was broken up he joined the 'Army of the South' in the Motril and Granada Front. This was a quiet Front where little was happening so when Jorge heard of the Fascist victory at Teruel and their advance to the coast he volunteered to go to the Levant Front in the spring of 1938. Here the next enemy attack was to be launched against the Republican city of Valencia. Near Saguntum he was twice wounded but refused to be treated for his injuries and was killed at the head of his Battalion, dying amongst the orange trees.[8]

Georges Kopp (1902-1951)

The Belgian born George or Georges Kopp was the Commander of the Centuria which contained the ILP contingent and he was eventually to rise to the rank of Major.[1] Kopp was forty-five years old when he came to Spain and, although physically fit, was a short corpulent man. His superior Gregorio Jorge was taller and slim and together they were called by the men 'Laurel and Hardy' after the two famous comedy film stars.[2]

Kopp was a native of Brussels and was a widower with four children. Having served in the Belgian Army he was a reservist officer and as such was forbidden to fight in another country's armed forces. By going to Spain he faced five years in jail with hard labour, plus a farther ten years for leaving the country without permission and for making explosives for the Spanish Republic. In Belgium he was paid a high salary as a chief engineer for an engineering company; however as a Socialist he used his training as a chemist to make explosives such as cartridges and bullets, using the company's state of the art laboratory, and often working late into the night. At first the engineering company were not suspicious as Kopp had often worked late in the past, inventing new products. Kopp claimed he produced enough explosives for seven million cartridges. He was also involved in organising arms, smuggling guns for the Spanish Republic and supplying explosives so that Republicans could make their own ammunition. Eventually his laboratory was raided; helped by left wing comrades, he evaded arrest by leaving on the same day for Paris. From there he travelled to Barcelona and volunteered to fight for the POUM militia.[3]

27. Georges Kopp. (NL)

Kopp was quickly chosen as a Centuria Commander leading between eighty and a hundred men in the POUM 'Miguel Pedrola'[4] Column. He eventually reached the rank of Major, the highest rank to which a militia officer could rise.[5] He was an impressive figure physically, being bigger than most Spaniards, and liked to cut a dash by riding a black horse and wearing a military uniform which included epaulettes.[6] He was noted for his efficiency, bravery and his coolness under fire.[7] Like most volunteers at the Front Kopp longed for something different to eat or to add to the rather boring rations, and so Eileen Blair (George Orwell's first wife) brought him some Lea & Perrins' 'Worcester sauce', which was a favourite of his.[8] Kopp criticised the inaction on the Aragon Front and the disorganisation of the militias to Orwell:

"This is not a war, it is a comic opera with an occasional death."[9]

Kopp was involved in military actions in Spain at Casetas and Huesca in October 1936, the Manicomio at Huesca in November 1936, Vedado Zucra in December 1936, Alcubierre in February 1937 and the Ermita Salas in April 1937.[10] He had served on the Aragon Front for nearly eight months and been wounded once when he went on leave to Barcelona with the ILP volunteers in late April 1937.

Here Kopp became involved in the 'May Days' events. Opposite one of the POUM buildings was a café occupied by police forces. When they clashed with POUM 'shock troops', Kopp told off the 'shock troops' and ordered them to avoid bloodshed.[11] He then went unarmed across to the police positions to organise a truce. When it was pointed out that there were two unexploded grenades nearby Kopp instructed the 'shock troops' to set them off by shooting them. He then left and ordered the POUM 'shock troops' to fight back only if attacked; otherwise they were to do nothing.[12]

Kopp returned to the Front near Huesca and was involved in a military action at Chimillas in June 1937.[13] George Orwell was wounded in the throat on this Front. Kopp, as his friend and as his commanding officer, wrote a detailed letter to Dr Laurence O'Shaugnessy (Orwell's brother-in-law) to enable Orwell to get proper care on his return to England.[14] In June 1937 Kopp was ordered to leave the Front by the 'Ministry of War'. The letter from the Ministry of War stated that his engineering skills were needed and he was to be transferred to another unit.[15] After visiting the 'Ministry for War' in Valencia and getting a new commission in the engineering regiment of the 'Army of the East' he returned to Barcelona to collect his belongings and was arrested on June 20th 1937.[16]

At first after his arrest Kopp was allowed visitors and was seen by Orwell a couple of times. From Kopp's hotel room Orwell retrieved the letter from the 'Ministry of War' stating the need for Kopp's skills in the engineers and awarding him his commission. He handed the letter over to the authorities but it made no difference and Kopp was not released. It is probable that Kopp was no longer allowed any visitors.[17] He was imprisoned with around hundred other POUMistas in a Communist 'cheka' in cramped and poor conditions. He was interrogated daily by NKVD agents (the 1930's version of the KGB) to get him to confess that the POUM were traitors and agents of Franco, and also that he was part of a plan to make POUM troops leave the Front so that it was open to the Fascists. It was claimed that Kopp was also tortured by being put in a darkened pit with rats biting his legs and by being threatened that he would be shot if he did not confess to being a traitor.[18] In a letter to the Communist journalist Frank Jellinek Orwell wrote that he believes Kopp was "shamefully treated" but hints that he might have been exaggerating about what happened to him.[19] One ILP volunteer actually claimed that he saw Kopp leaving the Fascist lines; the more likely explanation is that Kopp was returning from a patrol.[20]

Kopp managed to smuggle out a letter via a small boy but it never reached its intended recipient. Miraculously the letter reached the ILP in London and was printed in the *New Leader* of August 6th 1937. The letter was an English copy of a letter in Spanish that Kopp had sent to the Head of Police in Barcelona.[21] In the letter he told how he was sent a commission for the engineers but this was ignored. He goes on to describe the prison conditions: eighteen people shared a room designed only for three or four people, no exercise was allowed and food was at starvation levels. Finally he listed his service for the Spanish Republic in both Belgium and Spain and how he had commanded a Company, a Battalion and a Regiment.

In another letter to Eileen Blair Kopp again described his prison conditions. He was in a room ten feet by fifteen feet containing eighteen men. The prisoners were beaten by the guards and they were mixed in with common criminals. He wrote that he was planning a hunger strike as a protest at the way he and other political prisoners were being treated.[22] He wrote finally that his skills were needed at the Front, he wanted the chance to clear his name of any accusations and proclaimed his support for the anti-Fascist cause. The letters did not get him out of jail but may have saved Kopp's life. He was finally released on December 7th 1938. He had lost seven stones in weight, having entered prison weighting fifteen stones, and he had to walk with a stick.[23] He wrote to the Orwells from France on his release from prison asking if they could ask the ILP to lend him $50 to help him survive in France.[24]

In Spain Kopp seems to have become friendly with Orwell and his wife Eileen. He once drove Eileen back to Barcelona from the Front after she had visited her husband and again after he (Orwell) had been wounded in the throat.[25] In fact two of Orwell's biographers, Crick and Shelden, have suggested that Kopp had a more than friendly interest in Eileen Blair and may even have had an affair with her.[26] Shelden believes that Kopp was in love with Eileen Blair and that this was possibly reciprocated. He quotes a woman who knew Eileen well:

"Her eyes always lit up whenever Georges Kopp's name was mentioned, so there may have been some truth in the belief that she and Kopp had an affair."[27]

Some other members of the ILP unit believed something was going on and called it a "rotten business".[28] Kopp wrote from prison to Eileen and Orwell to try and get help to get himself released, it was through her efforts that his situation was publicised in the *New Leader*.[29] It has been reported that Eileen Blair was a little jealous when Kopp and his second wife had children and may possibly have been thinking of what might have been.[30]

When Kopp was released from jail he escaped to France and then travelled on to Britain and was nursed back to health by Laurence and Gwen O'Shaugnessy. Laurence was the brother of Orwell's wife, Eileen, and Gwen was Laurence's wife. When Orwell published *Homage to Catalonia* about his experiences in Spain, it was also translated into French. The translator suggested that George Kopp write a preface, which he did. Orwell was happy with what he had written but allowed the publisher to make the decision over whether to include the preface, and eventually it was omitted.[31]

When World War II began, Kopp went to France and volunteered for the French Army. In June 1940 he was wounded near Marne. After the defeat of France he lived in Marseille and made contact with Spanish Republican exiles. He joined the French Resistance and also had links with British Intelligence. When the Gestapo discovered his activities, he escaped from France by a plane organised by British Intelligence in September 1943.[32]

On his return to Britain he became a distant relative of Orwell by marrying Doreen Hunton, the sister of Gwen O'Shaugnessy, and later fathered three children with her.[33] Relations between Kopp and Orwell seem to have been less amicable in his later years and were not helped when he sold Orwell a lorry which proved unreliable.[34] His last few years were spent hill farming in Scotland where he died prematurely aged forty-nine in 1951, his life possibly shortened by his experiences in Spain and France.[35]

The most recent authorised biography of Orwell written by Michael Shelden casts doubts on several aspects of the George Kopp story.[36] Shelden completely rejects the story that Kopp was a Belgian reservist officer, a professional engineer, a devoted family man whose wife died in childbirth giving birth to the youngest of his four children and that he left Brussels because the authorities had discovered him making illegal munitions for the Spanish Republic. In fact, he says, Kopp was born in Russia and moved to Belgium when he was ten. He studied engineering at University but left in 1922 having not completed the course. He had five children with his first wife Germaine Warnotte, whom he divorced in 1934 shortly after the birth of their last child. He did work as an engineer in Brussels but there is no evidence he was producing illegal munitions for Spain. Equally there is no evidence that he was an officer in the Belgian Army. Other sources cite Kopp's as an unreliable witness when he claimed that while in prison he came upon a document that showed that fellow volunteer Bob Smillie had not died from appendicitis while in prison but had been kicked to death.[37] Kopp also claimed that he knew the Belgian Socialist Foreign Minster, a man called Spaark. This was found to be false, although Spaark did intervene to help get Kopp released from prison.[38]

Benjamin Levinski (Lewinski)

Kopp's second in command was Captain Benjamin Levinski, who arrived in Spain in August 1936. (Orwell refers to him as 'Benjamin' in *Homage to Catalonia*.) Levinski was a twenty-year-old Polish Jew who had grown up in Paris and worked as a fur coat maker.[1] Kopp put him in command of a hilltop position in November 1936. While commanding the hilltop position Levinski shot at some of the enemy in 'No Man's Land' but failed to kill anyone as the cartridge in his rifle was a dud; a clear example of the poor quality weapons the militia possessed.[2]

His appointment seems to have been more related to his linguistic abilities than to any military attributes he might have possessed. He spoke French, German, Italian, Catalan and English, although Orwell claimed his English was terrible.[3] Orwell describes Levinski at the Front:

> "He was a short youth of about twenty-five, with stiff black hair and a pale eager face which at this period was always very dirty."[4]

It was Levinski who made Orwell a Cabo, or Corporal, thanks to his language skills as he had picked up Catalan quickly.[5]

Levinski's most high profile act in Spain was his role in the night attack on the Fascists trenches at Ermita Salas where several ILP volunteers were wounded. For this attack Levinski was second in command to the Spaniard Gregorio Jorge. In the first exchanges of fire Jorge was wounded, effectively making Levinski the commanding officer for the rest of the action. In the fighting Levinski ordered Orwell to keep his head down, as Orwell was very tall, and actually pushed him down on another occasion.[6] In the rather fanciful *New Leader* account of the assault Levinski - described as a French Captain - rallies the ILP by calling out, "Are we downhearted?".[7]

Orwell describes Levinski in the raid on Ermita Salas thus:

> "Benjamin was kneeling on one knee with a pleased, devilish sort of expression on his face and firing carefully at the rifle-flashes with his automatic pistol."[8]

Levinski threw a grenade into the enemy trench and then ordered a charge. When the Fascists had retreated Levinski discovered a full ammunition box, which the ILP took back to their own lines. Eventually when the Fascists attacked in large numbers Levinski ordered a retreat back to their own positions.[9] After the 'May Days' events Levinski was made a Regular Captain in the POUM 29th Division.[10] As well as the raid on Ermita Salas described above, he also served on the Alcubiere Front and in an action at Mount Pocero.[11]

By all accounts Levinski was a brave soldier in Spain. What happened to Levinski after the POUM was suppressed is unknown; he may have been imprisoned like Kopp or he may have fled to France, but this is only conjecture.

* * *

Bob Edwards (1905-1990)

By the time he went to Spain, Bob Edwards was a member of the ILP National Administrative Committee (NAC) and was a national figure in the ILP. Bob Edwards was the Commander of the ILP contingent in Spain from January 1937 until he left to attend the ILP Easter conference in mid-March 1937.

28. Bob Edwards. *(ILP Archive)*

Edwards was born into a working-class Liverpool family and his father was a docker. His early influences were religion, Keir Hardie and pacifism. During the 1920's Edwards joined the ILP and its youth wing the 'Guild of Youth,' where he was involved in the disarmament movement. During the General Strike he was a TUC Congress) messenger. This involved delivering messages from the various unions to their leading body, the TUC. In the same year Edwards led a youth delegation to Soviet Russia, where he met and had discussions with Leon Trotsky.[1] Edwards says:

"...I disagreed with him as far as the role of the Soviet Union was concerned, and I thought at the time, although I was a very young man, that Stalin's policy was the correct one. [abandoning world revolution]"[2]

On his return Edwards wrote his first political pamphlet *Youth in Red Russia* where he emphasised the need for strong trade union links between the two countries and stressed that capitalism should not be allowed to overthrow the Soviet Union. At the end of the pamphlet Edwards' signature is first, as the delegation leader and chairman. Amongst the list of signatures is George Brown, who became a Commissar in the International Brigades and was killed at Brunete in July 1937. In the period 1926-36 Edwards was a leading member of the Socialist Youth International and later the 'London Bureau' Youth International. In 1927, aged just twenty-two, Edwards became Liverpool's youngest councillor, elected as a Labour Party candidate.[3]

Edwards was a keen supporter of the ILP's decision to disaffiliate from the Labour Party in 1932. In 1933 he became a member of the leading body of the party, the NAC.[4] In the same year Edwards married Edith May Sandham, who was an ILP councillor and the daughter of a prominent ILP member. Ironically it was his father-in-law whom he replaced on the NAC. He became the Divisional representative for Lancashire in 1934.

In the early 1930's Edwards was a keen supporter of the Revolutionary Policy Committee (RPC) group in the ILP, who wished to move the ILP towards a more revolutionary position. This group advocated greater links with the Communist Party, including joining the Comintern, the international Communist movement's organising body. The RPC sent Edwards and another man to Russia to ask the Soviets questions concerning how far the ILP would be allowed to keep its separate identity while joining the international Communist movement. The Soviets agreed the ILP could keep its name, organisation and officials but ruled that it must obey the policy of the Comintern. On their return, Edwards and his colleague wrote a pamphlet called *Revolutionary Unity*, which encompassed these points.

When it became known that two leading lights of the RPC were secret members of the Communist Party, the ILP NAC disciplined the members of the RPC including Edwards. Edwards was suspended and asked to declare that his main loyalty was to the ILP and not the Communist Party. Having given suitable assurances of his loyalty

Edwards' suspension was lifted. Although Edwards still favoured the RPC position, his public views from then on mirrored those of the mainstream of the party.[5]

Edwards wrote a brief account of his second visit to the Soviet Union.[6] He and his colleague were in Moscow for twelve days and met leading members of the Communist International including its leader, the Bulgarian Dimitrov. He had won international fame by his performance at his trial where the Nazis had accused him of burning the Parliament building, the Reichstag. Edwards also met Stalin and asked about missing international comrades who had disappeared in Stalin's purges of so-called traitors. He claimed that, because of this, his letters were opened and his camera was stolen while in Russia. Edwards describes his feelings on meeting Stalin:

"I was surprised when I met Stalin. He was a small man, half a head shorter than myself, and seemed a very modest man." [7]

Edwards says that it was he who argued for the ILP to remain a separate party, while his colleague in Russia, Eric Whalley, believed that the ILP should unite with the Communist Party. Whalley went on to join the Communist Party and was killed in Spain fighting in the International Brigades.[8]

In the same year Edwards was heavily involved in the 1934 national 'Hunger March', when unemployed workers converged on London from all over Britain to protest about their situation.[9] Edwards was living in Chorley, Lancashire, where the organised unemployed were members of the Communist-led National Unemployed Workers Movement (NUWM), but used the local ILP building for meetings. The ILP agreed that five workers from Chorley should take part in the 'Hunger March' to London and were provided with haversacks and army boots by the ILP. Although he himself was not unemployed, Edwards decided to take part in the march on behalf of the Chorley unemployed. The Lancashire contingent set off from Manchester three hundred strong, accompanied by a supporting lorry painted red. Edwards was elected their leader. Joining them on the march from Liverpool was councillor Jack Jones - future leader of the Transport and General Workers Union and another volunteer who went to Spain as part of the International Brigades. He was badly wounded during the Battle of the Ebro.

At Congleton in Cheshire the marchers were due to sleep in the

Town Hall; however they were told that they would not be allowed to do this. Furthermore they were told to march several miles to the local workhouse, having already marched many miles during the day. The marchers refused to walk and blocked the main road for an hour before buses were laid on to take them to the local workhouse. There they were given corned beef instead of cheese sandwiches for breakfast, a great luxury according to Bob Edwards! In London the various contingents united for several days. In order to raise awareness of the plight of the unemployed, the marchers would enter cafes and restaurants in Central London in groups of ten and then order a cup of tea each and proceed to unwrap their own food. Many cafes and restaurants gave them free food and cakes. Edwards claims that he saw the Minister of Transport and in return for paying ten shillings per man he agreed to arrange free rail tickets back to Lancashire for the marchers. In Parliament Edwards heckled the Prime Minster Ramsay MacDonald and was ejected from the building.[10]

In 1935 Edwards stood as an ILP Parliamentary candidate in the General Election at Chorley where he polled 1,365 or 3.3% of the vote, reflecting the ILP's weakness in Lancashire.[11] Reports say that Edwards began the campaign late and the local newspaper described the ILP's election campaign as "lacklustre".[12]

When Fascist Italy invaded an independent Abyssinia (now Ethiopia) in 1935-36 Edwards opposed the party leadership and supported sanctions against the Italian invaders.[13] By 1936 Bob Edwards, who had been a pacifist all his life, decided that the only way to defeat Fascism was by means of armed resistance. In his own words:

> "I had got rid of my pacifist ideas watching Fascism and all that it involved - the killing of some of my friends, the missing people in concentration camps, the danger of the Second World War, the destruction of democratically elected government by the revolt of an army based on Fascist ideas. So that by that time I had firmly come to the conviction that you had to do something about it in an armed way. You couldn't talk these people out of it, resolutions were meaningless, they needed fighting men..."[14]

Edwards' first involvement in the Spanish conflict was in September 1936 as one of two drivers who drove an ambulance with medical supplies from Britain to Spain. While in Spain Edwards visited the Front line and came back to Britain in October determined to raise a unit of soldiers to fight in Spain. By November the ILP NAC had agreed to his suggestion.[15] Fellow NAC member Fenner Brockway stated:

"On the initiative of Bob Edwards we mobilised a group of volunteer fighters of which Bob took command."[16]

Edwards himself said:

"The Spanish Government had no other means of defending themselves other than the workers' organisations. So they armed the political parties and the trade unions and they formed themselves into a militia to defend the democratic government of Spain. I persuaded the Council of the ILP, which was up to then pacifist, that it wasn't enough to be pacifist, that we should send a fighting force to Spain. Even though it was small it would be a gesture of international solidarity. I wasn't a military man but I was a good organiser."[17]

It was decided that only unmarried volunteers should be accepted to fight, although (as usual) the rules did not apply to Bob Edwards, who was himself a married man.[18] Edwards says that he was voted leader by the volunteers and given the rank of Captain by the POUM, even though he had no previous military experience - only an honorary rank of Lieutenant in the Russian Red Army given to him on his visit to Russia in 1926. Fellow volunteer Harry Thomas states in a letter to the Communist representative in Barcelona that Edwards was not the first choice leader, but became the unit's leader after the previous incumbent was send home because of drunkenness. Thomas further says that Edwards 'gazetted' himself as Captain, which possibly means that he appointed himself to the leadership.[19] In theory all the men could discuss all decisions, in practice Edwards and his NCOs made most of the decisions.[20] In a letter to his wife Edwards commented about his leadership:

"I am their leader not because I am Captain of the English Section and have the rights of leadership on paper, but because they respect my judgement and have confidence in me as a commander."

Fellow volunteer Thomas comments that Edwards would have made a better "Salvation Army leader" and goes on to describe his view of Edwards' leadership:

> "He lived a life of a snail, creeping out of his hole only to eat and wash, he evaded duty as our political leader and brought a Sam Brown belt (commonly worn by officers in Spain, designed for a pistol) and strutted about like an half paid officer, even our Spanish comrades made fun of him."[21]

In the letter to his wife he talked about rats in the trenches, the poor quality of the bread and coffee and the wet weather. He described problems with the men: some did not fit in and the later arrivals were the more troublesome but he still said they were a "damn fine lot without exception".[22] A few old soldiers in the unit were dismayed at being commanded by an amateur. Thomas - a World War I veteran – claimed that another volunteer disobeyed an order from Edwards, and the result was that he was disarmed, and a sentry instructed to shoot him if he deserted. The volunteer concerned did desert and joined another unit. Thomas further commented that things ran more smoothly after Edwards had left for Britain.[23]

In another letter home he stated that the Aragon nights were very cold in the mountains and asked if he could be sent a winter coat.[24] In a letter written in March Edwards described little happening except long-range rifle and artillery fire.[25] According to his own biographical notes Edwards was awarded the highest award given to a foreigner by the Republican Government when he was given the 'Commander of the Order of Spanish Liberation and Bar'.[26]

In Spain Edwards experienced the social revolution in Catalonia and saw it as a cause worth fighting for:

> "We were inspired by what we saw in Catalonia. The owners of the factories had left, and workers had to take over the factories. Landowners, always absentees, had left, and the land taken over by the peasants, and co-operatives formed. Hotels were taken over and councils set up to run them. There was workers' control throughout Catalonia, and equality of income. Everyone got ten pesetas a day, the General and the woman sweeping the streets. There was no black market. Prostitution was abolished. Bullfighting was abolished. It was a marvellous country to be in – for Socialists." [27]

While he was fighting in Spain Edwards was also a *New Leader* journalist and wrote several articles about the ILP Contingent for the newspaper. The first one came out in the *New Leader* of January 15th 1937 and was titled 'Why We Go'. In this article Edwards describes the large number of offers he had received from men who wanted to fight in Spain and the high calibre of the volunteers. He states that the time has come for the ILP to oppose Fascism by force of arms:

> "We then reached a stage when it became necessary for the Party to go further when it became necessary for us, despite our anti-war traditions, to give a practical expression to our adherence to Marxist revolutionary policy by enrolling volunteers to counter-balance the forces of International Fascism."[28]

In the following week's *New Leader* Edwards wrote an article called 'In Spain Today' which described the journey to Spain of the volunteers and their short military training in the Lenin Barracks.[29] His next article was written at the Front. Titled 'Trenches on the Black Mountain', it tells the story of a failed ambush on the enemy and a raid on the enemy HQ. Edwards says that a Fascist deserter had told him about a lake where they went fishing, so, armed with this information, part of the contingent attempted to ambush the enemy. The ambush failed when the enemy became suspicious. Annoyed at having missed the enemy in the ambush, Edwards' group made a raid on the enemy headquarters, where they fired many rifle shots at the Fascist HQ, before retiring to their own lines. This story has the flavour of 'comic book' action material, but there may be some truth in it. Volunteer Harold Thomas claims he never saw any deserters come over to the ILP force.[30] Edwards' next article, called 'ILP Contingent Under Fire on the Aragon Front', describes a major artillery attack on the ILP positions and the wounding of one of the contingent.[31] 'On the Aragon Front' consists mostly of a description of the conditions at the Front, but it also includes part of a letter sent by Georges Kopp to John McNair praising the ILP volunteers:

> "The English contingent is behaving splendidly. To illustrate the point, I want to tell you this. I thought of moving Bob's group to another strategic position for military reasons, but the Spanish comrades near them protested, saying they felt safe in their vicinity and did not want to have any other neighbours."[32]

Even bearing in mind the propaganda role of the *New Leader*, Kopp's letter shows that the ILP Contingent were valued as brave foreign fighters by the neighbouring militia forces.

Due to the quiet nature of the Front Edwards took part in many daring patrols in the 'No Mans Land' between the two forces. Edwards reported:

> "...we have on numerous occasions crept over the parapet and have managed to get very close to the Fascist lines."[33]

In Spain Edwards met the author George Orwell. Edwards described Orwell as being fearless under fire, but he was suspicious of his reasons for coming to Spain. Calling him a "bloody middle-class little scribe" and a "bloody scribbler", Edwards believed that Orwell had come to Spain primarily to write,[34] rather than fight. Michael Shelden believes that this criticism of Orwell is unjust, and that Edwards himself, although undoubtedly "a brave soldier", has exaggerated his own role in Spain. For instance, the article in the *New Leader* which describes the night attack on Ermita Salas contains a picture of Bob Edwards, identifying him as the leader of the ILP Contingent, but by this time Edwards had been back in Britain for over a month.[35] In Edwards' own account of his experiences in Spain he admits that he was indeed wrong about Orwell and came to believe that he went to Spain more to fight than to write.[36]

The first time that Edwards met Orwell, Orwell was with two young Spanish boys and their rather strange pet:

> "Behind them was a shaggy dog with 'POUM' painted on it. It made me roar with laughter. It was comic opera."[37]

When Orwell expressed a wish to join the International Brigades, Edwards pointed out to him the political dangers of doing so. Edwards explained he would be accused of being a Trotskyite and court-martialled and shot.[38]

On the Aragon Front one of the volunteers was wounded on a patrol so Edwards and Orwell strapped him to a donkey and headed towards the nearest First Aid post. They became lost and entered an enemy-held village, where enemy sentries saluted them. Rapidly realising their mistake, they retraced their steps to Alcubierre and reached their own lines unscathed.[39]

Orwell was not the only famous writer whom Edwards says that he met at the Front. He claims that the American adventurer and writer Ernest Hemingway paid them a visit. Hemingway apparently stayed for three days and complained that the food was vinegary and the bread mouldy. He took his boots off once and hopped around madly on one leg when a rat ran over his foot. Edwards also says that he introduced Hemingway to a small-time smuggler called Pablo, who later appeared in an exaggerated form in Hemingway's novel about the Spanish Civil War *For Whom the Bell Tolls*.[40]

At the end of March 1937 Edwards was recalled to Britain to attend the ILP annual conference. He was given permission to leave the Front and Spain but found the French border was closed, so he had to leave Spain secretly, crossing the Pyrenees on foot.[41] Edwards was not to return to Spain because of the ban on English volunteers going to Spain, and also probably because of the volatile political situation in Catalonia.[42] In a letter to the author Thwaites (9th December 1986), Edwards claims he tried to return to Spain and got as far as Perpignan in Southern France but did not try to re-enter Spain as the POUM had been declared illegal, this puts the date at June 1937. There is a possibility that he tried to enter Spain on one further occasion, presumably also without success.[43]

On his return to England Edwards wrote an article called 'Workers on Top in Spain' where he supported the POUM view that only the revolutionary forces could defeat Fascism. More interestingly, he describes in this article how he left Spain. Edwards was issued with a Spanish 'Nansen' passport, authorised by the Catalan Government, but was refused entry into France. He was forced to cross the Pyrenees twice because he was caught and returned to Spain by the French Border Guards, after his first crossing of the mountains in a snowstorm. The second attempt was successful, although Edwards did have to hide behind a hedge when a policeman on a bicycle came towards him.[44]

Edwards' reason for returning home was to address the Glasgow ILP National Conference on the Spanish situation. He was instructed that, on his way home, he should purchase a ship which was in Southern France, to get food into the Basque city of Bilbao which was being blockaded by Fascist warships. The ship was called the *Seven Seas Spray* and was captained by the famous Welsh blockade-runner Captain Owen Roberts. He was also to buy dried fish in Holland. The owners of the *Seven Seas Spray* refused to let it sail for Bilbao and Edwards did not visit Holland since the ILP no longer had a ship in which to put the food. When he arrived in England Edwards was interviewed in depth by the Special Branch about where he had been before being released.[45]

Back in Britain he travelled the country supporting the ILP policy on the Spanish Civil War, which on occasions led to friction with the local Communist Party.[46] He also wrote an article on Georges Kopp called 'Soldier of Socialism' which was based on conversations he had had with Kopp in Spain.[47] Edwards also supported Orwell's article in the *New Leader* refuting the claims of one ILP volunteer that the POUM were traitors.[48].

For a brief time after his return from Spain Edwards lived in the USA working with trade unionists and independent Socialists in that country.[49] At the start of World War II Edwards supported the official ILP policy that this war was an Imperialist war, and that the public should not support the Government. In December 1939 Edwards stood as the ILP candidate at the Stretford by-election, where he polled over four thousand votes. This amounted to approximately 15% of the vote against the Coalition Government candidate, a creditable performance by any standards. Edwards did not serve in the armed forces in World War II. He discovered he would not have been accepted for service because he had served as an officer in a foreign army.[50] In 1943 Edwards became the National Chairman (leader) of the ILP until 1948. He stood again in a by-election during the war; this time at Newport in Wales where he won over thirteen and a half thousand votes - over 45% of the vote - and almost won the seat.[51]

Bob Edwards was a trade unionist all his life and was elected General Secretary of the Chemical Workers Union from 1947-71. He left the ILP and was the Labour Party MP for Wolverhampton Bilston from 1955 until 1974, when the seat was abolished. In 1974 Edwards won the new enlarged seat of Wolverhampton South East, eventually standing down in 1987 as the oldest sitting MP in the House. He promoted ten private member bills as an MP, of which four became law. His greatest achievement here was the 'Clean Air Act'.[52]

Thanks to his experiences in Spain, Edwards was the MP whom Spanish dissidents automatically contacted for help. He received countless appeals for help from the International Brigade Association asking him to raise matters in the House or write to the Spanish authorities about such and such an imprisoned Communist or trade unionist. He first returned to Spain in 1959 where he was imprisoned and interrogated by Spanish police for ten hours, and then expelled from the country when it was discovered he had been sentenced to death in his absence in 1939. In 1975 he wrote to British Prime Minster Harold Wilson requesting that the British Government boycott Franco's funeral. Wilson's reply agreed with Edwards' sentiments but he said that he had to send someone.[53] Bob Edwards died in 1990.

Eric Blair (George Orwell) (1903-1950)

The writer and novelist George Orwell is probably the most well known British person who fought in the Spanish Civil War. While in Spain he was known by his real name, Eric Blair. He wrote a controversial account of his experiences in Spain called *Homage to Catalonia* which has received as much criticism as it has praise. Orwell joined the ILP Contingent in Spain, having originally journeyed there alone. He eventually became its leader after Bob Edwards returned home, and received a near fatal throat wound while at the Front.

There has been a mass of biographies written about Orwell, the most critically acclaimed being those written by Bernard Crick, D. J. Taylor and by Michael Shelden.[1] I will make no attempt to give a detailed account of Orwell's life before and after going to Spain. I will cover his time in Spain in more detail; in particular I have used reports made about him by other members of the ILP Contingent.

Eric Arthur Blair was born on June 25th 1903 in India. His father worked in the Indian civil service. In 1907 the Blair family returned to live in Britain although his father returned to work in India. The family lived in Henley-on-Thames and Orwell attended the local Anglican convent school. In 1911 Orwell was sent away to a boarding school called St Cypian's in Eastbourne, which he attended until 1916. During World War I (1914-18) Orwell wrote two patriotic poems, which were published in the local Henley newspaper. In 1917 Orwell entered Eton and wrote satirical pieces and short stories for a variety of college magazines. Orwell left Eton at Christmas 1921 and at around the same time the family moved to Southwold on the Suffolk coast. Strangely Orwell, unlike most Eton ex-scholars, decided not to go to university and instead joined the Indian Imperial Police in Burma in 1922. He served as an Assistant District Superintendent and later as a Headquarters Assistant. He left the police officially in 1928 but had returned home on leave in August 1927 and decided not to return to Burma.[2]

From the autumn of 1927 through to 1928 Orwell lived in a poor area of London and would spend the next five years exploring and getting to know the lives of the poor and the exploited. In 1928 he went to live in Paris in a working-class area. While living in Paris Orwell had several articles published in the professional press for the first time and in December 1928 his first professional article called *A Farthing Newspaper* appeared in a British magazine. In February 1929 Orwell fell ill for the first time with pneumonia and spent several weeks in hospital. During 1929 he wrote several short works and a couple of novels but none have survived. For around ten weeks in autumn 1929 Orwell worked as a dishwasher and kitchen porter in a luxury Paris hotel. In 1930 Orwell returned to Britain and stayed at his parents' house in Southwold where he did his writing. From time to time he lived as a tramp and in working-class districts in London. During the summer holidays of 1930 and 1931 he tutored some schoolboys. He wrote occasional articles during the period 1930-35, mainly for the *Adelphi* magazine. By 1930 Orwell had completed his first version of *Down and Out in Paris and London* and by 1931 he had started *Burmese Days*. In 1931 he spent some time in London and also worked in Kent as a hop-picker.[3]

In 1932 Orwell became a teacher at a small private boys' school. A publisher rejected his first version of *Down and Out in Paris and London*, but the left wing publisher Victor Gollancz accepted an abbreviated version. During the school holidays Orwell edited *Burmese Days*. Gollancz published *Down and Out in Paris and London* in 1933. Orwell continued to teach but changed schools and taught mixed-sex classes. At the end of 1933 Orwell fell ill with pneumonia again. This time he was seriously ill enough to have to go into hospital, and he had to give up teaching. In 1934 Orwell finished a novel called *A Clergyman's Daughter* and *Burmese Days* was published.

Orwell returned to Southwold after his illness, but in October he moved to London and worked as a part-time assistant at a bookshop. *A Clergyman's Daughter* was published in 1935 and Orwell had begun a new work called *Keep the Aspidistra Flying*. In this year he met his future wife Eileen O'Shaughnessy, who was a university student studying for a Master's degree. Victor Gollancz published *Keep the Aspidistra Flying* in 1936 and also commissioned Orwell to write about depressed areas in Northern England. By the end of the year Orwell had handed in his completed manuscript of *The Road to Wigan Pier* to Gollancz, and also found time to marry Eileen O'Shaughnessy in June that same year. Ironically, before he left for Spain, Orwell had reviewed for Gollancz the book *Walls have Mouths*, about the experiences of Wilfred McCartney, who had been jailed for ten years for spying. He was the first Commander of the British Battalion of the International Brigades in Spain.

In December 1936 Orwell left to go and fight in Spain. On his way to Spain he stopped off in Paris and visited the famous American writer, Henry Miller, who gave him a corduroy jacket to wear in Spain.[4]

When he arrived in Barcelona Orwell visited John McNair in the ILP office, carrying a letter from Fenner Brockway recommending him to McNair. According to McNair Orwell gave two reasons why he had come to Spain:

"First to assist actively the Republicans and the second to gather material for a book I propose writing on the Fascist revolt."[5]

Orwell himself claimed he would be of best use to the 'workers cause' by 'being a fighter at the front'. Orwell biographer D. J. Taylor also believes that Orwell's main reason for going to Spain was to fight Fascism:

"Orwell had a much more definite purpose in mind. He wanted to fight".[6]

Orwell told McNair that he had some military experience from his time in Burma as a policeman. McNair took him to the Lenin Barracks and introduced him to the POUM headquarters staff. Orwell spoke Spanish well and knew enough French to be able to understand Catalan. When McNair returned to the Lenin Barracks two days later Orwell had been made a Sergeant and was drilling the young recruits. The Spanish attempted to get Orwell drunk on their red wine but they failed as he had been used to drinking similar wine whilst living in Paris. When asked by McNair why he wrote under the name 'George Orwell' instead of his real name, he replied that he thought George was a more working-class name than Eric, and that the Orwell was a river in Suffolk. To the ILP Contingent Orwell was always known as Eric Blair.[7]

After being in the line for three weeks Orwell was sent to join the newly arrived ILP volunteers. In his time with the ILP Contingent Orwell became a Political Commissar (thanks to his ability to speak Catalan) and effectively became the leader of the ILP Contingent after Bob Edwards had left Spain for the ILP Easter conference.[8]

While fighting in Spain he suffered from regular cold infections, a septic hand and was shot in the throat by an enemy sniper and nearly killed.[9] In April 1937 Orwell's wife, Eileen Blair, became McNair's Secretary after the previous holder of the post had gone to the Front as a nurse.

Having served 115 days at the Front, Orwell returned on leave to Barcelona with the other ILP volunteers. Orwell describes his time at the Front as anything but heroic:

"the mingled boredom and discomfort of stationary warfare"

and

"and at the time this period seemed to me to have been one of the most futile of my entire life."

On his return to Barcelona Orwell fell ill due to eating and drinking too much. Within days of his return to Barcelona Orwell became involved in the street fighting during the 'May Days' events, although the only shot he fired was an attempt to blow up an unexploded grenade in the street. He first knew there was trouble when a bullet came through the window of the Hotel Continental where he was staying. During this time he wrote to the publisher Gollancz saying he had not finished the introduction to *The Road to Wigan Pier* because he was 'rather occupied', and also commented that he planned to return to the Front and to return home in August and write another book.

On his return to the Front he received his near fatal injury and was sent to hospital. His injury seems to have been caused by his own carelessness. He had a habit of smoking a cigarette as dawn rose, which meant his head and shoulders gave off a silhouette against the parapet making him visible to enemy snipers. The trenches were designed for volunteers much shorter than Orwell. He was discharged from the front due to his serious wound and returned to Barcelona. The first thing Orwell did was to try and help obtain the release of George Kopp, who had been arrested. This was a brave and also foolhardy thing to do, since he was risking imprisonment because the POUM had now been declared illegal. There was also a warrant to arrest Orwell and Eileen as 'Trotskyists and ILP agents of the POUM', and they could have been shot if captured. To avoid arrest Orwell pretended to be a middle-class gentleman during the day and slept rough in Barcelona at night, before he eventually left Spain by train with Eileen, McNair and the young volunteer Stafford Cottman. They were fortunate that the Border Police did not realise that they were wanted men or that the 29th Division from which Orwell had been discharged was actually the POUM Division.[10]

The ILP Contingent leader, Bob Edwards, describes Orwell's appearance in the cold mountains on the Aragon Front:

> "I'll never forget my first sight of him. A big man, you know, with big boots, the biggest boots I'd ever seen, corduroy trousers, and he had a balaclava hat down over his ears (it was blessed cold up there, and he suffered from bronchitis). He had a scarf round his neck, up to his eyes, and an old Winchester rifle on his shoulder, and two hand grenades hanging from his belt."[11]

Edwards believed that Orwell possessed almost reckless courage and gives one example when a Spanish machine gun crew refused to take cover when under fire, even though their own gun was no longer working. Orwell stood up with them to save their Spanish dignity. Orwell used to creep out into 'No Man's Land' to steal potatoes while under fire, believing he was out of range and therefore safe from being hit.[12] He also led the occasional night patrol and would crawl within a few yards of the enemy trenches without being spotted.[13] One ILP volunteer remembers Orwell as a disciplinarian who wanted the British volunteers to act more like soldiers.[14] At the Front Orwell suffered because of the cold and always had a 'dew drop' hanging from his nose. Bob Edwards again:

> "He suffered very badly in the mountains because it was bitterly cold. You'd lift a blanket over him and he was like a board, he was frozen. My hands are frost bitten still because I left the skin of my hand on the barrel of a rifle it was so cold. I had to wash them in hot olive oil to get the circulation going. And Orwell suffered a lot but he never complained. He was a very courageous chap."[15]

As well as the cold, Orwell hated the rats in the trenches (a fear he gave to his hero Winston Smith in *1984*!). If we are to believe Bob Edwards, he caused a panic when he shot one, which led to the Fascists bombing and firing at ILP positions thinking they were about to be attacked.[16]

Orwell was involved in the attack on Ermita Salas, the one major military action of the ILP Contingent, and in Edwards' absence he may have been the leader of the fifteen ILP volunteers who took part in the attack. During the attack he seems to have been cool under fire, but was told to keep his head down. He chased the fleeing enemy down a communication trench with a bayonet and is reported to have shouted, "Come on you bastards". Chapter Seven of *Homage to Catalonia* describes the attack in detail. It was also reported in more dramatic fashion in the *New Leader*. The following section emphasises Orwell's role:

> "'Charge!' shouted Blair.
> 'Over to the right and in!' called Paddy Donovan.
> 'Are we downhearted?' cried the French Captain Benjamin.
>   In front of the parapet was Eric Blair's tall figure coolly strolling forward through the storm of fire. He leapt at the parapet, then stumbled. Hell, had they got him? No, he was over, closely followed by Gross, of Hammersmith, Frankfort, of Hackney, and Bob Smillie, with the others right after them.
>   The trench had been hastily evacuated. The last of the retreating Fascists, clothed only in a blanket, was thirty yards away. Blair gave chase, but the men knew the ground and got away. In the corner of the trench was one dead man; in a dug-out was another body." [17]

Except for the occasional patrol, the attack on Ermita Salas was the only real military action in which Orwell took part. It was chaotic, with the ILP volunteers suffering several wounded men. The commanding officer, Jorge (Roca), was also wounded in this action. Reports suggest that Orwell was strongly involved in a successful assault but ultimately the attackers had to retire with a captured box of ammunition.

Some of the ILP volunteers disliked certain aspects of Orwell's personality, his background and his views; and they questioned his motives for being in Spain, but to the majority of volunteers he was a popular member of the unit. Edwards records that Orwell was always 'scribbling' in the trenches and did not mix well with the other volunteers, preferring to remain alone and read Shakespeare and Charles Reade's *Hard Cash*. One volunteer believes that other volunteers saw this as acting in a 'highbrow' way. On another occasion he sang the 'Eton Boating Song' while on guard duty. One volunteer took exception to the statement in *The Road to Wigan Pier* that 'working class people stank'. His upper middle-class accent and his easy certainty during debates also upset some volunteers. Orwell lacked any particular political ideology, being vaguely left wing, which annoyed some of the more revolutionary members of the unit. Several volunteers were angered when Orwell expressed a desire to join the International Brigades.[18] In a report written by the British Battalion Commissar Tapsell, Orwell is listed as wanting to leave the POUM militia and in addition he had a personal chat with Tapsell about whether his connections with the ILP Contingent would affect his chances of joining the International Brigades. D. J. Taylor claims Eileen Blair was offered some sort of Executive function within the International Brigades and Orwell may have been accepted for the International Brigades straight away but for his poor health.[19] Tapsell describes Orwell as follows:

"The leading personality and most respected man in the contingent at present is Eric Blair. This man is a novelist who has written some books on proletarian life in England. He has little political understanding and he is not interested in party politics, and came to Spain as an anti-Fascist to fight Fascism." [20]

To a Communist Party member like Tapsell this is a criticism but it shows Orwell as a true anti-Fascist volunteer not someone in Spain purely to write a book. Also, while he was in Barcelona, Orwell met another British member of the International Brigades - a Doctor called Kenneth Sinclair-Loutit - in a café where together they discussed the war and politics.[21]

Orwell escaped to Britain in July 1937 and within a few weeks of being back in the country he began work on his account of his time in Spain. Victor Gollancz refused to publish this work, and the *New Statesman* rejected his review of *The Spanish Labyrinth*. Both believed that Orwell's criticism of the Communists in Spain was undermining the Republican cause and splitting the Left. Orwell was able to express his views on Spain through smaller publications and in the ILP newspaper the *New Leader*. Back in Britain he went to Bristol to support fellow volunteer Stafford Cottman who was being called an 'agent of fascism' and being harassed by local Communists. Orwell stated he would sue if he was called the same. In August he attended the ILP Summer School at Letchworth along with other volunteers. He was asked to contribute to a publication called *Authors Take Sides on the Spanish War*. Many of the most famous living authors supported this publication and wrote almost entirely in favour of the Spanish Republic, but Orwell rudely refused to contribute:

"Will you stop sending me this bloody rubbish. This is the second or third time I have had it. I am not one of your fashionable pansies like Auden and Spender, I was six months in Spain, most of the time fighting. I have a bullet-hole in me at present and I am not going to write blah about defending democracy or gallant little anybody."

Homage to Catalonia finally found a publisher called Warburg, who was happy to publish Orwell's account of his time in Spain. Orwell completed *Homage to Catalonia* in January 1938 and it was published in April of that year. In its first year of publication it only sold seven hundred copies.

However in March 1938 Orwell fell ill with a tubercular (TB) lesion in one lung and went into a sanatorium in Kent until September. During this time he was forbidden to write anything other than the occasional review and had to turn down the offer to write a novel. In June 1938 he joined the ILP as the political party closest to his own Socialistic views. His reasons for joining the ILP was a rejection of 'quietism' where merely being a sympathetic Socialist was not enough. Orwell felt the need to be an active Socialist and anti-Fascist, although his piece on Pacifism for an ILP pamphlet was turned down as unsuitable. A benefactor gave Orwell three hundred pounds in order to regain his health in a warm climate and in September he and his wife left England for Morocco, staying there until March 1939. In Morocco he wrote *Coming up for Air* which Gollancz agreed to publish. On his return to Britain Orwell began work on *Inside the Whale*. When World War II broke out Orwell supported the British Government, but he was rejected for armed service because of his poor health. He left the ILP because of its anti-war stance in the autumn of 1939.[22]

During Christmas 1939 and into January 1940 Orwell was ill with influenza. In 1940 *Inside the Whale* was published by Victor Gollancz. During World War II Orwell worked for the BBC as a broadcaster and wrote articles for the Socialist journal *Tribune*. He was an enthusiastic supporter of the Home Guard.[23] During the war Orwell completed his allegorical novel *Animal Farm*, which was published in 1945. This sets the Russian Socialist Revolution and its aftermath and betrayal by Stalin's Communists (as Orwell saw it) in a farm, ending with the once-revolutionary pig leaders being no different from the capitalist humans they had overthrown. This work made Orwell internationally famous. In 1949 he published what is perhaps his most famous novel, *1984*, in which a future Britain is depicted as a totalitarian police state controlled by 'Big Brother' and his thought police.

Orwell's last years were blighted by ill health. His wife Eileen had died of cancer in 1945 and he lived a lonely existence on an isolated Scottish island for a time. Some of the last photographs of Orwell were taken by prominent British Anarchist, Vernon Richards, who Orwell had first met in 1938 through their interest and involvement in the Spanish war. In his final years he married Sonia Brownell. He died in London on January 21st 1950 aged forty six when a lung haemorrhaged, ironically while planning a visit to Switzerland, hoping the mountain air would be good for his health. D. J. Taylor comments:

> "Spain it can safely be said was the defining experience of Orwell's life."[24]

NCOs

Bill Chambers (?-1937)

Bill Chambers was a working-class cockney from London who was middle aged by the time he fought in Spain. In the ILP he served as a Corporal. He had previous military experience from fighting in World War I, and possibly also saw Army service in peacetime:[1]

> "...Bill Chambers: a fine Londoner with years of war experience"[2]

With the other NCOs and the Commander, each day Chambers would discuss the previous day's events, and plan duties and fatigues such as fetching the food.[3] When the

29. Arthur Chambers. (NL)

Fascists bombarded the ILP positions in the Aragon Mountains with major artillery, the ILP expected them to follow up with an attack, but nothing happened. Chambers and Bob Edwards formed a patrol with another volunteer and entered the valley between the two positions to try and discover if an attack was happening. Halfway between the two lines they occupied a deserted hut and listened and waited for a long time before returning to their own lines. A second patrol discovered that the Nationalists had abandoned any plan to attack their position.[4] In Spain he quarrelled bitterly with Orwell possibly over differing political views and Orwell's desire to join the International Brigades. In addition he teased Orwell about being afraid of rats.[5]

According to fellow volunteer Harry Thomas, Chambers was appointed a Sergeant on the second day in the Lenin Barracks. According to Thomas, here he rowed with the then leader of the ILP volunteers, W. B. Martin, over a 'foolish order' and resigned as Sergeant, possibly accepting the role of Corporal at the Front. Thomas goes on to say that Chambers later fell out with Bob Edwards, refused an order and stated he was going to join another unit. He was disarmed and a sentry told to shoot him if he tried to desert. Chambers ended up deserting regardless, and joined a Spanish unit instead.[6] Chambers joined a CNT Anarchist unit on the Aragon Front named after the Italian Anarchist 'Malatesta'. In July 1937 he was reported missing, but was confirmed killed the following month. His CNT regiment had taken part in a major attack on the Aragon and had suffered heavy losses. They had captured some enemy trenches but had been repulsed attacking against another line of trenches. In between the captured trenches and the enemy held trenches were many wounded men crying out in agony. Chambers volunteered to go and try to help rescue these men. While doing so he was shot dead by an enemy sniper. At the 1937 ILP Summer School at Letchworth there was a two minute silence to remember Arthur Chambers and the other ILP member to die in Spain, Bob Smillie.[7]

John or Michael 'Paddy' Donovan (1907-1971)

Donovan was from Cork in Ireland and he worked as a fitter. He had previous military experience serving in the Irish Free State Army. At first he tried to join the International Brigades but was turned down. Robson, the Communist Party's recruiter for the International

Brigades, told him that they had 'no room for O'Duffy (Irish Fascist leader) Fascists' and said he should try elsewhere. This decision was based on the fact the Communist Party supported the view of the IRA for a unified Ireland, rather than the Irish Free State's acceptance of a partitioned Ireland. So having been turned down for the International Brigades, Donovan joined the ILP Contingent and left with his fellow volunteers for Spain in January 1937. Due to his previous military experience he was made a Sergeant in the ILP unit.[1]

ILP leader Bob Edwards described Donovan as:

"...a tower of strength and of working-class common sense and beloved by the boys. He is also our military instructor and is my pal and dug-out companion." [2]

Donovan later also shared a dug-out in the mountains with Orwell and complained about the strong black shag tobacco Orwell smoke because it filled the dug-out.[3]

Donovan was seen as a one of the non-political members of the unit - more of a professional soldier than a political man.[4] Crick speculates that he was

"perhaps there for the job and the scrap".[5]

Conversely, Bob Edwards describes Donovan as a Socialist.[6] Donovan was one of the leading figures in the trench raid at Ermita Salas (the one major military action involving the ILP volunteers). In the attack on the trench Donovan shouted to the excitable (and extremely tall!) Orwell to keep his head down. He also told the volunteers to attack the right of the trench, as this was the best place to break in.[7] Once the trench had been secured Donovan was sent back for orders. He returned to order the ILP and Spanish volunteers to retreat. When Orwell wanted to go back to the enemy trench to get a telescope, Donovan told him "Bollocks the telescope!" and to hurry up. Under fire from both sides the volunteers retired to their own lines with Donovan holding open a gap in the barbed wire for Orwell to get through.[8] After the action Donovan was one of those men praised and named by the ILP Commander Georges Kopp as having "behaved exceptionally well" and "splendid action".[9]

After the 'May Days' events, Donovan claims that members of the

British Communist Party contacted him in Barcelona with criticisms concerning John McNair, the ILP representative in Barcelona. In the criticism McNair was accused of delaying the giving of passports to ILP volunteers who wished to go home, of neglecting the wounded and generally letting down the volunteers who were dissatisfied with his efforts. More importantly, Donovan states that he was asked to sign an open letter to the remaining ILP volunteers still at the Front appealing to them to join the International Brigades. He refused to do this since the Communists had been publicly calling the POUM a 'Fascist' Party. Donovan refutes all the charges made by the Communists and says that McNair was well respected and supported the ILP volunteers exceptionally well. Donovan also said that he did not want to join the International Brigade because if he was called a Fascist by the Communist Party in London, he would just as likely be called one in the International Brigades around Madrid.[10]

Nevertheless, Donovan did not return to the Front with the ILP volunteers after the 'May Days' events. Instead he joined the Anarchist 'Death Battalion', which included a contingent of Italians, and served with them until July 1937. In that month he was repatriated to Britain.[11] There is a possibility that Donovan returned to Spain in February 1938 and joined the International Brigades and deserted later in the year, possibly because of problems over his previous service in the ILP Contingent.[12]

We have two pictures of Donovan with the ILP Contingent: one from the Orwell archive where he is eating food with a group of volunteers. He is of medium build and average height, wearing a peaked cap and militia uniform with boots.[13] In the second picture from the Bob Edwards archive it is again mealtime and he is sitting crossed legged. He has thick, dark hair and is wearing a militia uniform with what look like puttees (like bandages wrapped around an arm or leg) around his lower legs.[14]

On his return to Britain Donovan attended the ILP Summer School at Letchworth in August 1937. On August 5th he was involved in a session discussing the Spanish War.[15] In the *New Leader* report on the Summer School they describe Donovan as:

"...an Irish proletarian, plain-spoken, with qualities both of fun and indignation."[16]

Later in 1937 Donovan, in company with many other ILP volunteers, signed an article condemning the views of fellow volunteer Frankford. He had suggested there were some treasonous relations between the POUM and the Fascists also involving Georges Kopp.[17]

During the winter of 1937-38 Donovan was unemployed and Orwell, keen to start writing again, employed him as a labourer-cum-gardener Donovan remained a loyal member of the ILP up and till his death in London in 1971.[18]

Thomas 'Buck' Parker (1909 - ?)

Buck Parker, as he was known in Spain was born in 1909, originated from South Africa and later lived in Liverpool. Before he went to Spain he was living in Golders Green, London, working as a mechanic. He served as a corporal in the ILP Contingent.[1] As a corporal Parker met each morning with the other NCOs and Bob Edwards to discuss events and plan the day's duties.[2] In the *New Leader* Bob Edwards refers to:

"...young Parker, still in his thirties, quiet, cool and very efficient." [3]

During the action in which the POUM militia (containing the ILP volunteers) advanced their lines forward towards the enemy trenches in April 1937, Parker was shot in the top of the thigh and wounded. Parker himself says that it was close to being a 'DSO'; a parody of the British 'Distinguished Service Order' medal, but actually an abbreviation of 'Dick Shot Off'![4] According to the *New Leader*, Parker was part of a special group of ILP volunteers who formed a special 'Shock Section' due to their military expertise and went in advance of the contingent.[5]

After being wounded Parker wrote an appeal for aid from his hospital bed in the *New Leader*:

"On January 19th 1937, the ILP contingent left London for Spain, to assist our Spanish comrades in the struggle against international Fascism.

We were then, and we are now more than ever, prepared if necessary to lay down our lives to smash the forces of Hitler, Mussolini and Franco.

The Fascist-trained fighting troops are equipped with every modern implement of war, supplied to them by the different capitalist arms manufacturers of the world. In the fighting lines of the workers we cry for arms. Alas! The ears of those who should hear this are heavily sealed with the diplomatic lies of national dictators and ambassadors.

At the present moment we, the workers of the world, are winning on all fronts. The battles are heavy, the casualties are many.

This struggle is also your struggle. Are you doing your part? The help we most need today in Spain is in the way of medical supplies. You can do your part by sending your financial assistance to the ILP offices." [6]

This is a well-written piece of propaganda, but it also shows clearly Parker's anti-Fascist views.

Parker also visited Orwell before he was wounded, when Orwell was in hospital recovering from a poisoned hand. Orwell comments that Parker looked surprised when he saw that Orwell had margarine, clearly something unavailable at the Front.[7] In a letter to the Communist journalist Frank Jellinek in December 1938, Orwell tells him not to believe what he had been told about the ILP militia by Buck Parker. This could indicate a belief by Orwell that Parker was untrustworthy or a liar.[8] In a meeting with other volunteers and John McNair on April 28th 1937, Parker vocally aired his view the ILP Contingent was being used purely as a propaganda tool by the POUM; this may be because he was a Communist or had Communist views.[9] Maybe after he returned home he was hostile to the POUM/ILP and that was why Orwell told Jellinek don't believe anything Parker said about the ILP unit.

The only other thing that is known about Parker was that he was in Barcelona during the 'May Days' and volunteered to guard a POUM held building because he had had a good night's sleep the previous night.[10] In May 1937 he was once again in a Barcelona hospital.[11]

In a picture from the Orwell archive Parker is shown smoking a cigarette during a meal at the Front. He is quite short with dark hair, wearing militia clothes and a beret.[12]

He returned from Spain on either the 21st or 29th May 1937.[12]

* * *

Notes

Rovira

[1] Wilebaldo Solano, Rercuerdo de Josep Rovira
www.fundanin.org/solano.htm
This is the major source I have used for the life of Rovira. It is in Spanish but is also available in a translated form.

[2] Victor Alba and Stephen Schwartz, *Spanish Marxism versus Soviet Communism: A History of the P.O.U.M.* (Oxford, Transaction Books, 1988) p51

[3] Alba and Schwartz, op cit., p21

[4] Ibid, p92

[5] Ibid, p111

[6] Ibid, p114

[7] Ibid, p154, Hugh Thomas, *The Spanish Civil War*. 3rd edition revised. (London, Penguin, 1986) p547, 677, Pierre Broue and Emile Temime, *The Revolution and the Civil War in Spain* (London, Faber and Faber, 1972) p142, 222

[8] Thomas, op cit., p703-704, Alba and Schwartz, Ibid, p226

[9] Alba and Schwartz, Ibid, p243

[10] Ibid, p243

[11] Ibid, p255

[12] Ibid, p197

[13] Solano, op cit., p3

Jorge

[1] Josep Pane, Gregorio Jorge, l'heroi desconegut
www.fundanin.org/pane.htm
This article is the major source on Jorge, the text is in Catalan and was very kindly translated for me by Philip Mahon. It is not possible to give page references as his translation was on four pages and the original article was six pages long.

[2] George Orwell, *Homage to Catalonia: And Looking Back on the Spanish War* (London, Penguin, 1988) p84-98

[3] Pane, op cit.

[4] Ibid

[5] Orwell, op cit., p80

[6] Ibid, p81-82

[7] Pane, op cit.

[8] Ibid

Kopp

[1] *Revolutionary History, The Spanish Civil War: The View from the Left* (London, Socialist Platform, 1992) p242-252. This volume contains a chapter written by Don Bateman on the life of Kopp.
[2] Pane, op cit.
[3] NL 13.08.37, Peter Davison (editor), *Orwell in Spain: The full text of Homage to Catalonia with associated articles and letters from the Complete Works of George Orwell* (London, Penguin, 2001) p150-151
[4] Miguel Pedrola. He was a militant of the POUM Youth organisation, killed in action near Huesca in 1936.
[5] Orwell, op cit., p175, Davison, op cit., p325
[6] Orwell, Ibid, p21, Andy Durgan, *International Volunteers in the POUM* Militias http://libcom.org/history/international-volunteers-poum-militias p6
[7] Durgan, op cit., p6
[8] Davison, op cit., p10
[9] Ibid, p54
[10] Ibid, p325
[11] T. R. Fyvel, *George Orwell: a personal memoir* (London, Weidenfeld and Nicolson, 1982) p75
[12] Orwell, op cit., p123-125
[13] Davison, op cit., p325
[14] Ibid, p18-22
[15] Orwell, op cit., p191
[16] Ibid, p199-200, Davison, op cit., p324
[17] Orwell, Ibid, p207-214
[18] Davison, op cit., p325
[19] Sonia Orwell and Ian Angus (editors), *The Collected Essays, Journalism and Letters of George Orwell: Volume 1 An Age Like This 1920-1940* (London, Penguin, 1970) p405
[20] NL 24.09.37, Bernard Crick, *George Orwell: A Life* (London, Secker & Warburg, 1981) p232
[21] Davison, op cit., p223-224
[22] Ibid, p227-228
[23] Ibid, p324, Orwell and Angus op cit., p409, 421, Durgan, op cit., p13
[24] Crick, op cit., p252
[25] Ibid, p218, 224
[26] Ibid, p221, Michael Shelden, *Orwell Authorised Biography* (London, Politicos, 2006) p298-300
[27] Shelden, op cit., p298-299
[28] Ibid, p298

[29] Ibid, p299
[30] Ibid, p413
[31] Davison, op cit., p29, 330
[32] Durgan, op cit., p13-14
[33] Crick, op cit., p347, Shelden, op cit., p298
[34] Crick, Ibid, p352, 355, 358
[35] Revolutionary History, op cit., p242-252, Durgan, op cit., p21
[36] Shelden, op cit., p297-301
[37] Gidon Cohen, *The Failure of a Dream: The Independent Labour Party from Disaffiliation to World War II* (London, Tauris, 2007) p187-188, Tom Buchanan, *The Impact of the Spanish Civil War on Britain: War, Loss and Memory* (Brighton, Sussex Academic Press, 2007) p98-121, John Newsinger, The Death of Bob Smillie, *The Historical Journal*, 41, 2, 1998, p575-578
[38] Cohen, op cit., p187-188

Levinski

[1] Shelden, op cit., p279, Durgan, op cit., p22
[2] Orwell, op cit., p24
[3] Ibid, p23
[4] Ibid, p23
[5] Shelden, op cit., p279-280
[6] Orwell, op cit., p86-88
[7] NL 30.04.37
[8] Orwell, op cit., p89
[9] Ibid, p84-99
[10] Ibid, p175, Shelden, op cit., p312
[11] Durgan, op cit., p22

Edwards

[1] There are two major sources for the life of Bob Edwards. The first is an interview by the Imperial War Museum in 1980. The interview is two hours long reference 4669/4. The second major source is the Bob Edwards personal papers held in the Labour History Archive and Study Centre, 103 Princess Street, Manchester, M1 6DD.
[2] Bob Edwards Papers, op cit.
[3] Imperial War Museum, Bob Edwards interview op cit., Bob Edwards Papers, Ibid.
[4] Cohen, op cit., p47
[5] Ibid, p88-90
[6] Bob Edwards papers, op cit.

[7] Ibid
[8] Ibid
[9] Cohen, op cit., p128
[10] Bob Edwards papers op cit.
[11] F. W. S. Craig, *Minor Parties at British Parliamentary Elections 1885-1974* (London, MacMillan, 1975) p41
[12] Cohen, op cit., p224
[13] Ibid, p174
[14] Imperial War Museum, Bob Edwards interview
[15] Peter Thwaites, The Independent Labour Party Contingent in the Spanish Civil War, *Imperial War Museum Review*, 1987 p52, Fenner Brockway, *Towards Tomorrow* (London, Hart-Davies, MacGibbon, 1977) p119
[16] Brockway, op cit., p119
[17] Imperial War Museum, Bob Edwards interview
[18] Thwaites, op cit., p53
[19] Ibid, p55, 60, Marx Memorial Library, International Brigade archive, Box C 13/12, H P Thomas letter
[20] Ibid, p55
[21] Bob Edwards papers, op cit. MML Thomas letter, op cit.
[22] Ibid
[23] Crick, op cit., p215, MML Thomas letter, op cit.
[24] Bob Edwards papers, op cit.
[25] Ibid
[26] Ibid
[27] Stephen Wadhams, *Remembering Orwell* (Harmondsworth, Penguin, 1984) p75-76
[28] NL 15.01.37
[29] NL 22.01.37
[30] NL 19.02.37, MML Thomas letter, op cit.
[31] NL 26.02.37
[32] NL 05.03.37
[33] Shelden, op cit., p282
[34] Crick, op cit., p216, 436-437, Wadhams, op cit., p78-79
[35] Shelden, op cit., p290
[36] Bob Edwards papers, op cit.
[37] Wadhams, op cit., p78
[38] Ibid, p85
[39] Bob Edwards papers, op cit.
[40] Ibid
[41] Thwaites, op cit., p56

[42] John McNair, *Spanish Diary* (Stockport, Independent Labour Publications, ND) p22
[43] Bob Edwards papers, op cit. National Archives, Cat no. KV/5/12 MI5 List of individuals who travelled and returned from Spain 1936-39
[44] Ibid, NL 02.04.37
[45] Bob Edwards papers, Ibid
[46] Hywel Francis, *Miners Against Fascism: Wales and the Spanish Civil War* (London, Lawrence and Wishart, 1984) p114-115
[47] NL 13.08.37
[48] NL 24.09.37
[49] Bob Edwards papers, op cit.
[50] Craig, op cit., p41
[51] Ibid, p42
[52] Bob Edwards papers, op cit.
[53] Ibid

Blair (Orwell)
[1] The three major biographies written on Orwell are by Michael Shelden, op cit. and by Bernard Crick, op cit. and Taylor, D. J. *Orwell: the life* (London, Vantage Books, 2004)
[2] Orwell and Angus, op cit., p594-596
[3] Ibid, p596-597
[4] Ibid, p597-599, Taylor, op cit., p200-1
Wilfrid MacCartney was the first Commander of the British Battalion of the International Brigades. He had previously been imprisoned for ten years for spying. He left Spain in mysterious circumstances when he was wounded accidentally by a gun being passed to him and returned to Britain in February 1937. Henry Miller (1891-1980) Famous American writer and painter, who lived in Paris in the period 1931-39.
[5] McNair, op cit., p14. Taylor, ibid, p194
[6] Taylor, ibid, p195, Spanish Revolution, Vol 2, No 2, February 3rd, 1937 http://contentdm.warwick.ac.uk/cdm/compoundobject/collection/scw/id/7116/rec/2
[7] McNair, op cit., p14-15,
[8] Thwaites, op cit., p55-56, 60
[9] McNair, op cit., p21, Davison, op cit., p18-22, Taylor, op cit., p211
[10] McNair, Ibid, p24-27, Orwell, op cit., chps 10-14, Christopher Hall, *'Disciplina Camaradas': Four English Volunteers in Spain 1936-39* (Pontefract, Gosling Press, 1994) p108. Taylor, ibid, p208, 215, 217, 220, 225-6, 231
[11] Wadhams, op cit., p78, Taylor, ibid., p202 (Orwell was seen in a hotel

foyer with his giant boots around his neck, by ILP activist Jenny Lee and later Labour MP)

[12] Ibid, p78-79, Hall, op cit., p48, Taylor, ibid, p211
[13] Wadhams, Ibid, p80
[14] Ibid, p83
[15] Imperial War Museum, Bob Edwards interview, op cit.
[16] Wadhams, op cit., p79, 84
[17] NL 30.04.37, Shelden, op cit., p287, Taylor, op cit., p214
[18] Wadhams, op cit., p79-86, Taylor, ibid., p211. Charles Reade (1814-1884). English novelist and dramatist.
[19] Marx Memorial Library, International Brigade Archive, Box C 13/7a 'Report on the English Section of the POUM'. Taylor, ibid, p219
[20] Marx Memorial Library, International Brigade Archive, Box c 13/7a, op cit.
[21] Taylor, op cit., P225, Dr Kenneth Sinclair-Loutit (1913-2003).
He was a trainee doctor when he left for Spain in August 1936 and was administrator of the first British Medical Unit. He left Spain in December 1937 to complete his medical studies.
[22] Orwell and Angus, op cit., p599-601, Taylor, ibid, p245-6, 248, 252, 256-7 W H Auden (1907-73) and Stephen Spender (1909-95) were both left wing and homosexual poets. Both visited and supported Republican Spain. Spender's then boyfriend Tony Hyndman served in the International Brigades. Orwell's comments here are clearly homophobic.
[23] Home Guard. This was a volunteer defence force raised to support the Regular Army if the Germans invaded Britain during World War II. In its early days training in guerrilla tactics was led by Tom Wintringham, a former leader of the British Battalion of the International Brigades assisted by ex International Brigaders and Spanish Republican exiles. Before long the Government feared that the 'Reds' were trying to train a revolutionary army and took over the training of the volunteers.
[24] Orwell and Angus, op cit., p601, Crick, op cit., chps 12-17, John Ramsden, *The Oxford Companion to Twentieth-Century British Politics* (Oxford, Oxford Univ. Press, 2005), p488. Taylor, op cit., p201, 330.
Vernon Richards (1924-2001) was a British Anarchist who edited 'Spain and the World' during the Civil War.

Chambers

[1] Cohen, op cit., p181, Hall, op cit., p75, NL 19.02.37
[2] NL 19.02.37
[3] NL 19.02.37
[4] NL 26.02.37

[5] Orwell, op cit., p104
[6] MML Thomas letter, op cit
[7] NL 06.08.37, NL 13.08.37, Cohen, op cit., p186, Thwaites, op cit., p60, Taylor, op cit., p246, Durgan, op cit., p19. Cohen, and Andy Durgan in correspondence with author believes Chambers was killed in 1938. Chambers is listed in the Tapsell report as one of the volunteers who had left the ILP Contingent to return home, Marx Memorial Library, International Brigade Archive, Box 13/7a, op cit. Jim Carmody in correspondence with the author says a William Chambers left Valencia for England in April 1937.

Donovan

[1] Marx Memorial Library, International Brigade Archive, Box C 13/12 John Donovan letter 27.05.37, Jim Carmody correspondence, National Archives, op cit., List of International Brigaders with annotations given to author by Local History Group, Author unknown.
R W Robson, was a Scotsman and World War I veteran. He was the London District Organiser of the Communist Party and vetted volunteers going to Spain. He described in detail to the potential volunteers the horrors that awaited them in Spain.
Eoin O'Duffy (1890-1944) He was the leader of the Irish Fascist 'Blueshirts'. He led a contingent to Spain of a few hundred men to fight for Franco, but after achieving little returned home after less than six months in Spain.
[2] NL 19.02.37
[3] Crick, op cit., p216-217
[4] Ibid, p216-217
[5] Crick, Ibid, p217
[6] NL 19.02.37
[7] Shelden, op cit., p286-287, NL 30.04.37, Cohen, op cit., p182
[8] Orwell, op cit., p95-96
[9] McNair, op cit., p20, Buchanan, op cit., p100
[10] NL 11.06.37, Thwaites, op cit., p57, 61. Donovan is listed in the Tapsell Report as a volunteer who wished to leave the POUM militia, Marx Memorial Library, International Brigade Archive, Box 13/7a, op cit. It is possible Tapsell was one of the Communist Party members that wanted him to denounce McNair. Tapsell saw McNair as an obstacle to recruiting the members of the ILP Contingent into the International Brigades, Marx Memorial Library, International Brigade Archive, Box 13/10, 'Report on the position with regard to the ILP Group'. MML Donovan letter, op cit.

[11] Ciaran Crossey, "We Intend to Show the World", (Belfast, Belfast and District Trades Union Council, 2007) p12, List of International Brigaders, op cit., National Archives says left Spain 29.05.37.
[12] List of International Brigaders, Ibid, National Archives says left Britain for Spain 05.02.38.
[13] Thwaites, op cit, p55
[14] Bob Edwards papers, op cit.
[15] Shelden, op cit., p308-309, Crick, op cit., p233
[16] NL 13.08.37
[17] NL 24.09.37
[18] Crick, op cit., p237, McNair, op cit., p20, Durgan, op cit., p19, Taylor, op cit., p330

Parker

[1] Orwell and Angus, op cit., p298, Durgan, op cit., p22, National Archives, op cit., correspondence Jim Carmody
[2] NL 19.02.37
[3] NL 19.02.37
[4] Orwell, op cit., p80-81, Cohen, op cit., p182, Thwaites, op cit., p60, Davison, op cit., p30
[5] NL 23.04.37
[6] NL 30.04.37
[7] Orwell and Angus, op cit., p298
[8] Ibid, p405
[9] Marx Memorial Library, International Brigade Archive, Box 13/7a, op cit, National Archives Archive says he had a Communist International card.
[10] NL 21.05.37
[11] Marx Memorial Library, International Brigade Archive, Box 13/7a. op cit.
[12] Thwaites, op cit., p55
[13] National Archives, op cit.

* * *

CHAPTER 9

British and Irish Members of the ILP Contingent

30. George Orwell and Eileen O'Shaughnessy on the Aragon Front near Huesca, 13th March 1937. *(UCL)*

Pictured are members of the ILP Contingent and some of the fearless Spanish machine gunners who Orwell says once disdained to take cover when under fire when their gun jammed in the open. The machine gun pictured is a Hotchkiss Model 1914. The ILP volunteers in the picture include:

Far left, standing is **John Braithwaite**; Third from the left kneeling in beret is American **Harry Milton**; Fourth from the left looking down is **Charles Justessen**; Next to him is **Philip Hunter**; Next to him is **Reg Hiddlestone**; Next to him is **George Orwell**; Orwell's wife **Eileen O'Shaughnessy** is to the right of Orwell. Second from the right, behind the militiaman with his hands in his pockets, is **John Agnew**.

John Agnew (1900 - ?)

Born in 1900, John Henry Agnew came from Blackpool, Lancashire, and was a miner. He had previous military experience, having served in the British Army. He left for Spain with the other ILP volunteers on January 10th 1937, departing from Newhaven and landing in Dieppe.[1]

The only other information available on John Agnew is that he appears in the photograph from the Orwell archive where a group of ILP volunteers are grouped around a Hotchkiss machine gun at the front taken on 13th March 1937.[2] Agnew is a head shorter than Orwell, which must make him about five feet seven or eight inches tall (see page 171). He left Spain for home in late May 1937.[3]

Lewis Ernest Avory

Lewis Avory was an ILP member who joined the POUM Lenin Division, at a date which is unknown. It is possible he joined the ILP Contingent either in Barcelona or at the Front at some stage. No further information is known about this volunteer.[1]

William Bennett

William Bennett was a Scottish volunteer.[1] Peter Thwaites identifies one of the volunteers pictured in a photograph in the Bob Edwards archive as Bennett.[2] Bennett is sitting down at mealtime talking to Buck Parker. He is wearing white canvas shoes, probably Spanish alpargatas, puttees, corduroy trousers and shirt, and is bare-headed, with dark hair. He appears to have a drink in one hand and a cigarette in the other. He looks in his mid-twenties. After his return to Britain he became a plasterer and was a prominent member of that trade union.[3]

John, or Jock, Braithwaite, or Branthwaite (1914 - ?)[1]

John Braithwaite (the more common use of his name) was a Scottish working-class volunteer from a mining family. At around twenty-two years old he was one of the youngest volunteers and left for Spain with the main group of volunteers in January 1937.[2] He may have been a member of the ILP or its 'Guild of Youth' prior to going to Spain but certainly became a member of the ILP on his return to England.

Braithwaite says that from time to time Orwell, as one of the leaders, told him to smarten up to show the Spanish that the unit had discipline. Braithwaite remembers discussing Orwell's book *The Road to Wigan Pier* with other volunteers. He believed that Orwell was not a snob and that he did not believe that working-class people stank. He also talked with Orwell, and no doubt with other volunteers, about having a coffee in the enemy-held town of Huesca after its capture; unfortunately this never occurred.[3]

In Spain Braithwaite was a highly politicised volunteer, like the other ILP volunteers.

"We'd been arguing politics a lot, day and night...."[4]

The best depiction of Braithwaite in Spain is in the Orwell archive, where some volunteers are grouped around a Hotchkiss machine gun.[5] Braithwaite is on the extreme left wearing boots, puttees, corduroy trousers and a thick jumper, and is holding a Mauser rifle. He is of average height - around five feet seven or eight inches tall - and has lightish hair colour (see page 171).

Braithwaite was in Barcelona when the 'May Days' events took place but there is no account of his actively being involved. His introduction to the 'Civil War within a Civil War' was dramatic:

"We were sitting there, and a shot came through the window. We all ducked."[6]

John McNair wrote in the *New Leader* about the 'May Days' events and refers to Braithwaite singing a tune in his office.[7]

After the 'May Days' Braithwaite returned to the Front and was near Orwell when Orwell was shot and wounded by an enemy sniper on May 20th. He helped Orwell climb on to a donkey and, along with other volunteers, took him to the hospital at Sietamo. He had earlier warned Orwell about keeping his head down but Orwell ignored this piece of good advice because he believed that the enemy were too poor a marksman to hit him. Braithwaite visited Orwell in hospital and shortly afterwards had a second spell of leave. In Lerida POUM sympathisers warned him that if he was going to Barcelona he should destroy his POUM uniform and any POUM related papers he possessed, as the POUM had now been outlawed. In Barcelona, Braithwaite met Orwell again, and did not even book into a hotel in case it was discovered he was linked with the POUM. Unlike most of the ILP volunteers, Braithwaite did not even have a passport, having travelled to Spain on a Thomas Cook's weekend ticket to Paris! When he visited the British Consulate to help to get him out of Spain they refused to help him.[8]

Braithwaite escaped from Spain by taking a boat to Marseille in July1937.[9]

On his return to Britain he attended the ILP Summer School at Letchworth in 1937[10] with other volunteers. The *New Leader* describes Braithwaite at the Summer School as:

"Jock Braithwaite, a young strong worker, bubbling over with life."[11]

He was also one of the signatories who condemned Frank Frankford's accusations that the POUM and ILP had fraternised with the enemy.[12] Braithwaite tells an intriguing story (if it is true) about visiting Orwell at his house and possibly giving Orwell the idea for his later work *Animal Farm*:

"I remarked once, casually, 'Well, I don't know about you, Eric, but I see you've got some animals here. I wonder if we handed over the reins of government to the animals, if they'd do any better?'"[13]

He was also surprised when visiting Orwell that he was expecterd to wear formal evening attire for dinner.[14]

He later settled in Toronto in Canada, before returning to live in Dorset in the south west of England in his last years.[15]

Harvey Buttonshaw (1912/15 - 1990's)

In the sources Harvey Buttonshaw has been called both Archie and Harvey and described as both Australian and American. He was most likely British and born in 1914 in Plymouth. He was by profession a poster artist. He left for Spain in January 1937 with the main body of the ILP volunteers.[1] Buttonshaw served on the Aragon Front up to the 'May Days' and visited Orwell in hospital when he had an infected hand. He appears in a photograph taken at the Front with a shell burst in the foreground; unfortunately his appearance in the picture is badly blurred.[2]

Like the vast majority of the ILP volunteers Buttonshaw was involved in the 'May Days' events in Barcelona. He was at the POUM headquarters when Kopp asked for two volunteers to mount a guard on a building controlled by the POUM. Buttonshaw and another ILP volunteer left to guard this building.[3]

There have been two interviews with Buttonshaw where he gives different stories of his life. The first account of Buttonshaw's life is related by the Australian academic Amirah Inglis.[4]

Inglis states that Buttonshaw was born in Australia in 1912.[5] He was a poster artist by profession. In 1936 he was in London and joined the ILP Contingent there. Inglis says Buttonshaw was politically an Anarchist. Buttonshaw saw the Civil War in Spain as:

"...a free civil conflict, not a war of the bosses."[6]

Buttonshaw relates that he travelled by train from London to Barcelona. He received basic military training in Barcelona and then in the countryside, which included lots of "dashing about" but no rifles.[7]

At the front Buttonshaw drew a self-portrait that shows him as a young thin man wearing a beret and sporting a moustache.[8] After serving on the Aragon Front, he was in Barcelona during the 'May Days' where he tells of fighting the Government forces and their Communist allies:

"We fought the Commies in the streets of Barcelona, holed up in the National Theatre firing from the windows high up across to the bastardos in a tower across the Rambla del Flores. This was the end of the revolution; once more force reigned."[9]

This is the only known case of an ILP volunteer openly taking part aggressively in the 'May Days' against the Government and Communist forces.

Buttonshaw remained in Barcelona when the 'May Days' were over. He was arrested and then expelled from Spain. In France his Anarchist friends could not find him work so he joined the French Foreign Legion.[10]

During World War II Buttonshaw deserted the Foreign Legion in North Africa, helped by men of the RAF. He was imprisoned on Gibraltar until it was established that he was not an enemy spy. From there he went with the RAF to Ireland to draw maps and then trained in England to be a rear gunner on a Lancaster bomber.[11]

Looking back at his experiences in Spain Buttonshaw commented:

"It was the opportunity to bring down Fascism, which I detested. I would not have missed it. I'm very glad, that I had the opportunity to join those gracious folk willing to give their life not for a country, but for an ideal."[12]

The other interview with Harvey Buttonshaw is by the Anarchist Joseph Toscano in the 1980's.[13] Toscano believes that Buttonshaw was born in England in 1915, and returned to the Front after the 'May Days' with the reduced ILP Contingent. In this version Buttonshaw says that it was he who told Orwell to keep his head down just before he was wounded.[14]

After the ILP Contingent and the POUM 29th Division was disbanded, Buttonshaw joined an Anarchist unit and continued to fight in this unit until the collapse of Catalonia in 1939. After fleeing to France he was imprisoned in a concentration camp. Republican soldiers who fled into France, when Catalonia was being overrun by the Nationalists, were put into camps on open beaches with little or no facilities and were guarded by French Senegalese soldiers behind barbed wire. Buttonshaw managed to escape and eventually joined the French Foreign Legion.[15] Although both Inglis and Toscano agree that Buttonshaw did join the French Foreign Legion at some time, Inglis has a picture of Buttonshaw in the uniform of the Foreign Legion dated 1938, one year earlier than the fall of Catalonia to the Nationalists in 1939. Toscano's account also has Buttonshaw deserting the Foreign Legion by crossing the Sahara desert and, luckily, meeting British servicemen. Of the two stories I lean towards Inglis' account as it is reported that Buttonshaw left Spain in July 1937.[16]

Toscano says that Buttonshaw joined the Merchant Navy on his return to England. In 1949 he left the Merchant Navy to work in Australia, where he married and eventually settled there until his death in the 1990's. In later years Buttonshaw made contact with the Australian Anarchist movement.[17]

Les Castle

The only known information about this volunteer is that he eventually disagreed with the leadership of the ILP Contingent and the policy of the POUM. He went to Barcelona in May 1937 and tried to join the International Brigades but failed when it was discovered the representative from the British Battalion had left the area and returned to his headquarters.[1] What happened to Castle after this date is unknown.

William Clarke (1900/1 - ?)

Evidence for William Clarke being a member of the ILP Contingent is slight but two sources mention he deserted the International Brigades to join the POUM/ILP forces. Fellow International Brigader, Jack Coward states:

> "Bill Clarke, a Liverpool southender, actually deserted the Brigade to join the POUM."[1]

Clarke was thirty six, married with three children when he went to Spain. He left a job as a clerk and he was a member of the Transport and General Workers Union (T&GWU). He was a Socialist and was a member of a left wing group in the Labour Party called the 'Socialist League'. He had previous military experience having served in the British Army either in peace time or in the last year of World War I. He arrived in Spain and joined the International Brigades in January 1937 and fought at Jarama the following month. The last time his wife knew his whereabouts was a letter sent by him in March 1937. His wife wrote to the Foreign Office trying to find his location possibly as late as 1940.[2] Maybe he was killed in action, or became a POW or deliberately disappeared or returned home at a later date the answer is unknown? He appears in no list of International Brigades dead and if he had been killed fighting in the ILP Contingent or other Republican unit the *New Leader* would have published it.

Arthur Clinton (1907 - ?)

Arthur Clinton was from Swinton in the North West of England (Lancashire) and was nicknamed 'Lanky'- possibly a reference to his height or his county of origin.[1] Clinton was a member of the Pendlebury (Salford) branch of the ILP and left with the bulk of ILP volunteers in January 1937.[2]

Clinton was the 'joker' of the Contingent. Bob Edwards told *New Leader* readers that Clinton helped to keep up the spirits of the volunteers on the journey from Paris to Perpignan across France, southwards towards the Spanish frontier. The volunteers were suffering from lack of sleep due to overcrowding on the train and the long duration of the journey:

> "Very soon we discovered a number of humorists in our ranks, and notably our good comrade, Clinton, from Pendlebury, whose droll, Lancashire humour never failed to keep the men in good spirits."[3]

> "Arthur Clinton is a member of the Pendlebury (Manchester) branch of the ILP. He is known as 'Lanky' and has endeared himself to everyone by his good spirits and irrepressible humour".[4]

On the Aragon Front a particularly heavy artillery bombardment by the Fascists took place. The Contingent was expecting an attack, so when nothing happened a patrol was sent out to check if the enemy had advanced. This patrol included the Commander, Bob Edwards, NCO Chambers and Clinton. They went into 'No Man's Land', occupied a hut used by sheep for shelter and waited. They listened for a long time before returning to their own lines with the news that it looked like the Fascists were not going to attack.[5]

Clinton was one of the volunteers who were wounded in Spain. There are conflicting accounts of how he came to be wounded: possibly by enemy shelling, or by a stray enemy bullet while in the trenches, or during an attack on an enemy position known as the Manicomio.[6] Orwell believes that a stray bullet smashed Clinton's left shoulder and disabled his arm. Orwell met Clinton again in the Sanatorium Maurin (the POUM hospital), where Clinton was in plaster in a wire contraption known as 'the aeroplane' because it looked like an aeroplane's wing.[7]

Before he was wounded in March 1937 Clinton had sent a letter to the ILP offices in London. In the letter he says that he is anxious to attack the enemy. He describes the ILP Contingent's position in the lines as about three kilometres from Huesca, and says that in some places their trenches are only two hundred yards from the enemy. He describes how he was caught with some Spaniards in a Fascist artillery barrage and claims that only five of eighteen German-made shells exploded. Clinton believed this was because of sabotage by German anti-Fascist workers. He also describes how the volunteers lacked arms and munitions, and gives his views on how the

Republicans could win the war:

> "The lads here say that we cannot lose if the Government of Spain puts a rapid move on to get munitions, train volunteers and attack."[8]

He was still in hospital in Barcelona in May 1937.[9] After he left Spain he stayed briefly in touch with Orwell and was writing to members of his family in 1937-38. Orwell had planned for Clinton to recuperate at a shop of his, but this never came to fruition as the shop was sold to pay off debts.[10]

Tom Coles

Tom Coles originated from Bristol, although he may have been living in Worcester at the time he volunteered to serve in Spain.[1] He worked as a docker, lorry driver or labourer.[2] His journey to Spain unlike most of the volunteers had a degree of espionage about it. He left London after the other volunteers had left for Spain and journeyed to Paris on his own. At the Paris rail station he was told to look out for a man holding a particular brand of cigarettes and to make contact with him.[3] This he did and then he journeyed onto Spain and linked up with the rest of the ILP volunteers. Coles was one of the ILP volunteers who took part in the night attack on Ermita Salas and played a brave role. After the volunteers had abandoned the enemy strongpoint and returned to their own lines, Coles was one of the missing volunteers. He returned to his own lines about an hour later. Coles had stayed behind to help another volunteer, badly wounded with a shattered arm, get back to his own lines. This suggests that he could have been a 'First Aid' man or a stretcher-bearer. Of course, he may have been neither and stayed behind purely to help a wounded comrade escape from the enemy.[4]

But in time Coles disagreed with the policies of the POUM and the ILP and decided to join the International Brigades. Unfortunately, when he tried to make contact with its representative in Barcelona he had already returned to their headquarters in Albacete. Determined to continue fighting Fascism, Coles joined the PSUC (Catalan Communist) forces and once again found himself on the Aragon Front at Alcubierre. While fighting with the PSUC he received two flesh wounds and returned to Britain in late 1937 or early 1938.[5]

Coles was one of the men who signed an article condemning Frankford's allegations that the POUM and ILP had fraternised with the Fascists.[6] Coles was in Spain fighting for a Communist unit at the time, which may cast doubts on whether he had actually agreed to have his name used in support of this article.

Jock, or John, Connor

Jock, or John, Connor, a Scot from Glasgow left Britain in December 1936 and joined the POUM militia and then the ILP Contingent. He later left the ILP volunteers and went on to join and fight in the International Brigades, returning to Britain in September 1938.[1]

Stafford Cottman (1918 - 1999)

Staff Cottman was born on March 6th 1918 in Southampton and was the youngest ILP Contingent member, aged only eighteen.[1] Fenner Brockway described him in 1937:

> "...a boy of eighteen with the heart of a giant."[2]

His father was Captain of the only Russian oil tanker in England. He died in a car crash, leaving Staff's mother to raise Staff and his two brothers alone in an artistic household with Socialist views.[3] During Staff's childhood the family moved to London and finally Bristol. Staff left school when he was fourteen, as he needed to earn money for his family. An unusual aspect of Staff's childhood was his attendance at the 'Socialist Sunday School' in Barking in London. Here they were taught Socialism, internationalism and the horrors of the industrial revolution. They read poetry by Edward Carpenter and books by Charles Kingsley (of *The Water Babies* fame), both writers being supporters of Socialist ideas. They also went camping and took part in political demonstrations. Staff's favourite saying from his time at the Socialist Sunday School was:

> "Observe and think in order to discover the truth. Do not think that he who loves his own country must hate or despise other nations, or wish for war, which is a remnant of barbarism."[4]

31. Stafford Cottman. *(NL)*

As a teenager Cottman joined both the ILP 'Guild of Youth' and the Communist YCL (Young Communist League),[5] attracted by the anti-Fascism of the two organisations. He realised the full horrors of the Nazi regime in Germany when in 1933 he attended a meeting where German refugees were present and Nazi implements of torture were displayed. In Bristol Staff took part in an attempt to disrupt a 'Blackshirt' (British Union of Fascists) meeting and was thrown down the steps of Colston Hall.[6]

Cottman was aware of constant Fascist aggression at this time, particularly Mussolini's invasion of Abyssinia in 1935. He had been involved in numerous anti-Fascist meetings and demonstrations, and it was a natural step for Staff to volunteer to fight in the Spanish Civil War after further Fascist aggression in Spain:[7]

> "My political concerns were more instinctive than analytical. I felt a personal disgust that Franco should get military aid from Hitler and Mussolini, whilst Britain and France agreed on a non-intervention policy, which starved the rightful Government of Spain of arms and meant Spanish workers bled to death. Surely it must be wrong to do nothing. So I volunteered to fight for the Spanish people on the side of the elected Government."[8]

Staff saw adverts for volunteers in both the *New Leader* and the Communist paper the *Daily Worker* and applied to both to go to Spain. It is possible he was rejected for the International Brigades as being too young.[9] The ILP replied first, so Cottman went to its Head Office and spoke with Bob Edwards who was more interested in his Socialist views than his lack of military experience.[10] Cottman commented:

> "They asked whether I had military experience with their tongue in their cheek, because what sort of chap would they get with military experience, because there wasn't much military experience to be had? The only experience of guns I'd ever had was at fairgrounds where you set them up and had a shot."[11]

Cottman was accepted for the ILP Contingent and travelled to Spain in January 1937.[12] On the way to Spain Staff and the other volunteers were entertained by an anti-Fascist artist in the border French town of Perpignan:

> "There was a comedian performing in a little restaurant. He had a false Hitler moustache and he was singing humorous songs, which were taking the mickey out of the Fuhrer. The French people were delighted by this type of humour." [13]

In Barcelona Cottman found a city in the throes of revolution, with the colours of the revolutionary parties displayed everywhere. When asked for his identity in Barcelona Cottman showed his British passport. The Anarchist official spat on it, due to Britain's non-intervention policy. Dismayed, Staff handed in his passport to the British Consulate and used instead an Anarchist trade union card, which was readily accepted by officials.[14] Staff particularly remembers the noise of the city:

> "All the various political groups in Catalonia had large brass bands and numerous banners, which were brought to demonstrations, two or three times a week. Everybody seemed to enjoy the noise, display and fun. The bands played 'The Marseillaise', 'The Internationale' and a rousing Anarchist marching song 'Hijos del Pueblo' or 'Sons of the People'. Our contingent was met at the station and marched to the Hotel Falcon, the POUM headquarters in Barcelona, amid cheers and enthusiasm and with banners and a brass band." [15]

In Barcelona Cottman and the other ILP volunteers received two weeks' rudimentary military training in the Lenin Barracks. Staff stated that, although the training was inadequate, it was enough to get by. The weapons they received were old and poorly maintained. Cottman was armed with an 1890's Mauser rifle and wore black boots to the knees, corduroy breeches, an army jacket and a poncho for use in poor weather.[16] On the way to the Front Staff witnessed a civil wedding which had been illegal before the revolution:

> "I remember a wedding ceremony at the town hall in Lerida. I remember the fuss a mother was making about her daughter not being properly married in a church by a priest. She was laughingly reassured by a cheerful crowd that her daughter, who had gone through a civil marriage service, was quite content and indeed married."[17]

Cottman served at the Front from January through to April 1937, when he was sent to the Maurin Sanatorium in Barcelona to help him recover from suspected TB.[18] He describes his fellow volunteers as mainly working-class men, a few intellectuals and political men, with few having military experience, but describes most of them as "a little offbeat".[19] Their Spanish comrades could also on occasions be "offbeat":

> "They were very slap-happy about guns and bombs in a way that could be frightening."[20]

Staff remembers sleeping in caves in the mountains of Alcubierre, which were remarkably comfortable, although he had a personal dread he would awaken one day facing an enemy bayonet. He also recalled a skirmish involving four Moroccans (elite mercenaries fighting for the Fascists) caught in 'No Man's Land', where they shot one Moroccan dead. The body remained lying on the ground for several days. On the Aragon Front Staff saw a Spanish youngster being shot and falling forward over the sandbags. Cottman dropped his rifle to go to the young man's aid and then realised he too could be shot, so he remained in cover till the 'First Aid' group arrived to carry away the young man. Staff claimed that he fired few shots in Spain because the enemy were too far away and ammunition was in short supply. He also said that what shots he did fire, he never saw anyone fall as if hit.[21] While near Huesca Cottman was bombed by Italian planes, which he said were camouflaged to blend in with the sky because you could hear them but not see them.[22]

Staff Cottman is pictured in the *New Leader* along with other ILP volunteers who took part in the attack on the Fascist trench at Ermita Salas. It is possible that he took part in this attack but there is no mention of him in the accounts in the *New Leader* and in Orwell's *Homage to Catalonia*.[23]

The food at the Front was poor, Cottman declaring that he left Spain hating rice, sardines and olive oil, although the sweetened coffee and bread were much better. Staff recalls that the volunteers regularly talked about capturing Huesca and drinking a coffee there:

> "It became a joke that we looked forward to the day when we would capture the town and drink coffee at our leisure. This was never to be the case and in fact it took me forty-six years to have the pleasure of drinking coffee in Huesca in 1983. This was thanks to the BBC and I enjoyed a coffee with Nigel Williams, writer and director of the Arena programme and Orwell enthusiast."[24]

While at the Front Cottman received a letter from the Barking 'Guild of Youth', asking him if he needed anything. He replied that chocolate was in short supply and what there was did not taste as good as the English version. He later received several tea chests of chocolate. He ate a bar with John McNair in Barcelona and then sent the rest to the local hospitals.[25]

In May 1937 while on leave in Barcelona, Staff met the future German Chancellor, Willy Brandt. Brandt informed Staff that the troops they were facing on the Aragon Front were young Spanish conscripts and not the German and Italian Fascists he had hoped to fight. Cottman was deeply shocked and felt like returning home, since he had not come to Spain to fight conscripts.[26] Staff found that his Anarchist identity papers were less acceptable now and so he requested that his passport be returned. He found his British passport was now treated with greater respect than his Anarchist papers. He witnessed furious arguments between drivers and the police, as they were being forced to give back vehicles they had seized at the beginning of the war. Government permits were replacing trade union ones as the revolution was being overturned.[27] While in Barcelona Staff met the International Brigades Commissar Tapsell who tried to get him and other ILP men to join the British Battalion.[28] Staff claims that like Orwell he wanted to join the International Brigades but after the 'May Days' this was not possible:

"With all the political suspicion we had and hostility towards their methods and so on, we recognised that's where the fighting was, that was the place under attack and we had a comradely responsibility to help. Here we were on the Aragon front with very little happening, you saw the enemy miles over there as a little moving dot on the landscape. You didn't feel as though you were making a useful contribution in the Spanish war."[29]

Cottman further believed that Tapsell had been sent to investigate the 'May Days' events on behalf of the British Battalion.[30]

Staff was in Barcelona during the 'May Days' events. He left the Maurin Sanatorium (where he was recovering from tuberculosis) to help his comrades and was put on guard duty on the roof of the Hotel Falcon where McNair claimed it was healthier for him![31] At the Hotel Falcon he was given a couple of hand grenades due to lack of rifles:

"Now these grenades were the dangerous Spanish phosphorous type grenade, which you lit before throwing. They were always considered as much more of a hazard to the user than the recipient."[32]

Staff slept on the roof of the POUM headquarters for three nights until the fighting started to die down.[33] Cottman remembers hearing shooting, and that one of the ILP volunteers who refused to be involved got arrested for buying a large quantity of beer. After the 'May Days' Cottman decided not to return to the Front as the 'writing was on the wall'. Anyone with any links with the POUM could be arrested or worse.[34] After the 'May Days' events Cottman returned to the Maurin Sanatorium and was there when a police raid took place looking for POUM sympathisers. Staff and another ILP volunteer fled and avoided capture.[35]

As members of the POUM were arrested, Cottman and the others made visits to the British Consulate for help.[36] Staff was living in the same hotel as McNair, and when the police raided McNair's room he asked Staff to warn other foreign Socialists in Barcelona who supported the POUM. Staff did this.[37] One of these foreigners was Willy Brandt. He refused Staff's offer to come to England, and was in despair because working-men were fighting each other. Cottman and Orwell destroyed some documents that may have been incriminating to those people mentioned. Staff helped another volunteer, who had not paid his hotel bill, by smuggling his luggage out of the hotel. When this volunteer was arrested two days later because of his POUM card, Staff tried to get him released from jail but was unsuccessful.[38]

Staff Cottman left Spain in June 1937, along with Orwell and his wife and McNair. During the day Cottman, McNair and Orwell pretended to be British businessmen, while at night they slept rough.[39] The British Consulate eventually got their passports in order but the slow process meant they missed the train to the frontier. Luckily, the Anarchist owner of a restaurant close to the station allowed them to sleep in his house till morning.[40] They caught the next train and decided that everyone should read a book on the train, and pretend to be wealthy businessmen or tourists. Staff read John Masefield's poetry. The group's luck held once more when police checked their papers and passports and failed to recognise that the 29th Division mentioned in Orwell's Discharge Papers actually meant the POUM.[41]

While in Spain Staff wrote an article as a member of the YCL with the Head of the ILP 'Guild of Youth', Bob Smillie, called 'Unity in the Trenches'. In this article they report Communist slanders against the POUM, but the writers claim the POUM still had faith in the Communist Movement. They praise the revolutionary organisation of the militias and the ILP volunteers, while unity between Socialists and Communists is seen as the key to winning the war. The article was published after Smillie's death and was already out of date since Regular armed forces were replacing the militias on the Aragon Front. The YCL publication *Challenge* refused to publish the article.[42]

On his return to England Cottman wrote letters to try and obtain Georges Kopp's release from prison and wrote two published articles supporting the ILP/POUM position and their role in the 'May Days' events in Barcelona. He even sent a pro-POUM/ILP article to the Communist *Daily Worker* which was, unsurprisingly, not published. He became involved in 'Aid Spain' Movement, attending meetings, taking part in door-to-door collections and visiting the Basque refugees in Street, Somerset.[43] Staff was expelled from the YCL and his house was picketed by local Communists. They accused him of being in the pay of Franco, of receiving gold from Franco, being a Fascist agent and being involved in a Fascist uprising.[44] Local Communists kept a watch on his house and even questioned people who entered his house. In the 1980's his friend Don Bateman organised a meeting with Staff and some old YCL comrades who were sorry for their earlier actions towards him.[45]

Along with other volunteers Cottman attended the ILP Summer School at Letchworth.[46] He spoke for a few minutes and was described in the *New Leader* as:

"Stafford Cottman, very young, frail in body and yet with a spirit of steel" [47]

Cottman also joined other ILP volunteers in condemning the views of fellow volunteer Frankford who claimed the POUM fraternised with the Fascists.[48]

At the outbreak of World War II Cottman declared himself a conscientious objector because of his experiences in Spain and the appeasement policy of the British Government. But the success of Hitler's armies made Cottman change his mind and he joined the RAF and became a rear gunner.[49] During his time with the RAF he met his future wife Stella, who was also in the armed forces. He and Stella later had a daughter. After the war the Cottmans moved to Ruislip in Surrey where Staff worked in air traffic control at London airport. There he was an active trade unionist and became a Labour Party member. In Spain Staff had become a friend of George Orwell, once even reciting the Eton boating song for Orwell, much to the famous author's amusement and remained his most loyal friend from the Spanish War, even trying to visit him days before Orwell's death in January 1950.[50] Staff and Stella later moved to Bath where Staff, now aged seventy, almost won a safe Conservative council seat because of his local standing.[51] Throughout his life Cottman stayed a committed Socialist and Internationalist. In 1968 he and Stella were in Czechoslovakia during the 'Prague Spring' when Czech leader Dubcek attempted to liberalise the Communist state but was overthrown by Soviet tanks.[52]

Cottman returned twice to Spain after the Civil War, firstly for a holiday in 1960, then in 1983 as a guest of the BBC while they were making an *Arena* documentary on George Orwell.[53] In Cottman's last years he became friendly with the film director Ken Loach and helped him with his researches for his critically acclaimed film *Land and Freedom*. Many believed that the film's main character was based on Stafford Cottman [54]. By the time the film was premiered in London, Staff Cottman was too ill and frail to attend, so Ken Loach arranged a special screening in Bath with Staff as the guest of honour. His wife, Stella, wrote:

"He watched it in silence and then said 'George Orwell always said, 'the truth about what happened to the Republican cause in Spain will never be told', but now it has been." [55]

When honorary Spanish citizenship was granted to ex-International Brigaders, attempts by Staff's friend Don Bateman to obtain it for Staff were unsuccessful. Stafford Cottman died on September 19th 1999.[56]

Charles Doran (1893/4 - 1974)

Doran was born in Dublin but moved to Glasgow in 1915 and was a labourer, where he returned after fighting in World War I. He joined Guy Aldred's Anti-Parliamentary Communist Federation, which was actually an Anarchist group; however Doran joined the ILP in the early 1930's, and was still an ILP member while fighting in Spain.[1]

Once in Barcelona several ILP volunteers were regularly drinking too much wine. These actions angered Doran who believed they should be setting a better example to the Spanish people. Possibly Doran was tee-total? Doran discussed this drunkenness problem with a female Scottish Anarchist called Ethel MacDonald who was involved in radio propaganda for the Spanish Anarchists in Barcelona:

> "Charlie Doran is sitting here at present telling me all about Glasgow and Lanarkshire. He came the day before yesterday with the ILP section from London and he is attached to the POUM. Why does someone not impress on the British volunteers not to get drunk when they arrive here? There is always that tendency. Perhaps it is because they are unaccustomed to wine. Doran was very indignant at the idea of volunteers for freedom getting drunk, and I sympathise with his feelings." [2]

He returned to Britain in July 1937 using an Emergency Certificate. Doran was one of the signatories to the letter that denounced the views of Frankford (that the POUM/ILP had fraternised with the Fascists at the Front).[3] Doran also was convinced Bob Smillie had been murdered by the Spanish authorities.[4] During the period 1938-9 he corresponded with Orwell, but after this date the letters ceased. As late as December 1938 he was convening a fund raising Flag-Day for Spain, organised by the Partick (Glasgow) ILP branch.

Doran went back to his Anarchist roots in World War II when he joined an anti-militarist Anarchist group led by Willie MacDougall, an opponent of the war. He wrote for the group's newspaper, which was called the *Pioneer News*.[5]

In the Spanish national archive there is a document relating to Doran, written by the Republican secret police. In this document they say that Doran was an ILP man serving with the POUM militia on the Huesca Front. He is described as a "confirmed Trotskyist" who had dealings with the FAI and POUM youth organisations. The document states that in December 1936 Doran wrote an article in which he condemned the 'Moscow Trials' and defended Trotsky and the old Bolshevik, Radek.[6] In the Edwards archive there is a picture of Doran in Spain. He is pictured at the Front, along with Edwards, Orwell and Donovan, and he is holding a tin plate, apparently about to eat. Doran is kneeling and wearing boots and puttees, corduroy trousers, a checked jacket or thick woolly shirt and a woolly hat. He has a thin build and a sharp nose.[7]

- Evans

We have no known first name for this volunteer. Evans came from Sunderland in the North East of England. He worked as a docker, lorry driver or labourer.[1] During his time in Spain he disagreed with the ILP leadership and the policy of the POUM. In May 1937 he tried to join the International Brigades but narrowly missed making contact with its representative in Barcelona, who had returned back to his base area. Having failed to join the International Brigades he joined the PSUC (Catalan Communists) Battalion and served on the Aragon Front in areas where the ILP Contingent had previously been based. While fighting for the PSUC he was seriously injured and was invalided home.[2]

James Farrell (1904 - ?)

James Farrell was born in Dublin in 1904, later moving to Dundee.[1] Farrell claimed to have been involved in the Irish Republican movement from the age of eleven. He was a cadet in the British Army from 1917, and served in Russia against the new Bolshevik Government in the period 1917-18. Farrell finally left the Army in 1920, having also served in Germany and India. By the end of his time in the Army he had risen through the ranks to become a Warrant Officer. When he returned to Ireland Farrell became involved in the Republican movement again, and served with the IRA during the Irish Civil War against the Free State Government. He was appointed a Lieutenant in the 5th Western Flying Column, probably due to his previous military experience. In 1930 Farrell joined the Irish Communist Party (the CPI) and remained a member until 1934, when he migrated to London and worked as a motor engineer until 1936.

In October 1936 Farrell left London to go to Spain to:

"help to fight for the rights of the Spanish people." [2]

Farrell fought in the militias before he joined the ILP Contingent and served with them until May 1937. After the 'May Days' he returned to England. He returned to Spain in December 1937 and this time he joined the British Battalion of the International Brigades. For political reasons, Farrell's International Brigades file says very little about his previous time in Spain; he would have been viewed as politically suspect if it were generally known that he had served with the now-suppressed POUM.

Along with other British volunteers in the International Brigades, Farrell was captured in March 1938 by the Nationalists at Calaceite and made a prisoner of war. He was not released and repatriated until February 1939. This volunteer has also been known as P. H. O'Farrell and James Forcell but they all seem to be the same person.[3]

Frank Frankford or Frankfort (1913 - 1990's)

Frank Felix Alexander Frankford is one of the major dissenting voices, or mavericks, in the ILP Contingent.

It was Frankford who denounced the POUM/ILP militia in a *Daily Worker* interview in 1937. He claimed that they did little to further the war effort, fraternised with the enemy and even agreed a truce with them. He never recanted these views, even after the war. Unlike most of the volunteers he also loathed George Orwell.

Frankford was born in Slough, in South East England, on September 7th, 1913, into a middle-class Jewish family. His father was a factory owner. In 1927 he ran away from home to London, where he

32. Frank Frankford. *(NL)*

held a variety of jobs. In the 1930's he became politically active in the Bethnal Green, Whitechapel and Hackney areas of London, joining the Communist Party and that party's unemployed movement the National Unemployed Workers Movement (the NUWM). He was involved in physical clashes with the British Union of Fascists (BUF) in Whitechapel. He left the Communist Party of Great Britain and joined the ILP because he was fed up with his fellow Communists:

> "not having any opinion, 'till they'd read the next day's *Daily Worker* [the British Communist daily newspaper]." [1]

When the Spanish Civil War broke out Frankford was involved in several 'Aid Spain' meetings where he helped to raise money for the POUM. During these 'Aid Spain' activities he met the prominent ILP member and future fellow volunteer, Bob Smillie. Even though he had no previous military experience, Frankford volunteered to fight in Spain When he applied to the British authorities for a passport (to get to Spain) he claimed that he wanted a passport in order to watch the Dutch royal wedding, despite being a staunch Republican.[2]

Frankford said that when he arrived in Spain, many Spaniards believed that he and his companions were Russians because of the new high leather boots they were wearing. Frankford arrived in revolutionary Barcelona and was greatly moved by what he saw:

> "You would insult the barber if you offered him a tip. The waiters wouldn't accept tips - that's something! And they didn't. If you asked someone the way, they'd take you on the bus and pay your way. There was this sort of spirit. And when we went to the Front for the first time we were marching down to the station to catch the train, and we had this terrific crowd and bands playing. I'll always remember that."[3]

Frankford underwent 'British style' military training: advancing, throwing yourself to the floor, firing, getting up running and then down on the ground again. The Spanish thought that this was a cowardly way to fight, and had to be given leaflets showing them that people who stood up to shoot were more likely to be shot themselves![4]

On his arrival at the Front he was given an 1895 cavalry carbine, most likely an 1896 Mauser carbine. Frankford found the quality of ammunition very poor. Most cartridges were old ones made from refills from other older cartridges, which caused rifles to jam regularly whenever anyone tried to fire them.[5] Frankford believed that he and the other volunteers were achieving little militarily at the Front, but that their physical presence was helping the fight against Fascism:

> "All of us in Spain felt we were part of a world-wide opposition to Fascism. The only real good we did was to show our Spanish comrades that the workers of the world supported them."[6]

Unlike many other ILP/POUM volunteers Frankford found the food at the Front adequate, saying that there was enough food to make it unnecessary for Orwell to go foraging for more, and there was always plenty of wine. The standard of discipline at the Front seems to have rankled with Frankford more than the standard of the food. Frankford and another volunteer were sent to get supplies, but they stayed away from the Front for several days and were not disciplined on their return. Frankford also mentions another breach of discipline, which is not mentioned by any other volunteers. He says that groups of ILP volunteers regularly visited brothels. (This could have occurred when the volunteers first arrived in Barcelona, or when they were on leave in April – May, or possibly before they left for home.[7] Many volunteers were young men so this might be true, but volunteers had very little time in Barcelona to actually visit brothels. I suspect it was Frankford and his friend who are the likely brothel visitors during their time in Barcelona.)

Frankford was one of the fifteen ILP volunteers who took part in the night attack on the enemy strongpoint of Ermita Salas, following Orwell and two other volunteers into the enemy trench.[8] Like the rest of the volunteers Frankford was in Barcelona during the 'May Days', but was not actively involved in any fighting.[9] He stated there was a truce each day so everyone could go to the market to get food.[10] Frankford describes the chaos of the 'May Days' through his eyes:

"We didn't really know what was going on. I was with Tanky, there was a lot of dashing about, lorries floating about, people waving rifles, you'd hear the odd shot, they started blocking off roads. People starting digging up the cobbles on the Ramblas and making barricades across the road. The 'Moka Café' was taken over by some of the Guardia (police), who also had guns trained on us. But they couldn't get out of there because they were under our guns. On the other hand we couldn't get any beer because there was a curfew on. So we had a sort of an agreement, made over the phone I think, that we wouldn't fire on each other providing they gave us some beer."[11]

After the 'May Days' Frankford returned to the Front with the reduced ILP Contingent and, like several other volunteers, he claims that he was talking to Orwell when the famous writer was shot.[12] Frankford had a very low opinion of Orwell and in one case even accused him of being a Fascist:

"Basically his attitude was Fascist, he didn't like the workers... I don't care what he says and what he's written, when you spoke to him he didn't like them, despised them. That was why I could never understand what he was doing there. In fact we said to him that he was a man of the right and not of the left and that he had never thrown off his Burma police attitude. I'm sure he despised us all, which was why we disliked him... As far as he was concerned, we were a load of nits. We probably were a load of nits, but no need to have adopted that attitude."

and further adds:

"You always got the impression that he felt Socialism was alright as long as the workers didn't run it."[13]

His usual phrase of abuse for Orwell was "supercilious bastard"![14]

He was particularly offended by Orwell's book *The Road to Wigan Pier* and its depiction of the working-classes. Frankford strongly believed Orwell went to Spain as a journalist.[15] However Frankford's views were not shared by the majority of the volunteers, who elected Orwell as their leader after Bob Edwards left for home. Ironically, Frankford shared with Orwell the (ultimately fruitless) desire to join the International Brigades. He said that he wanted to join the International Brigades to prolong his stay in Spain but nothing came of this wish.[16]

Frankford claims that when he was back in Barcelona in June 1937 his POUM connections gave him no problems with the authorities,[17] but he claimed that the police spotted him reading an English book and drinking beer in a café, and arrested him on the accusation that he was a spy.[18] Frankford was actually arrested in Barcelona for not having his papers. He told the police that he had been robbed the previous day of everything, including his passport.[19] He was jailed for some time as the police suspected Frankford of knowing something about the theft of some paintings from a church; although he was never charged with anything.[20] It has since been discovered that Frankford's record in the Secret Police archives states that he had been unfairly detained and had a good service record.[21]

Frankford's release was organised by a Communist radio broadcaster, Sam Lesser, a former International Brigades veteran, to whom he gave an interview. The interview appeared in an edited version in the *Daily Worker* of September 14th 1937 (it also appeared in *Treball* and *Volunteer for Liberty*).[22] In this interview Frankford levels seven charges against the POUM:

1. That a cart each night travelled between the POUM lines and the Fascist lines.
2. Georges Kopp was seen once coming from the enemy lines.
3. The POUM were defeatist.
4. During the 'May Days' the POUM had access to many hidden weapons.
5. It was a crime for the POUM to rise against the Government.
6. At the Front there was open fraternisation between POUM and Fascist forces.
7. The POUM were glad to get rid of Frankford because of his views.

This interview was condemned and refuted point by point, firstly by John McNair and secondly by Orwell and many other ILP volunteers in the ILP newspaper, the *New Leader*.[23]

After the interview with the *Daily Worker* reporter Frankford was deported from Spain, and had to beg money from the British Consul in Paris to help him get home. He had also contracted jaundice, probably brought on by his imprisonment.[24] In Paris he received further support from the French Communist Party (PCF) who had read his article in *Treball* condemning the POUM. They supplied him with a ticket home, clothes and £5![25] He returned to England on September 4th 1937 and, remarkably, received financial assistance from the ILP on the 7th of that month.[26]

Fenner Brockway described Frankford's visit, where he says he withdrew his allegations:

> "A few days later the boy arrived in London and came at once to McNair at the ILP Head Office. He broke down crying and begged forgiveness. He had been imprisoned in Barcelona and had been presented with the document to sign as a condition of freedom."[27]

Frankford's accusations in the *Daily Worker* interview were untruthful; even the *Daily Worker* had to change certain 'facts' two days later. However, Frankford disagreed with Brockway's description of his visit, and said that he never wept or asked for forgiveness. He said that he agreed to give the journalist an interview but claimed that he never signed any statement. In various interviews later in his life Frankford showed little remorse about his actions, even saying they were 'quite legitimate in politics'. He said that he also did not repudiate the *Daily Worker* article because there was some 'hanky panky' that has never been explained.[28] Thwaites, on the other hand, believes that Frankford repudiated all his former comments in an interview with him in 1986, where he stated that he never saw a Fascist newspaper in the POUM trenches. He still believed he heard a cart crossing between the lines at night, but he attributed this to troops from the same family or area, forced to serve on opposing sides, communicating with each other and he saw nothing sinister in this.[29] In 1998, although now very old and with a poor memory, Frankford told an interviewer that he did break down before Brockway and begged forgiveness but he was now unsure if his accusations made in 1937 were true.[30]

In a letter to the Communist journalist Frank Jellinek, Orwell tells him not to believe any statements about Spain by Frankford.[31]

During World War II Frankford did not hold pacifist views and served in the armed forces.[32] Later he wrote to the right wing *Daily Telegraph* in 1979 to refute a story that Orwell was shot in Spain by another leftist group.[33]

George, or Albert, Gross (1906 - ?)

George Gross was a member of the ILP who came from Hammersmith in London. He was an electrician of Russian extraction. We know little of his time in Spain, although we do know he was one of the fifteen volunteers who took part in the night attack on the enemy position of Ermita Salas. In the attack Gross was one of three volunteers who followed Orwell into the enemy position. According to fellow volunteer Harry Thomas, Gross was on sentry duty the night Chambers deserted. Thomas claimed he asked Gross why he had not shot Chambers as instructed by Bob Edwards. Gross answered he had no intention of carrying out that order.[1]

He left Spain using an Emergency Certificate because he had no passport. On his return to England he was one of the volunteers who signed a rebuttal to the accusations of Frankford in his *Daily Worker* interview.[2] In World War II Gross served in the armed forces and set up an ILP branch representing ILP members in the Armed forces,[3] even though the ILP held a pacifist position on the War.

A Communist called Colin Siddons serving in the Armed Forces during World War II was involved in editing an unofficial newspaper called *Into Action* for his fellow soldiers. He came into contact with a Private Albert Gross. Siddons describes Gross as a left-winger, pre-war ILPer and a Trotskyite. Gross did not support the Communist unofficial newspaper and hence was condemned as a Trotskyite. Siddons, who is undoubtedly a hostile source, describes Gross as follows:

> "His strong point - a great platform speaker, with every trick, inflexion, oratorical gesture. His weak point: inability to hold private conversations with anyone. Every private discussion becomes a public meeting with himself on the rostrum. His vanity makes him a figure of fun among the men. He is an obsessive card player; nearly all his spare time is taken by cards. His key political

line is that Germany and the United States are both on the verge of proletarian revolution."[4]

The above sounds like a description of an isolated man having to defend his political views vigorously against a group of Communist opponents.

Reg Hiddlestone or Hiddleston

33. Reg Hiddlestone. *(NL)*

Hiddlestone was the marksman of the Contingent and described as the best shot. He was also a member of an elite 'shock' unit that led the way in any attack. There are suggestions he was the unit's chief sniper and may have killed several enemy soldiers in this way.[1] Hiddlestone was one of the contingent volunteers who took part in the attack on Ermita Salas and went missing after he had received several wounds in the attack, possibly because he was leading the way:

"Hiddlestone had received a dreadful wound - a bullet which travelled right up his left arm, breaking the bone in several places; as he lay helpless on the ground a bomb burst near him and torn various other parts of his body." [2]

Somehow Hidddlestone managed to get back to his own lines an hour later. At first he crawled on his back. One version of the story says that he then met a wounded Spaniard and together they helped each other to return safely to their own positions. Another version has fellow ILP volunteer Coles helping Hiddlestone to get back to his own lines. Hiddlestone recovered from his horrific wounds and returned to action on the front line.[3] He talked later about his care and treatment by Spanish doctors:

"The Spanish people are the best in the world. Never have I seen such comradeship, honesty and decency. I would like nothing better than to go and live my whole life with them, to share their joys and sorrows, because we are one."[4]

After the suppression of the POUM Hiddlestone preferred not to return home and joined another Republican unit, remaining in Barcelona until only a few hours before the city fell to Fascist forces. He returned to Britain in February 1939, making him one of the last ILP volunteers to leave Spain.[5]

In the photograph from the Orwell archive Hiddlestone is standing next to Orwell. He is a young man in his early twenties, a good head shorter than Orwell, and is bare-headed. He is wearing a buttoned long-sleeved shirt and his legs are obscured by the machine gun[6] (see page 171).

A letter from Orwell written in 1938 to the Communist journalist Frank Jellinek mentions Hiddlestone as someone who can be trusted, but one who may misunderstand things. Perhaps Orwell believed that he was not very intelligent?[7]

Philip or Phillip Hunter

Philip Hunter was from London and a member of the Dartford ILP branch. He was injured in the leg in April 1937 shortly before the night attack at Ermita Salas.[1] There is no explicit mention of Philip Hunter taking part in the night attack on the enemy positions at Ermita Salas; however his picture is shown in the *New Leader* article about the attack. Then again, Bob Edwards' picture also appears in the article and he was back in England at the time and so very definitely did not take part in the action! It is possible that Hunter did not take part in the

34. Philip Hunter. *(NL)*

attack because he was still suffering from his leg wound.[2]

Hunter is fifth from the left in the photograph from the Orwell archive. He is a tall man, about six feet tall, and only his head and shoulders are visible. He is wearing a garment with a collar: either a shirt or zipped jacket, and is wearing a woolly hat. He appears to be in his mid to late twenties.[3] (see page 171).

Back in England at the end of May 1937 Hunter was one of the signatories to the letter condemning the slanders made by Frank Frankford about the POUM and ILP volunteers.[4]

Urias, or **Uriah, Jones (1907 - ?)**

Urias Jones was an unemployed miner from Tumble in the Gwendraeth Valley in South Wales and had also served in the British Army. His family were devout Baptists, although by the time Jones volunteered for Spain he was no longer a Christian. He subscribed to, and was a reader of, the *New Leader*, and he was an ILP sympathiser. However he was not a Party member and in fact was moving towards joining the Communist Party.

For three years before he went to Spain Jones attended National Council of Labour Colleges (NCLC) evening classes. In these classes political and trade union activists were taught Marxism, Socialist theory, economic theory and history by tutors who were quite often members of the Communist Party. Jones claimed that he was taught Marxism by local Communist militant Jack Jones, who later went to Spain himself, fighting in the International Brigades, and returned to Wales to become a high-ranking Miners' Union official. (This Jack Jones is not to be confused with the better-known Liverpudlian Jack Jones, who also fought in Spain with the International Brigades and later became leader of the Transport & General Workers' Union).

When he saw the advertisements for volunteers in the *New Leader* he wrote in asking for further details. He went to the ILP Head Office in London where he was interviewed by Fenner Brockway, the General Secretary of the ILP, and accepted as a volunteer. Jones' reasons for going to Spain were to fight Fascism and to help install a Socialist Government. He says that he left for Spain at Christmas time 1936 and served in Spain until early 1938.[1]

Jones served at first in the ILP Contingent on the Alcubierre and Aragon Fronts, but soon began to disagree with the style of leadership of the Contingent, and had political differences with many of the other volunteers. He supported the Communist philosophy, which was to win the war first, and then introduce the revolution afterwards, and to regularise the militias into a professional army. So Jones decided to join the International Brigades. He failed to make contact with them so he joined the Catalan Communist forces of the PSUC instead and became a member of that political Party. He served with the PSUC for seven or eight months on the Aragon Front in areas like Alcubierre near where he had served with the POUM. By the end of his time serving with the PSUC forces he had learnt the Catalan language well enough to be understood by the locals. When Jones decided to leave Spain he needed help from both the British and French Consulates.[2]

35. Urias Jones. (NL)

A picture of Jones appears in the *New Leader* article on the attack on Ermita Salas, although there is no explicit mention of his taking part so it is not clear whether he was involved or not.[3] When Jones' family saw this photograph in the *New Leader* they feared the worst, that he had been killed or wounded.[4]

Despite Jones' political differences with his fellow volunteers, he was one of the men who signed the article condemning Frankford's slanders about the POUM and ILP volunteers.[5] At the time this article was written Jones was serving with the PSUC and was a member of the Catalan Communist Party, so he may have been motivated to sign by a sense of fairness. On the other hand it is possible that his name was added to the list of signatories without his knowledge. Certainly in later life Jones was hostile towards the views of the POUM and the ILP and strongly supported the Communist position on the Spanish Civil War. He went so far as to state that he would have preferred to have volunteered to fight in the International Brigades rather than the ILP unit.[6]

When Jones returned to Wales he stopped subscribing to the *New Leader* and joined the Communist Party. He served in the armed forces in World War II after being called up in 1942. After the war he returned to his old job as a miner, but was forced, like many miners, to retire early on the grounds of ill-health.[7]

Julius

The only information we have about this volunteer is that he is mentioned in the Tapsell Report as a volunteer who wishes to leave the POUM militia.[1]

Charles Justesen, or Justessen (1903 - ?)

36. Charles Justessen. *(NL)*

Charles Richard Justesen was a member of the ILP; his local Branch was Cheetham in Manchester. By birth he was probably Jewish. He worked in the garment trade and was a trade union organiser in the Waterproofing union. He left England to later settle in Australia.[1] All we know about Charles Justesen's time in Spain is that he served in the ILP Contingent and returned to Britain safely. He left Britain with the main body of ILP volunteers in January 1937 and left Spain in May 1937.[2] He may have been involved in the attack on Ermita Salas, since Justessen appears in a photograph alongside the account of the attack in the *New Leader*, but he is not mentioned in the accounts of the *New Leader* or of Orwell. We know that some of the volunteers in the picture are not mentioned in the article, and one pictured volunteer was actually in England at the time! On his return to Britain he was one of the signatories to the article condemning the allegations of fellow volunteer Frankford.[3]

Robert MacDonald

Robert MacDonald was from Derry in Northern Ireland. He went to Spain and served in the POUM/ILP force.[1] The only other information we have about this volunteer is that he was arrested in Valencia in June 1937 and repatriated back to Derry.[2]

Hugh McNeil (1896 - ?)

37. Hugh McNeil. *(NL)*

We have very little information about Scottish volunteer McNeil. He was a member of the Independent Labour Party in Glasgow, although he may have been secretly a Communist, as he possessed a Communist International Card.[1] His picture appears in the *New Leader* article describing the night attack on Ermita Salas, although there is no mention of him in the article or in Orwell's account of the attack, so it is not certain if McNeil took part in the action.[2] He was a member of the ILP Contingent and returned to Britain sometime in June 1937.[3]

Douglas Moyle (1910 - 1990's)

Douglas George Francis Moyle had been a sailor and a technician of some sort before he went to Spain, and it is likely he was an ILP member or sympathiser, although he travelled to Spain with a Communist International card. He left London for Spain in January 1937 with the majority of the ILP volunteers.[1]

Moyle describes a night patrol with Orwell:

"We went out on a brilliant moonlight night. He assured me that although it was a moonlight night there was no need to creep about and that no one would see us even if we stood up and walked naturally. And it was quite true. I felt immediately I could trust him. I knew he had plenty of experience already of night patrolling.

We approached the Fascist parapet to within about thirty yards and kept our heads down for the last few paces before dropping into a hollow behind a low ridge. He told me to stay there until he returned but to have a couple of hand grenades ready just in case. Then he moved off into the night and seemed to be getting even closer to the enemy's lines. I was dead scared at first because I could hear Fascists talking quite clearly, but they were completely unaware of our presence. Then, after about fifteen to twenty minutes, he returned and we walked away without any trouble at all." [2]

Moyle took part in the assault on Ermita Salas, handing Orwell a grenade to throw into the enemy position. Moyle entered the captured enemy position and seized a telescope but it was unfortunately left behind in the retreat after the attack had failed. Moyle was one of the two English volunteers who responded, along with three Spanish volunteers, to the Section Commander Kopp's request for five volunteers to go and find the missing men. The Fascists had re-occupied the position, fired on the five volunteers and threw a grenade, forcing them to retreat. The missing men later made their own way back to the lines.[3]

Moyle was in Barcelona during the 'May Days' and spent most of his time on guard duty on a roof opposite a café occupied by Spanish police.[4] During his time in Spain the Spanish Secret Police got hold of a letter written by Moyle to Orwell.[5] He met with the British Battalion Commissar in Barcelona and is listed as one of the ILP volunteers who wanted to leave the POUM militia.[6] When he heard about the death of Bob Smillie, Moyle wrote to the *New Leader* describing Smillie as the "best man" in the ILP unit. In a pamphlet in honour of Bob Smillie, Moyle further comments:

"He never shirked his responsibilities, of which he had more than his fair share. No task was too lowly, no task too difficult."[7]

Back in Britain he visited Orwell at his house in the Hertfordshire countryside, and in August 1937 Moyle attended and spoke at the ILP Summer School at Letchworth.[8] In the *New Leader* account of the volunteers speaking at the ILP Summer School, Moyle is described as:

"...a technician, a fine combination of character, sincerity and clear thinking."[9]

A photograph of Douglas Moyle taken at the ILP Summer School shows him standing with McNair and Fletcher (from the ILP office in Barcelona), Cottman, Braithwaite and Orwell (see page 246).[10] Moyle was one of the ILP volunteers who signed the article condemning Frankford's slanderous allegations that the ILP and the POUM had been pro-Fascist.[11]

After Spain Moyle kept in contact with Orwell and was writing to him as late as 1949.[12] Although not recording his experiences in Spain, Moyle was happy to be interviewed on more than one occasion by scholars concerning his experiences with Orwell in Spain. In 1984 he was a guest of honour at an Orwell Conference where he was described as:

"Douglas Moyle, a retired (and retiring) veteran of the Spanish Civil War." [13]

He stayed a lifelong friend of fellow volunteer Stafford Cottman and was still alive in the 1990's. In 1994 Douglas Moyle wrote to the author to say how he had enjoyed the book *Disciplina Camaradas* and gave this view on the Spanish Civil War:

"Often during the first half of World War II Churchill said that that war need never have happened. How right he was and how different the future may have been if the Spanish Civil War had been settled differently." [14]

Patrick O'Hara (1898 - ?)

An Irishman from Ballymena in county Antrim, but living in London working as a kitchen porter, Patrick Hugh O'Hara was the ILP Contingent's First Aid man in Spain, because he had some previous medical experience or medical knowledge. He left for Spain with the main body of volunteers in January 1937.[1]

He performed his duties bravely during the night attack on Ermita Salas; tending the wounded and being shot at by his own side:

"A number of wounded, English and Spanish, were lying outside. Patrick O'Hara, a Belfast Irishman who had some training in first-aid, went to and fro with packets of bandages, binding up the wounded men and, of course, being shot at every time he returned to the parapet, in spite of his indignant shouts of 'POUM'!"[2]

The *New Leader's* account of the action commends O'Hara's bravery. He was one of the first men to enter the enemy position and he then left the position to bandage two wounded men in the open while under fire. Back inside the enemy parapet, he shouted out to ask whether anyone else needed treatment. The *New Leader* said that he ministered to the wounded:

"With great bravery and coolness he achieved this difficult task."[3]

By May 1937 he was planning to return to England. A Hugh O'Hara returned to Britain from Spain in September 1937.[4]

John Ritchie (1889 - ?)

John, or Jock Ritchie as he was known in Spain, was an ex-boxer from Glasgow, originally from Turfholm, Lesmahagow in Lanarkshire and travelled to Spain in January 1937 with the main body of volunteers.[1] He was poorly educated, and was frequently drunk.[2] Other volunteers found it very difficult to understand what he was saying in his strong Glaswegian accent.[3]

When Ritchie was at the front with the ILP Contingent he was visited by the ILP representative David Murray, who related their meeting to the *Lanark Gazette* who published these words about Jock Ritchie:

"The familiar accent of Lanarkshire was heard in the trenches of the Aragon front when a Motherwell man, Mr David Murray, visited Jock Ritchie, ex-amateur heavyweight boxing champion of Scotland. 'Big Jock' was very calm and collected and as a bullet smashed into a sniper's post in a tree just overhead he remarked laconically 'they always shoot high anyway'. As they talked about the country, the besieged town of Huesca could be plainly seen about 500 yards away. Much nearer than that could be observed a line of loop-holed sandbags, in one of the enemy's positions. As a matter of fact at the point where Jock was anxiously awaiting his dinner, the rebel trenches were only a few yards away, well within a good biscuit or rather bomb toss."[4]

He was one of those volunteers who returned to the Front in a much-reduced ILP Contingent[5] after the 'May Days' events. He met with Tapsell in Barcelona and was one of the volunteers who wished to leave the POUM militia.[6] When he returned to Britain in August 1937 Ritchie signed the article condemning the slanders of Frank Frankford.[7]

Robert ('Bob') Smillie (1916-1937)

Robert Ramsay Smillie was born on June 18th 1916 in Larkhall in Scotland[1] into a highly politicised family. His grandfather had been a leading coal mining trade union leader and later a Labour Party MP. His father was a Scottish farmer and Chairman of the Scottish ILP.[2] ILP leader James Maxton described the family's political pedigree in his eulogy after Smillie's death:

> "We knew the stock from which he came. We saw his father and mother living a strenuous existence on their little farm in Lanarkshire, toiling early and late on the soil, but still with surplus energy to devote to the Socialist Movement, to the unemployed, to the improvement of the conditions of the miners living around them. We knew his grandfather – that strong leader of the miners, who pioneered their organisation first in Lanarkshire, then in Scotland and Great Britain, finally to become a great International working-class figure. We knew his grandmother, a great woman who to this day at advanced years maintains a spirit of sturdy independence, and staunch adherence to the worker's cause."[3]

Bob Smillie himself was a national ILP figure even though he was only twenty. He had been involved in the 1935 Scottish unemployed hunger marches in the Lanarkshire section and was Chairman of the ILP youth wing, the 'Guild of Youth'. He had been appointed to the 'Guild of Youth' leadership to prevent it being controlled by either YCL supporters or Trotskyites, and to make it more loyal to the adult party.[4] He was a noted debater and platform orator and was earmarked as a future leading figure in the ILP.[5] He was also one of the youngest ILP members to campaign for the ILP to send an armed contingent to Spain.[6] Fenner Brockway praised his Socialist beliefs after his tragically premature death in Spain:

"The death of young Smillie affected me deeply. Without exception he was the finest lad I knew in our Movement. Socialism was his life and his own character reflected all that is best in Socialist spirit." [7]

Smillie gave up his studies at Glasgow University to go to Spain in October 1936. He was a trained chemist and could speak both French and Spanish adequately.[8] He was twenty when he went to Spain, initially to help the Republican war effort by setting up an armaments factory (possibly in conjunction with Georges Kopp). This was unsuccessful.[9] After the failure of the factory enterprise Smillie stayed in Barcelona to help John McNair in the ILP office. Here he carried out administrative duties and later he represented the youth wing of the 'London Bureau'. McNair and Smillie spent New Year's Eve together in Barcelona working in the ILP office then going out for a meal. They ended the night drinking whisky and singing Scottish songs, even though, as McNair commented, Smillie rarely drank alcohol.[10] Smillie was a keen supporter of the POUM youth wing, the JCI, and supported its stance of social revolution over democratic revolution. While on the Aragon Front he wrote an article with fellow volunteer and YCL member Stafford Cottman calling for the unity of all anti-Fascist forces to win the war. He also clearly states his faith in the ILP stance of supporting the Revolution to win the war:

38. Bob Smillie. (NL)

"However, it was the revolutionary workers that beat the Fascists, here in July, and it is the revolutionary workers who will hold the conquests of the revolution. We in the English contingent are helping them to do that by fighting Fascism on the Aragon front."[11]

The article was published after his death. He also saw similarities between revolutionary Barcelona and the ILP stronghold of Glasgow.[12] When the ILP Contingent arrived in Barcelona in January 1937

Smillie volunteered to join them. Before he joined the ILP Contingent Smillie had attended a funeral of a leading POUM youth member killed in action, along with fellow 'Guild of Youth' executive member Jennie Lee (future Labour MP and wife of Aneurin Bevan, the famous left wing 'firebrand' Labour MP). The politically charged and emotive funeral may have finally convinced Smillie to join the other British volunteers at the Front. He had earlier been horrified at the atrocities committed by enemy forces when they had captured Irun and Badajoz and massacred thousands of Republican prisoners.[13] He joined the ILP Contingent along with two American volunteers (Milton and Stearns) having persuaded McNair to release him from his political role in Barcelona.[14]

39. Bob Smillie and John McNair in the POUM offices in Barcleona, 1936-1937. (NL)

When the ILP volunteers were based in the Alcubierre Mountains, Smillie was one of the volunteers who shouted political slogans through a megaphone to try to entice enemy troops to desert. As he spoke good Spanish he was seen as the best volunteer to do this! He also volunteered to be the Contingent's cook, which involved twelve hours of labour a day, while he also continued to take part in patrols and carrying out sentry duty.[15] John McNair visited Smillie on the Aragon Front and asked him which guard duty he liked best. Smillie replied that he preferred the 5.00 – 7.00 a.m. duty because he could watch the dawn light up the Pyrenees in the distance.[16]

In the attack on Ermita Salas his bravery was commented on by his Commanding Officer.[17] The Section Commander, Georges Kopp, praised the performance of all the ILP volunteers who took part in the action but picked out three men for special mention:

"Among them I feel it my duty to give a particular mention of the splendid action of Eric Blair, Bob Smillie and Paddy Donovan who behaved exceptionally well."[18]

Orwell describes Smillie in action during the attack on the enemy position:

"Bob Smillie, the blood running down his face from a small wound, sprang to his knee and flung a bomb."[19]

In the attack Smillie, supported by two other British volunteers, followed Orwell into the enemy position. They took part in its capture and helped to hold it temporarily against enemy counter attack until they were forced to retreat.[20] Orwell described Smillie as the best of the ILP volunteers, as did Douglas Moyle, another member of the ILP Contingent.[21] After Smillie's death Orwell wrote about his personal qualities:

"Bob Smillie was only twenty-two years old and physically he was one of the toughest people I have met. He was, I think, the only person I knew, English or Spanish, who went three months in the trenches without a day's illness"

and

"Here was this brave and gifted boy, who had thrown up his career at Glasgow University in order to come and fight against Fascism and who, as I saw for myself, had done his job at the Front with faultless courage and willingness..."[22]

George Kopp in a letter to his parents paid tribute to Smillie as a soldier:

"You have by this time heard of the sad and untimely fate of your son, Robert. He was one of the most gallant soldiers in the regiment which I commanded. It is a duty and a privilege to express to you my sympathy, and to assure you that Bob always carried himself bravely and courageously in and out of the firing line. You can be proud of him."[23]

Like other ILP volunteers Smillie was involved in the 'May Days' events and found himself defending the POUM headquarters building. In an article about the 'May Days' McNair refers to Smillie by name and this may have made him known to the Spanish authorities. McNair describes him as having been on guard duty and fast asleep in a chair.[24]

In May Smillie was given permission to visit Paris for a meeting of the youth wing of the 'London Bureau' and to go from Paris to Britain and deliver a series of propaganda lectures. Buchanan believes that Smillie signed up to fight at the Front for three months and was then supposed to return to Britain on a propaganda tour.[25] He set out for home on May 10th and on May 11th he was arrested by police at the Spanish frontier for not having his papers. It is possible he was seen as a deserter, although he was discovered carrying a POUM badge and his connection with the POUM would not have done him any favours at this point.[26]

He was sent to Valencia and imprisoned, and from there he managed to get a note to McNair on May 12th. A businessman and family friend called David Murray was sent to Valencia to make contact with Smillie. He was a fellow ILP member and spoke good Spanish. Smillie believed that the police had been waiting for him in some pre-arranged trap. Murray believed he was arrested for having no proper papers. Smillie was carrying a report of the 'May Days' events written by McNair (which he managed to destroy), letters from ILP volunteers and an article written by Orwell. He was also carrying two discharged bombs to use in his propaganda lectures, which led to him being charged with carrying arms.[27]

When questioned by the police Smillie freely admitted the discharged bombs were his and that he had been involved in the 'May Days'. Unfortunately his openness meant that the secret police became involved, and his imprisonment became more serious. Smillie also had the POUM newspaper *La Batalla* delivered to him in prison, which would have further incriminated him as a foreign Trotskyite in the eyes of the secret police.

Tragically, Smillie fell ill in prison and died of peritonitis on June 11th 1937.[28] In chapter five I have discussed the controversy surrounding his death, including whether Smillie was actually murdered or died of neglect. Tom Buchanan, who wrote the major work on his death, believes that "...the full facts of Bob Smillie's death may never be established."[29]

Attempts by Smillie's father, Alex, to get David Murray and the ILP NAC to publish in full Murray's report of Bob Smillie's death proved unsuccessful and continued to fuel speculation that he had been murdered, or, at the least, the Spanish Authorities were guilty of manslaughter.[30] In its final report on Smillie's death the *New Leader* paid him the following homage:

> "All the evidence we have seen from any and every source proves conclusively that not only was Bob absolutely innocent of any charge which warranted his being arrested and imprisoned, but that during his whole imprisonment he remained what we have always known him to be, namely, an utterly fearless, honest and intelligent Socialist. Bob Smillie gave his life in the service of the workers."[31]

John Milnes Alan Smith

John Smith left for Spain with the main body of ILP volunteers in January 1937 sailing from Newhaven and landing in Dieppe. The only reference to him in Spain is when British Battalion (International Brigade) Commissar Walter Tapsell lists a Smith as an ILP unit volunteer who was about to or had returned home. John Smith returned to Britain in Mid-May 1937.[1]

'Tanky' (James Cope)

'Tanky' seems to be a nickname of the Welsh volunteer James Arthur Colin Cope from Cardiff.[1] Tanky had some previous military experience, either as a veteran of World War I or in the British Army in peacetime:

> "Our ILP contingent was a very mixed group...one had deserted from the British tank corps, he was so enthusiastic to fight in Spain."[2]

'Tanky' had deserted from the Royal Tank Corps at Bovington in Hertfordshire, in December 1936 to go to Spain.[3] Tanky's friend in Spain, Frank Frankford told an interviewer in 1998, that Tanky had served in the Tank Corp in World War I (hence the nickname 'Tanky'). By 1998 Frankford was a very old man with a poor memory according to the interviewer, so he may have been mistaken.[4] It is just possible that Tanky served from World War I through to 1936 in the Army but this seems very unlikely. Another ILP volunteer says that Tanky told him he was wanted for stealing cars in South Africa and had had a variety of short-term jobs including fairground work on the dodgems prior to coming to Spain.[5] Tanky left for Spain with the main group of ILP volunteers in January 1937.[6]

Tanky was probably chosen to take part in the night attack on Ermita Salas because of his military experience. In the attack reported in the *New Leader* his rifle jams and he shouts for a replacement rifle. Perhaps he demanded a rifle because he was a better shot than most of the men in the unit, due to his military experience, but this is only conjecture.[7]

In Spain he was a friend of Frank Frankford, and together they left the Front without permission for a few days. They brought food in a local village and in Barbastro where they were drunk for three days. This shows Tanky's disdain of military discipline.[8]

He was in Barcelona during the 'May Days' events and did guard duty with Frankford opposite the Moka Café held by Spanish police. Along with Frankford he wanted to join the International Brigades as a way of staying longer in Spain, but nothing came of this wish.[9] He returned to the Front with the reduced ILP Contingent but was back in Barcelona by June. Here it is alleged that he became mixed up in some very shady dealings when he and Frankford were offered some paintings stolen from a church. While trying to organise a buyer for them, Tanky was arrested.[10]

It is likely he was released with the aid of either the *Daily Worker* journalist, Sam Lesser, that had helped Frankford or the British authorities. On his return to Britain in July 1937 he returned to Bovington and was arrested for desertion and imprisoned.[11] A report from 1938 says a James Arthur Cope had fought and been wounded in Spain.[12]

* * *

Harry Parry Thomas (1894 - ?)

Harry Parry Thomas was a Welshman from Carreglefn in Anglesey, he later moved to Liverpool and had served in World War I in the King's Liverpool Regiment, rising to the rank of Sergeant. By profession he was a seaman and was living in London when he volunteered to join the ILP Contingent.[1]

Thomas wrote a detailed letter to the Communist Party representative in Barcelona in May 1937 in which he explains why he joined the ILP group and talks about his experiences with the ILP Contingent. It seems Thomas was a Communist Party member and was in trouble for leaving with the ILP volunteers so the thrust of the letter is to denigrate the ILP Contingent.[2]

According to Thomas he visited Harry Pollitt, the British Communist Party leader, and asked to join the International Brigades. He was told he could go with the next draft of volunteers. He claims he received a letter a few days later stating it was not possible for the next draft to leave just yet and he should wait. So instead he volunteered and was accepted for the ILP Contingent. He then re-visited Pollitt to tell him what he had done, Pollitt advised him to be careful as the ILP were "only messers".[3]

Thomas travelled on a weekend ticket to Paris and the journey was straightforward. He claims the volunteers expected to go on to Madrid. Once on the front lines, Thomas and other volunteers opened fired on the enemy, but were told to stop as it 'may provoke the enemy'. Thomas claims that this was the general rule during all the time he was at the Front, though a more likely explanation is they were told this to prevent them wasting ammunition as it was in limited supply. Thomas states they later moved to a mountain top position where the enemy positions were four kilometres away. Possibly because of his previous military experience he formed part of a covering group of volunteers who advanced eighty yards ahead of the main body of volunteers when one night their positions were moved forward 830 yards and new trenches dug. Thomas comments that he expected trouble but nothing happened. He suggests that this might have been because of some agreement between the two sides. Another explanation could be the lack of ammunition and numbers on the enemy side. After this he spent his time at the Front swimming in a nearby river and sunbathing and saw their presence with the POUM militia as a 'farce'.[4] He took part in the attack on Ermita Salas where he was wounded. In the *New Leader* Thomas was reported as shouting "I'm hit", which suggests that he suffered a bullet wound.[5]

Thomas comments sarcastically that in three and a half months in Spain his only military action lasted three quarters of an hour. His wound was serious enough for him to be hospitalised.[6]

Thomas writes of his experiences of the 'May Days' events, while on leave from the front in Barcelona. He recounts seeing barricades in the streets, much firing and bombs going off and seeing dead bodies. He recalls being told to stay in their hotel and not being rung by the POUM or given any instructions by them. He met fellow volunteer Douglas Thompson in the streets. At a barricade Thompson was allowed to pass freely but Thomas was held and searched for arms before being allowed to go free. His hotel room was searched by Government supporters and they found a bayonet with a scabbard and a club which he had had in the trenches. On discovering these items the patrol threatened to shoot both Thomas and the Spanish comrade with whom he was sharing the room. They were arrested and taken to a checa where there were fifty men seated and an old man cross-examined them. On being spoken to in Catalan, Thomas replied:

"'Hombre', I replied, 'H. P. Thomas no savvee.'"

He was made to write down his personal and political details and was then released.[7]

Thomas ends his letter to the Communist representative in Barcelona saying he left the POUM/ ILP forces because everyone was saying they were Franco's 5th Army, and asking why it was that the POUM claimed they were the 'spearhead of the revolution' but took no action. Thomas states he was not a politician but was a strong anti-Fascist.[8]

He left Spain in late May 1937 and returned to Britain. His name appears in the *New Leader* article condemning Frankford's anti-POUM allegations. Maybe once back in Britain he had changed his mind after a period of reflection or his name was added without his knowledge.[9]

* * *

Douglas Thompson (1894 - ?)

Douglas Herbert Thompson was a Londoner from Golders Green and left for Spain with the majority of the ILP volunteers in January 1937.[1]

On the Alcubierre Front Thompson went out on a night patrol with Orwell to see if the Fascists were intending to follow up a major bombardment of the ILP positions with an attack. The patrol discovered there were no Fascists in 'No Man's Land' and that they were still in their own positions, so they were able to report the enemy were not preparing to attack their positions.[2]

Thompson took part in the night attack on Ermita Salas and was wounded in the action but bravely carried on fighting rather than have his wound treated.[3] Orwell describes him firing at the enemy:

> "Douglas Thompson, with a wounded arm dangling useless at his side, was leaning against the parapet and firing one-handed at the flashes. Someone whose rifle had jammed was loading for him." [4]

In the *New Leader* account of the attack, Thompson exclaims, "I've caught one" and refuses to receive treatment. Further on in the story Thompson is helping to build a new parapet to give cover from enemy machine gun fire. He is carrying sandbags one-handed, which suggests he most have been a large man or at the very least an incredibly strong man. Then as in the Orwell account he orders another volunteer to load his rifle while he fires it one handed.[5]

After he was wounded Thompson was sent to a hospital in Tarragona and then onto to Barcelona, when the 'May Days' events began. In Barcelona he met Orwell in the street and asked him what the shooting was all about. He decided he would remain neutral as his arm had not healed properly, and retired to his hotel room. Unfortunately his hotel was in an area controlled by the Government forces and was raided. Thompson was arrested and jailed for eight days. He was kept in a cell that was so full he was unable to lie down to sleep.[6] He may also have been arrested because he had a large quantity of beer in his room, which he had bought to help him get through that troubled period. During the May Days he also came across fellow volunteer Harold Thomas in the streets.[7] The British Consul intervened to secure Thompson's release from prison.[8] After his release from jail he returned to hospital for treatment before returning to England in late May 1937.[9]

Harry Webb

Harry Webb was from Chelmsford in Essex and arrived in Barcelona in March 1937 wishing to volunteer for ambulance work. He had no desire to fight Fascism in the armed struggle, as he was a member of the Society of Friends (a Quaker). On arrival in Barcelona he met the ILP representative, John McNair. While they were drinking coffee and discussing Webb's request to join the ILP Contingent they were arrested by Spanish police and taken to a large prison. McNair and Webb received no reply as to why they had been arrested and began to shout loudly and kick the cell door to gain the attention of the guards. Around an hour later prison warders arrived at their cell and McNair told them he knew very important people including the Catalan President, Companys. Fearful of this the warders told the Prison Governor. The next day McNair and Webb were taken before the Prison Governor, who released them. On their release they were met by the POUM leader, Andreu Nin, and then taken to meet the POUM Executive.[1]

Nothing more is heard of Webb until the wounding of Orwell. He may have briefly gone to the Front or met up with the ILP volunteers when they were on leave in Barcelona. We have information about only one ILP volunteer who deliberately stayed out of the 'May Days' events in Barcelona, so it is likely Webb was involved somehow; however, as a Quaker it is very unlikely that he was involved in a military capacity. We know that Webb returned with the reduced ILP Contingent to the Front after the 'May Days' events.

At the Front Webb became a stretcher-bearer and was present when Orwell was shot in the throat by an enemy sniper. Orwell describes Webb helping him after he had been shot:

> "Harry Webb, our stretcher-bearer, had brought a bandage and one of the little bottles of alcohol they gave us for field-dressings...I felt the alcohol, which at ordinary times would sting like the devil, splash on to the wound as a pleasant coolness." [2]

He returned to Britain in late October 1938 having been a member of the Spanish Medical Aid Committee.[3]

* * *

David Wickes (1901 - ?)

David Leslie Wickes was a Londoner. He had been a member of the Labour Party since 1928 and was a member of the left wing Socialist League at the time he went to Spain. He was a language teacher and spoke four languages; English, French, German and Spanish. According to the Moscow archives he served with the ILP medical unit in Spain before transferring to the International Brigades.[1]

During the 'May Days' events Wickes was arrested and, possibly as a condition of his release, he agreed to work for Communist Intelligence. In a secret report on the Blairs and fellow ILP volunteers, David Wickes is listed as the Albacete (Headquarters of the International Brigades) contact.[2] One Orwell biographer claims that Wickes attempted to join the International Brigades before he joined the ILP unit and was turned down, although Communist Party leader Harry Pollitt instructed him to join the ILP unit and spy on their activities.[3] In an article on spies who may have shadowed the Blairs in Spain by Robert Stradling, Wickes is named in a list of five, although Stradling comments:

> "There is evidence- though by no means conclusive in every case- that all these men were working for various Communist-run intelligence outfits in Spain."[4]

After the 'May Days' Wickes joined the International Brigades. First he worked in Albacete as an interpreter with the Canadian 60th Battalion. He was promoted to Assistant Battalion Paymaster and in October 1937 was wounded in the attack on Fuentas de Ebro. In the Moscow archives there are several concerns about his previous ILP associations. This view was vindicated when he refused to take part in a firing squad in April 1938 which was to execute two American volunteers.[5] A report in the Moscow archive about him states:

> "Activity appears good, but has a tendency to take up Trotskyist positions and should be watched for that reason."[6]

Wickes also believed many good soldiers and those with military experience were being ignored for leadership positions in the International Brigades in favour of those with good Communist credentials.[7]

Wickes left Spain in December 1938 and on his return to London he became Honorary Secretary of the Basque Children's Committee in London.[8]

Robert ('Bob') Williams

Bob Williams was a Welshman, originally from the Rhyl area in North Wales.[1] By profession he was a labourer, docker or lorry driver[2] and was one of the older volunteers, aged in his thirties. Physically he was a tall man.[3] Williams was not a member of the original ILP Contingent but joined them in Spain. He was married to a Spanish woman and living in Spain at the time the ILP volunteers arrived. William's wife had been involved in suppressing the military rebellion in Barcelona and showed Orwell how to put on his military leather cartridge boxes. Like Orwell Williams was already at the Front with the POUM militia when the ILP volunteers reached the Front.[4]

Williams served with the POUM militia on the Alcubierre Front along with his brother-in-law Ramon and Orwell. They shared the same dug-out under fire. When the ILP Contingent arrived at the Front all three of them joined the British ILP volunteers.[5]

During the Civil War Williams was wounded three times and hospitalised through illness.[6] He broke his ankle in February 1937 during enemy shelling.[7] Later he served with the Catalan Communist PSUC forces and fell sick at the Front and was hospitalised.[8] When he returned to Britain he met Orwell:

> "Two friends have just got back from Spain. One is a chap called Robert Williams who has come out with his guts full of bits of shell." [9]

The timing of these injuries means they must have been received while Williams was serving with the PSUC unit.

Williams was in the Sanatorium in Barcelona recovering from a broken ankle when it was raided by police. Williams and another ILP volunteer fled into hiding. There is conflicting evidence of what happened next to Williams. One story says that he was arrested by the Spanish authorities and spent several months in jail. During this time he smuggled out a letter to Eileen Blair, Orwell's wife telling her Georges Kopp was still alive.[10]

Another story says that Williams had a disagreement with the leadership of the ILP Contingent after Bob Edwards had left for Britain. He was said to have disagreed with the revolutionary policy of the POUM. He decided to leave the POUM and join the International Brigades but missed their British representative when he visited Barcelona.[11] Along with three other disillusioned ILP volunteers Williams then joined the Catalan Communist PSUC armed forces. He served with the PSUC forces for several months on the Aragon Front, where he fell sick and was later invalided home after being wounded.[12]

There are problems with both accounts. If Williams had been in hospital since February then it would have been difficult for him to fall out with the ILP leadership. If he was imprisoned for several months, then when did he join the PSUC military unit? He was definitely suffering from wounds on his return to Britain when Orwell met him, so he must have served in the Republican forces at some time. Perhaps his jail term was only for a short period and it was assumed that, because he was still in Spain, he must be in jail rather than fighting for another unit.

Williams did not return to Britain until December 1938.[13] A *New Leader* article reports that he arrived safely in Britain with his wife and child. On the day they left Barcelona it suffered seven air raids. The *New Leader* says this about Bob Williams:

> "Bob was wounded three times on the Aragon Front, and proved himself to be during the whole campaign one of the most courageous fighters on behalf of the Spanish workers."[14]

Williams and his family were sent to the ILP Basque refugee home at Street in Somerset to recover from their ordeal.[15]

Mike Wilton or Milton

Mike Wilton was an intellectual from Oxford who disdained politicians and politics, and because of this may have had Anarchist leanings. He liked poetry; his two favourite poets being the French poet Baudelaire and the English poet Swinburne. In Spain he wore his knee length boots in a bohemian style, opened so they looked like seventeenth-century riding boots.[1]

Before he joined the ILP Contingent it is possible that Mike Wilton served in the Catalan militia forces that unsuccessfully attacked the rebel-held island of Majorca in August 1936.[2] After this he left Spain and travelled to Morocco where he worked for the British Embassy before returning to Spain to join the ILP volunteers.[3]

Mike Wilton served in the ILP Contingent in the period up to the 'May Days' events and also in the period after. He was still at the Front as late as July 1937.[4] He and with two other volunteers visited Orwell in hospital when he had an infected hand.[5]

He took part in the night attack on Ermita Salas in April 1937. He was one of the volunteers who occupied the captured enemy trench, and had a close shave with an enemy bullet:

"'Hang it, that last shot took my hat off', yelled Mike Wilton."[6]

He was in Barcelona in late May 1937 and met with Tapsell the British Battalion Commissar where he is described as one of the volunteers who desires to leave the POUM militia.[7] On his return to Britain he was one of the signatories to the article which condemned Frankford's slanders against the ILP and POUM.[8]

FOREIGN VOLUNTEERS IN THE ILP CONTINGENT AND MEDICAL PERSONNEL

Louis Levin (1906 - ?)

Dr Louis Levin from New York in September 1936 became a member of the Scottish Ambulance Unit, having joined this unit in Glasgow, although he did not go with them to Spain. Politically he may have been a Communist as he later travelled to Spain with a Communist International card. This may have been his reason for not going to Spain with the Scottish Ambulance Unit as they were set up as a non-political unit. Levin then left for Spain with the ILP volunteers in January 1937.[1]

On arrival in Barcelona Dr Levin offered his services to the POUM but was officially attached to the ILP Contingent. During the 'May Days' Orwell was recognised by an agitated American doctor, whose name he did not know. Orwell says that he had been at the Front with the ILP volunteers.[2] Another volunteer states it was an American doctor who treated Orwell when he had been shot in the throat. As there are no records of any other American doctors, we can presume that this unknown doctor is the same doctor that Orwell met in Barcelona [3] and is most likely to be Louis Levin.

W. B. Martin

In the accounts of his time in Spain Martin is always referred to by his initials 'W.B.'; his first name was William.[1] Although he was not a member of the ILP Contingent, he had been one of two drivers who drove an ILP sponsored ambulance to Spain in September 1936.[2] After delivering the ambulance he volunteered for artillery work as he had gunnery experience as an officer (Captain) in the First World War. Once he had demonstrated his skills he was put in charge of an artillery unit of sixty men consisting of POUM and Anarchist militia. This unit was the 6th Artillery Battery of the 1st Durutti Column.[3]

In a *New Leader* article Martin sent revolutionary greetings as a member of the ILP to his comrades in the ILP, and says that he was visiting Barcelona to try and procure more heavy artillery for his unit.[4] In a later article Martin states that his best friend at the Front is a Hungarian who served in the Austro-Hungarian forces during World War I on the German side. He says this man risked his life to save Martin'sl; and asks *New Leader* readers to send warm clothing for his unit members serving on the Huesca Front in winter, and to continue to raise money for the war effort.[5] He was later repatriated to Britain some time in 1937.

Fellow volunteer Harry Thomas claims that Martin was appointed ILP Contingent leader during the training in the Lenin Barracks in January 1937. Thomas goes onto to say that fellow volunteer Chambers resigned from being a Sergeant after being given an inappropriate ('daft') order by Martin. Martin was then removed from his command after being severely drunk on the way to the Front. This led to him being sent back to Britain, so possibly his return to Britain was late January 1937. No other source relates this story and Thomas was trying to impress the Communist Party representative in Barcelona by denigrating the ILP unit, so his evidence is potentially flawed.[6]

Once back in Britain he spoke about his time in Spain. In November 1937 he addressed the Ruislip-Northwood (south of England) Labour Party about his time in Spain:

"Over the top dressed in German field grey uniform (Nationalist troops) there was the nucleus of world war in Spain and the English working class should say it must stop since the beginning of the wars in Spain had been turned from a country of olive groves and vineyards into one of desolation and ruin by the rebel fascist forces who were backed by dictators. Unless that was stopped in Spain it would happen to this country." [7]

These were very prophetic words. Within two years Britain was at war with Nazi Germany.

Harry Milton (Wolf Kupinski)

Harry Milton was a thirty-year-old American who joined the ILP Contingent out in Spain. His real name was Wolf Kupinski and he was a member of a Trotskyite party called the American Revolutionary Workers' League.[1] He was described by another ILP volunteer as:

"...The one Trotskyist proud to boast of the association, and playing it as sort of trump card to end all discussion." [2]

Before he went to Spain Milton had exchanged letters with prominent American Trotskyites and even Trotsky himself.[3]

At the Front Milton had many political disagreements with other members of the ILP Contingent. He particularly disagreed with Orwell and his desire to join the International Brigades, calling Orwell "politically virginal".[4] On a train journey to Barcelona Milton tried his utmost to persuade Orwell to change his mind about joining the International Brigades, "Well, I blew my top." He even tried to frighten Orwell but the famous writer's views were not changed:

"They won't take you, but if they do, they'll knock you off.[5]

Milton describes his time at the Front and his views on the POUM militia:

"Our sector of the front was as quiet as a graveyard. We were miserably armed. The majority of the regiment was a bunch of kids. They were shooting each other accidentally. And we had only one real go at the enemy. It was the first time we went into action. It was a hellish business; the whole thing was botched up. I never expected to survive the Spanish experience. It would have been a disaster if we'd really gone into action." [6]

Although not mentioned as taking part in the night attack on Ermita Salas it sounds from this that he was involved in the action. His description above paints the action in a much less favourable light than the *New Leader* and Orwell.

During the 'May Days' Spanish police shot at Milton and he had to dive into a gutter to avoid their fire. He was only saved when POUM troops threw grenades at the police.[7] Orwell's account of the incident merely mentions 'an American' but Milton has confirmed that he was the American:

"The Civil Guards (Spanish police) had fled back into the café, but when the American came down the street they had opened fire on him, though he was not armed. The American had flung himself behind the kiosk for cover..." [8]

Milton served on the Aragon Front with the ILP Contingent both before and after the 'May Days' events. Milton was on guard duty when an enemy sniper shot Orwell and cut open his shirt to check where he had been hit. He also helped to get him onto a stretcher and helped to walk him around a mile to the nearest front line hospital.[9]

There is a picture of Milton at the front in the Orwell archive taken when Eileen Blair visited the front. It is a group photograph around a Hotchkiss machine gun. Milton is kneeling down holding a rifle in the photograph of ILP members taken on the Huesca Front. He is wearing boots, puttees, trousers, jumper and a beret (see page 171).[10]

When Orwell went to visit Kopp in prison he came across Milton, who had also been arrested. Both men pretended not to know each other in case they incriminated each other. Milton had previously managed to reach the frontier with the correct papers, but he was arrested trying to leave the country. When he was arrested he was wearing corduroy trousers, which showed he was an ex-militia man. This alone may have been enough to get him arrested, or perhaps he was known as a foreign Trotskyite and ex-POUM militia member. Another ILP volunteer says that Milton had fled Barcelona without paying his hotel bill so perhaps he was wanted for a criminal offence?[11]

Milton describes the prison conditions in a letter to an American comrade:

"The conditions here in jail beggar description, a long damp stone room about hundred persons in it."[12]

He was imprisoned with Georges Kopp for a time, helping him out financially (probably to buy food).[13] He was finally released in August 1937 after pressure from the American Consulate.[14] On his release he sent a letter to Orwell in which he stated that Kopp had been murdered by the Communists. This proved to be false.[15] After Spain Milton kept in touch with Orwell and stayed with him and Eileen at least once.

On his return to America he remained a devout Trotskyite for many years and served in the American Army during World War II.[16]

Ramon

Ramon was the brother-in-law of Bob Williams and joined the ILP Contingent at the same time as Williams and Orwell. His surname was possibly Fenellosa.[1] Before he joined the ILP unit Ramon had been in a non-international POUM unit along with Williams and Orwell. Orwell describes an incident where they were forced to dive into dug-outs to avoid enemy fire on the Alcubierre Front.[2]

It is likely that Ramon served with the ILP Contingent at least until they went on leave to Barcelona in late April 1937, as Orwell recalls that Ramon fell asleep on him and snored after the attack on Ermita Salas on April 13th 1937. Perhaps Ramon was one of the fifteen ILP or even Spanish volunteers involved in the night attack, hence his fatigue? Orwell further describes him as a young man, possibly aged in his early twenties.[3] Nothing further is known about Ramon. It is likely he stayed in Spain fighting with the POUM and probably later joining a non-POUM unit.

Orwell in a poem, written after Spain which praises an Italian militia man he had met in Barcelona, suggests Ramon was either later killed in action or executed. Orwell states:

> "And where is Ramon Fenellosa?
> The earthworms know where they are."[4]

Douglas Clark Stearns

He was a nineteen-year-old American from New York. He briefly served with the ILP Contingent before leaving to join an Anarchist militia column. He may have joined the American Abraham Lincoln International Brigade Battalion after his Anarchist unit was dissolved in July 1937. He survived the war and probably returned to the USA.[1] He is mentioned in the Tapsell Report as a ILP volunteer who wished to leave the POUM militia.[2]

Sybil Wingate

Sybil Wingate was a young middle-class woman from a famous family who offered her services as a secretary to John McNair in the ILP office. Wingate had been a member of the Labour Party and its left wing affiliated group the 'Socialist League'. As a member of this group she supported the recruitment of new professionals who were no better off financially than many of the working class.[1] She supported the 'Socialist League's' position on the 'League of Nations' (the forerunner of the United Nations) that it merely helped to perpetuate imperialism.[2] She had recently graduated from Oxford University and finished some research in Spain before offering her services to help the Republican war effort.[3] When the ILP Contingent were leaving for the Front in January 1937 Wingate decided to join some Spanish women who were going to the Front as nurses and stretcher bearers. After a short time Wingate was ordered to leave the Front Line because the Spanish Government no longer wanted women at the Front. Wingate ignored this order and, on a visit to the ILP Contingent, John McNair had to order her back to Barcelona.[4] McNair describes the meeting with a very unhappy Wingate:

> "It was in one of the villages that I found Sybil Wingate. She was not at all pleased to see me. She was dressed as a militiaman and looked as smart and capable as she was. "Why do you come worrying me

John? I'm very happy here. I like the men and I think I'm doing useful work." I agreed with her completely but had to insist and we arranged to go back the next morning to Barcelona."[5]

In April 1937 Wingate wrote for the journal the *Socialist Broadsheet* where she praised the Spanish Revolution:

"Things which in England are topics of academic discussion have become in Spain the material of daily life."[6]

She claimed there was unity in the fight against Fascism but admitted there were some disagreements between the different political groups. Her biggest criticism was directed against the Labour Party:

"To be a member of the British Labour Party is not a subject for pride in Spain today. If it had been left to the official party and trade union movement, there would not be one single English volunteer fighting in Spain".[7]

On her return to Britain Wingate was a member of the Labour Party's Spain Campaign Committee (SCC), which was involved in several major demonstrations and a rally at the Albert Hall in December 1937. Wingate resigned from the SCC in 1938 because it was becoming more interested in humanitarian aid than in campaigning for arms for Republican Spain.[8] At the 1939 Labour Party Conference Wingate delivered a withering speech condemning the Labour Party's lack of support for Republican Spain.[9] Her concluding remarks strongly condemned the British Government and the Labour Party Executive for the defeat of the Spanish Republic:

"Even now the National Executive has no conception of what it has done. It is quite smug, complacent, and pleased with its record. They say 'Very sorry boys'. We did our best but the Government would not do what you wanted, and so Spain is lost, and a million of our comrades are dead. Isn't it just too bad! But never mind, there may be a revolt against Franco tomorrow, and in the meantime you had better do what you can for the refugees and the survivors of the Brigade. Lord Halifax has told us recently that this Government has no Spanish blood on his hands. He took water and washed his hands and said: 'I am innocent of the blood of this just person'. We know what to think of that Pontius Pilate, but what are we to say of ourselves, of our own Movement, of our National Executive who by their betrayal during the first terrible year, and their obstinate refusal to take any effective action worthy of the situation afterwards, have cost us the key position in the fight against Fascism and sacrificed the lives of so many of our best and bravest comrades."[10]

During World War II her frustrations with the Labour Party saw her become one of the leading members of the Commonwealth Party.[11] One of the leading members of this party was former International Brigader and one of the leaders of the British Battalion, Tom Wintringham. After the war Wingate re-joined the Labour Party. She became a councillor for Holborn in London and worked as a senior civil servant.[12]

NOTES

Agnew
[1] National Archives cat no. KV/5/12, MI5 List of British Indivduals who travelled to and from Spain 1936-39, Author Correspondence with Jim Carmody. In the International Brigade archive Agnew is also known as James Mann, who fought at Jarama in February 1937 with the British Battalion and then in May 1937 told Tapsell he had served with the POUM/ILP at one time. Jim Carmody sees these two individuals as separate volunteers and I support this view.
[2] Andy Durgan, *International Volunteers in the POUM Militias*
http://libcom.org/history/international-volunteers-poum-militias
p18, Peter Thwaites, The Independent Labour Party Contingent in the Spanish Civil War, *Imperial War Museum Review*, 1987, p56
[3] In the Tapsell report Agnew is named as one of the ILP volunteers who was about to or had left for England. Marx Memorial Library, International Brigade Archive, Box C13/7a, 'Report on the English Section of the POUM'. National Archives, op cit.

Avory
[1] Correspondence with Jim Carmody.

Bennett
[1] Correspondence with Jim Carmody
[2] Thwaites, op cit., p55

[3] Bob Edwards papers, letter to the author Thwaites 27.01.87

Braithwaite
[1] Durgan, op cit., p19, Peter Davison (editor), *Orwell in Spain: The full text of 'Homage to Catalonia' with associated articles, reviews and letters from The Complete Works of George Orwell* (London, Penguin, 2001), p228
[2] Davison, op cit., p245, Jim Carmody correspondence, National Archives, op cit., D. J. Taylor, *Orwell: the life* (London, Vintage, 2004),p211
[3] Stephen Wadhams, *Remembering Orwell* (Harmondsworth, Penguin, 1984), p83-84, Taylor, op cit., p211
[4] Wadhams, op cit., p87
[5] Thwaites, op cit., p56
[6] Wadhams, op cit., p87, Taylor, op cit., p220
[7] NL 21.05.37
[8] Wadhams, op cit., p89-92, Taylor, op cit., p230-1
[9] Davison, op cit., p228, National Archives, op cit.
[10] Bernard Crick, *George Orwell: A Life* (London, Secker & Warburg, 1981), p233, Taylor, op cit., p246
[11] NL 13.08.37
[12] NL 24.09.37
[13] Wadhams, op cit., p100
[14] Taylor, op cit., p330
[15] Correspondence Stephen Wadhams to Stafford Cottman 24.01.84 and Stafford Cottman to Thwaites 13.01.87. Copies provided to author by Michael Eaude.

Buttonshaw
[1] Durgan, op cit., p8, Thwaites, op cit., p60, Gidon Cohen, *The Failure of a Dream: The Independent Labour Party from Disaffiliation to World War II* (London, Tauris, 2007), p180, correspondence with Andy Durgan.
Fellow ILP veteran Stafford Cottman in a letter to Thwaites 07.12.86 believed Buttonshaw's first name was Archibald, copy given to author by Michael Eaude. In his interview for the Imperial War Museum, Stafford Cottman believed Buttonshaw was American. IWM 9278/7, National Archives, op cit. Jim Carmody correspondence.
[2] Sonia Orwell and Ian Angus (editors), *The Collected Essays and Letters of George Orwell: volume 1: An Age Like This 1920-1940* (London, Penguin, 1970), p298
[3] NL 21.05.37
[4] Amirah Inglis, *Australians in the Spanish Civil War* (London, Allen & Unwin, 1987)
[5] Inglis, op cit., p219

- [6] Ibid, p117
- [7] Ibid, p138
- [8] Ibid, p155
- [9] Ibid, p154
- [10] Ibid, p167-169. In the Tapsell Report, Buttonshaw is listed as one of the volunteers who had either left or was about to return to England. Marx Memorial Library, International Brigade Archive, Box 13/7a, op cit.
- [11] Ibid, p202
- [12] Ibid, p217
- [13] Joseph Toscano, Articles on Harvey Buttonshaw in *Anarchist Age Weekly Review* 471 October 2001 and *Anarchist Age Weekly Review* 569 October 2003. www.takver.com/history/Buttonshaw_harvey.htm
- [14] Toscano, op cit.
- [15] Ibid
- [16] National Archives, op cit.
- [17] Ibid. Andy Durgan in correspondence with the author favours Toscano's account over Inglis'.

Castle
- [1] South Wales Coalfield Collection, Urias Jones interview, (09.10.74), AUD/177, Swansea University

Clarke
- [1] Jack Coward, *Back From the Dead* (Liverpool, Merseyside Writers, ND), p12. List of International Brigaders with annotations presented to author by Local History Group, Author Unknown.
- [2] Correspondence with Jim Carmody

Clinton
- [1] Cohen, op cit., p182, NL 26.03.37, www.wcml.org.uk/internat/spain.htm
- [2] NL 26.03.37, Jim Carmody correspondence
- [3] NL 22.01.37
- [4] NL 26.03.37
- [5] NL 26.02.37
- [6] Durgan, op cit., p19, Cohen, op cit., p182, Thwaites, op cit., p60
- [7] Crick, op cit., p224, Thwaites, Ibid, p61, *George Orwell, Homage to Catalonia: And Looking Back on the Spanish War* (London, Penguin, 1988), p71, 190
- [8] NL 26.03.37
- [9] Marx Memorial Library, International Brigade Archive, Box 13/7a, op cit. Tapsell also states he is of a Trotskyist persuasion and should not be

allowed to fight in the International Brigades. Jim Carmody correspondence, National Archives say left Spain May 37, Taylor, op cit., p228.

[10] Orwell papers: Eileen Blair papers K30, letter Arthur Clinton to Gwen and Eric (Laurence) O'Shaugnessy 1937/8. AIM 25,University College, London. Taylor, op cit., p218

Coles

[1] Durgan, op cit., p19; South Wales Coalfield Collection, Urias Jones interview, (09.10.74), AUD/177, Swansea University
[2] Bill Alexander, *British Volunteers for Liberty: Spain 1936-1939* (London, Lawrence and Wishart, 1982), p108
[3] Stafford Cottman, Imperial War Museum Interview. IWM 9278/7
[4] NL 30.04.37
[5] South Wales Coalfield Collection, Urias Jones interview, (09.10.74), AUD/177, Swansea University
[6] NL 24.09.37

Connor

[1] Correspondence with Jim Carmody. National Archives, op cit. List of International Brigaders.

Cottman

[1] Christopher Hall, *'Disciplina Camaradas': Four English Volunteers in Spain 1936-39* (Pontefract, Gosling Press, 1994), p14, Guardian, Obituaries 29.09.99
[2] Fenner Brockway, *Inside the Left: Thirty Years of Platform, Press, Prison and Parliament* (London, George Allen & Unwin, 1942), p303
[3] *Guardian*, Obituaries, 29.09.99
[4] Hall, op cit., p15
[5] Crick, op cit., p217
[6] Hall, op cit., p20
[7] Ibid, p22-23
[8] Ibid, p23
[9] Durgan, op cit., p19
[10] Thwaites, op cit., p60
[11] Imperial War Museum, Stafford Cottman interview, op cit.
[12] Hall, op cit., p28-29, National Archives,op cit.
[13] Imperial War Museum, Stafford Cottman interview, op cit.
[14] Hall, op cit., p91
[15] Ibid, p29
[16] Ibid, p33-34

[17] Ibid, p91
[18] *Guardian*, Obituaries, 29.09.99, Orwell, op cit., p190, Crick, op cit., p224, Taylor, op cit., p228
[19] Imperial War Museum, Stafford Cottman interview, op cit.
[20] Ibid
[21] Ibid
[22] Hall, op cit., p47
[23] NL 30.04.37
[24] Hall, op cit., p47
[25] Ibid, p48, Imperial War Museum, Stafford Cottman interview, op cit.
[26] Hall, Ibid, p87, Imperial War Museum, Ibid,
[27] Hall, Ibid, p91-92
[28] Ibid, p94. In the Tapsell Report, Cottman is listed as one of the volunteers in hospital. Marx Memorial Library, International Brigade Archive, Box 13/7a, op cit.
[29] Imperial War Museum, Stafford Cottman interview, op cit.
[30] Thwaites, op cit., p61
[31] NL 21.05.37
[32] Hall, op cit., p94
[33] Imperial War Museum, Stafford Cottman interview, op cit.
[34] Hall, op cit., p95
[35] Orwell, op cit., p199, Taylor, op cit., p230
[36] Ibid, p202, 205, Taylor, Ibid, p232
[37] John McNair, *Spanish Diary* (Stockport, Independent Labour Publications, ND), p24-26
[38] Wadhams, op cit., p92
[39] Orwell, op cit., p214-215
[40] Ibid, p216
[41] Hall, op cit., p108, Cohen, op cit., p185, McNair, op cit., p26-27, Crick, op cit., p225-226, Wadhams, op cit., p95-96, Davison, op cit., p24, Michael Shelden, *Orwell Authorised Biography* (London, Politicos, 2006), p309-310
[42] NL 25.06.37
[43] Hall, op cit., p108-109. Richard Baxell, *The Unlikely Warriors: The British in the Spanish Civil War and the struggle against Fascism* (London, Aurum Press, 2012), p197
[44] Cohen, op cit., p139, 184, Imperial War Museum, Stafford Cotman interview, op cit., Davison, op cit., p246-247, Crick, op cit., p230, Shelden, op cit., p309-310, Tom Buchanan, *The Impact of the Spanish Civil War on Britain: War, Loss and Memory* (Brighton, Sussex Academic Press, 2007), p228, Taylor, op cit., p246-8
[45] Hall, op cit., p112, Guardian Obituaries, 29.09.99
[46] Crick, op cit., p233

[47] NL 13.08.37
[48] NL 24.09.37
[49] Hall, op cit., p112, Thwaites, op cit., p61
[50] Crick, op cit., p404, Taylor, op cit., p55, 418
[51] Guardian Obituaries, 29.09.99
[52] Indpendent Obituaries, 03.11.99
[53] Hall, op cit., p117
[54] Cohen, op cit., p176
[55] Letter Stella Cottman to author 11.09.95
[56] *Guardian*, Obituaries, 29.09.99

Doran

[1] Davison, op cit., p247, Cohen, op cit., p180, Jim Carmody correspondence
[2] Daniel Gray, *Homage to Caledonia: Scotland and the Spanish Civil War* (Luath Press, Edinburgh, 2008) p78
[3] NL 24.09.37, Jim Carmody correspondence, National Archives, op cit
[4] Gray, op cit., p163
[5] Davison, op cit., p245-247, Shelden, op cit., p308-309, UCL Library Services Special Collections Orwell /C/4/E
http://www.ucl.ac.uk/library/special-coll/orwell.shtml
[6] Davison, Ibid, p24-27. In the Tapsell Report Doran is listed as a Trotskyite who should not be allowed to join the International Brigade. Marx Memorial Library, International Brigade Archive, Box 13/7a, op cit.
[7] Bob Edwards Archive, op cit.

Evans

[1] Alexander, op cit., p108
[2] South Wales Coalfield Collection, Urias Jones interview, (09.10.74), AUD/177, Swansea University

Farrell

[1] Robert Stradling, *The Irish and the Spanish Civil War 1936-1939: Crusades in Conflict* (Manchester, Mandolin, 1999), p268. Stradling calls him 'Forcell' but it is the same person. List of International Brigaders
[2] Main source for this volunteer correspondence with Jim Carmody and Dundee and the Spanish Civil War website.
http://groups.msn.com/DundeeandtheSpanishCivilWar/homepage.msnw
[3] Op cit. List of International Brigaders, National Archives says returned to Spain July 1937.

Frankford

[1] Imperial War Museum interview with Frank Frankford. IWM 9308/5
[2] Ibid, National Archives, applied passport 06.01.37.
[3] Wadhams, op cit., p76
[4] Ibid, p77
[5] Thwaites, op cit., p60
[6] Ibid, p59
[7] Imperial War Museum, Frank Frankford interview, op cit. Frankford and 'Tanky' brought eggs from a local village, bought a turkey in Barbastro and stayed there for three drunken days.
[8] Crick, op cit., p217-218, NL 30.04.37
[9] Thwaites, op cit., p60
[10] Imperial War Museum, Frank Frankford interview, op cit.
[11] Ibid
[12] Crick, op cit., p223
[13] Ibid, p439, Taylor, op cit., p211
[14] Imperial War Museum, Frank Frankford interview, op cit.
[15] Wadhams, op cit., p82-83, Taylor, op cit., p213
[16] Imperial War Museum, Frank Frankford interview, op cit. In the Tapsell Report Frankford is listed as a Trotskyite who should not be allowed into the British Battalion. Marx Memorial Library, International Brigade Archive, Box 13/7a, op cit.
[17] Imperial War Museum, Frank Frankford interview, Ibid, Thwaites, op cit., p61

[18] Jeffrey Meyers, Repeating the Old Lies,'*The New Criterion*', 1999, p77
http://orwell.ru/a_life/Spanish_War/english/e_olies
Imperial War Museum, Frank Frankford interview, ibid
[19] Imperial War Museum, Frank Frankford interview, ibid
[20] Ibid, Taylor, op cit., p248
[21] Correspondence with Andy Durgan.
[22] *Treball* was the newspaper of the Catalan Communist Party, the PSUC. The *Volunteer for Liberty* was the newsletter of the XV International Brigade. Frankford's hostile POUM article appeared in its 13.09.37 edition. Baxell, op cit., p196-7
Sam Lesser (1915-2010). He was one of the first British volunteers in Spain and was wounded at Lopera in January 1937. After being wounded he left the International Brigades to work as a radio broadcaster in Barcelona and later became a journalist for the Communist 'Daily Worker'.
[23] NL 17.09.37, NL 24.09.37

[24] Imperial War Museum, Frank Frankford interview, op cit
[25] Ibid
[26] NL 17.09.37, National Archives, op cit.
[27] Brockway, op cit., p317
[28] Cohen, op cit., p184-185, Thwaites, op cit., p61, Crick, op cit., p232-233, 439
[29] Thwaites, Ibid, p58, 61
[30] Meyers, op cit., p77
[31] Orwell and Angus, op cit., p405
[32] Thwaites, op cit., p61
[33] Crick, op cit., p439

Gross

[1] Shelden, op cit., p287, NL 30.04.37, Jim Carmody correspondence, National Archives, op cit., MarxMemorial Library, International Brigade Archives, Box C 13/12 H P Thomas letter.
[2] NL 24.09.37. In the Tapsell Report Gross is listed as a volunteer who had left for England or was about to leave Spain (May 1937). Marx Memorial Library, International Brigade Archive, Box 13/7a, op cit. Jim Carmody correspondence.
[3] Thwaites, op cit., p61
[4] Richard Kisch, *The Days of the Good Soldiers: Communists in the Armed Forces WWII* (London, Journeyman, 1985), p92

Hiddlestone

[1] NL 23.04.37
[2] Orwell, op cit., p98
[3] Ibid, p97-98, Cohen, op cit., p182, Thwaites, op cit., p60, Durgan, op cit., p21, NL 23.04.37, NL 30.04.37. According to the Tapsell Report he was still in hospital in May 1937. Marx Memorial Library, International Brigade Archive, Box 13/7a, op cit.
[4] NL 10.02.39
[5] Cohen, op cit., p185-186, NL 10.02.39
[6] Thwaites, op cit., p56
[7] Orwell and Angus, op cit., p405

Hunter

[1] Cohen, op cit., p182, Thwaites, op cit., p60, Durgan, op cit., p21
[2] NL 30.04.37. According to the Tapsell Report he was still in hospital in May 1937. Marx Memorial Library, International Brigade Archive, Box 13/7a, op cit.

[3] Thwaites, op cit., p56
[4] NL 24.09.37, National Archives, op cit.

Jones
[1] Hywel Francis, *Miners Against Fascism: Wales and the Spanish Civil War* (London, Lawrence and Wishart, 1984) p175; South Wales Coalfield Collection, Urias Jones interview, op cit, Jim Carmody correspondence, National Archives say Jones was back in Britain in May 1937, which puts some doubts on his oral testimony.
[2] Francis, op cit., p175; South Wales Coalfield Collection, Urias Jones interview, ibid. Durgan, op cit., p21. Jones met with the British Battalion Commissar Tapsell and is listed as one of the ILP volunteers who wanted to leave the POUM militia. Marx Memorial Library, International Brigade Archive, Box 13/7a , op cit. Probably Tapsell returned to Albacete (International Brigades HQ) before Jones could see him about joining the International Brigades.
[3] NL 30.04.37
[4] South Wales Coalfield Collection, Urias Jones interview, op cit
[5] NL 24.09.37
[6] South Wales Coalfield Collection, Urias Jones interview, op cit
[7] Ibid

Julius
[1] Marx Memorial Library, International Brigade Archive, Box 13/7a, op cit.

Justesen
[1] Salford Working Class Movement Library, Jim Carmody correspondence
[2] Durgan, op cit., p21. In the Tapsell Report he is listed as having left or about to leave for England (May 1937). Marx Memorial Library, International Brigade Archive, Box 13/7a, op cit., National Archives, op cit.
[3] NL 30.04.37, NL 24.09.37

MacDonald
[1] Ciaran Crossey, *No Pasaran: "We Intend to Show the World"* (Belfast, Belfast and District Trades Union Council, 2007), p6
[2] Correspondence with Jim Carmody.

McNeil
[1] Gray, op cit., p163, Jim Carmody correspondence, National Archives, op cit.
[2] NL 30.04.37

[3] Durgan, op cit., p22, National Archives, op cit.

Moyle
[1] Orwell, op cit., p131, NL 13.08.37, National Archives, Ibid, Jim Carmody correspondence.
[2] Wadhams, op cit., p80
[3] Orwell, op cit., p95-99, Crick, op cit., p217, Durgan, op cit., p22, NL 30.04.37, Taylor, op cit., p215
[4] Orwell, Ibid, p131
[5] Davison, op cit., p26
[6] Marx Memorial Library, International Brigade Archive, Box 13/7a, op cit.
[7] NL 25.06.37, We Carry on: Our Tribute to Bob Smillie http://contentdm.warwick.ac.uk/cdm/compoundobject/collection/scw/id/12169/rec/1
[8] Wadhams, op cit., p100, Shelden, op cit., p308-309, Crick, op cit., p233, Taylor, op cit., p246
[9] NL 13.08.37
[10] Thwaites, op cit., p58
[11] NL 24.09.37
[12] George Orwell, *Our Job Worth Living: 20: 1949-50: The Complete Works of George Orwell* (London, Secker & Warburg, 1999), p56
[13] C. C. Barfoot and Dominic Baker-Smith, *Between Dream and Nature: Essays on Utopia and Dystopia* (Amsterdam, Editions Rodopi BV, 1987), p106
[14] Letter Douglas Moyle November 1994 to author. In the letter he states Stafford Cottman had sent him a copy of *Disciplina Camaradas* which included an account of Cottman's time in Spain. Moyle commented that it had brought back happy memories.

O'Hara
[1] Cohen, op cit., p181, National Archives, op cit., Jim Carmody correspondence.
[2] Orwell, op cit., p91
[3] NL 30.04.37
[4] Tapsell Report, Marx Memorial Library, International Brigade Archive, Box 13/7a, op cit. National Archives, op cit.

Ritchie
[1] Gray, op cit., p146, National Archives, Ibid, Jim Carmody correspondence.
[2] Letter Stafford Cottman to Thwaites, ND. Copy provided to the author by Michael Eaude.

[3] Imperial War Museum, Frank Frankford interview, op cit.
[4] Gray, op cit., p146-147
[5] Durgan, op cit., p23
[6] Tapsell Report, Marx Memorial Library, International Brigade Archive, Box 13/7a, op cit., National Archives, op cit.
[7] NL 24.09.37, National Archives, op cit.

Smillie
[1] NL 25.06.37, National Archives, Ibid.
[2] Cohen, op cit., p147
[3] Ibid, p188
[4] Ibid, p147-148, 188
[5] McNair, op cit., p19, NL 18.06.37
[6] McNair, Ibid, p10
[7] Brockway, op cit., p303
[8] Buchanan, op cit., p98, 100, Orwell, op cit., p206, NL 09.07.37, National Archives, op cit.
[9] Buchanan, Ibid, p100, 226-227, National Archives, Ibid.
[10] McNair, op cit., p12, 15
[11] NL 25.06.37
[12] Buchanan, op cit., p228
[13] Ibid, p227, We Carry On, op cit.
[14] Thwaites, op cit., p54, Cohen, op cit., p180, NL 09.07.37
[15] NL 19.02.37, We Carry On, op cit.
[16] NL 09.07.37
[17] Thwaites, op cit., p56, Buchanan, op cit., p100
[18] McNair, op cit., p20
[19] Orwell, op cit., p94
[20] NL 30.04.37
[21] Orwell, op cit., p39, NL 25.06.37
[22] Orwell, Ibid, p206
[23] Gray, op cit., p159
[24] Buchanan, op cit., p102, NL 21.05.37
[25] Buchanan, Ibid, p100-101, 227, Orwell, op cit., p174
[26] Buchanan Ibid, p100-101, McNair, op cit., p19, NL 18.06.37
[27] Durgan, op cit., p11, Buchanan, Ibid, p106-107
[28] Ibid., p106-109, Cohen, op cit., p186-188
[29] Buchanan, Ibid, p121
[30] Ibid, p115
[31] NL 11.03.38

Smith
[1] National Archives, op cit., Marx Memorial Library, International Brigade Archive, Box 13/7a

'Tanky'
[1] Correspondence with Jim Carmody.
Robert Stradling, *Wales and the Spanish Civil War: The Dragon's Dearest Cause*? (Cardiff, Univ. of Wales, 2004), p186 lists a James Cope from Cardiff as fighting in the POUM. National Archives list him as James Arthur Colin Cope.
[2] Wadhams, op cit., p76
[3] Correspondence with Jim Carmody
[4] Meyers, op cit., p77
[5] Letter Stafford Cottman to Thwaites 07.12.86. Copy sent to author by Michael Eaude.
[6] National Archives, op cit.
[7] NL 30.04.37
[8] Thwaites, op cit., p60, Imperial War Museum, Frank Frankford interview, op cit.
[9] Imperial War Museum, Frank Frankford interview, ibid
[10] Meyers, op cit., p.77, Imperial War Museum, Frank Frankford interview, ibid. Taylor, op cit., p248 says "church".
[11] Correspondence with Jim Carmody, National Archives, op cit.
[12] National Archives, Ibid.

Thomas H. P.
[1] Ibid, Jim Carmody correspondence, MMLThomas letter, Thomas is listed as coming from Liverpool, as he was a seaman by profession it is likely his place of residence changed on a fairly regular basis. Francis, op cit., p175 *The Northwest and the International Brigades exhibition* held at the 'Peoples Centre' in Liverpool on 03.09.08, by Simon Hawkesworth and Dan Payne.
[2] MML, Thomas letter, Ibid.
[3] Ibid. Harry Pollitt (1890-1960) He was General Secretary of the British Communist Party from 1929-56 and visited the British Battalion in Spain on several occasions.
[4] Ibid
[5] NL 30.04.37
[6] MML,Thomas letter, Tapsell Report, a Thomas with no initial is reported as being in hospital. Marx Memorial Library, International Brigade Archive, Box 13/7a.

[7] MML, Thomas letter, Ibid.
[8] Ibid
[9] Ibid, Jim Carmody correspondence, National Archives, op cit., NL 24.09.37

Thompson
[1] NL 23.04.37, Jim Carmody correspondence, National Archives, ibid. Jim Carmody says he came from Twickenham.
[2] NL 26.02.37
[3] Cohen, op cit., p182, Thwaites, op cit., p60, Durgan, op cit., p23, NL 30.04.37
[4] Orwell, op cit., p93
[5] NL 30.04.37
[6] Orwell, op cit., p140-141
[7] Thwaites, op cit., p61, MML, Thomas letter
[8] NL 11.03.38
[9] Tapsell Report, has Thompson in hospital in May 1937. Marx Memorial Library, International Brigade Archive, Box 13/7a, op cit., National I Archives, op cit.

Webb
[1] McNair, op cit., p18-19, National Archives, Ibid.
[2] Orwell, op cit., p178
[3] National Archives, op cit. Spanish Medical Aid Committee. This organisation was founded on August 1st 1936 and raised money and sent medical personnel out to Spain throughout the entire period of the Civil War.

Wickes
[1] Richard Baxell correspondence, Baxell, op cit., p191, James K Hopkins, *Into the Heart of the Fire: The British in the Spanish Civil War* (Stanford Univ. Press, Stanford, USA, 1998) p150
[2] Robert Stradling, The Spies Who Loved Them: The Blairs in Barcelona, 1937, *Intelligence and National Security*, Vol 25, No 5, 638-655, October 2010, p648, Peter Davison (Editor), *Orwell in Spain*: The full text of Homage to Catalonia with associated articles, reviews and letters from the complete works of George Orwell (Penguin, London 2001), p26
[3] George Bowker, *George Orwell* (London, Little Brown, 2003), p220
[4] Stradling, op cit., p647
[5] Baxell, op cit., p191, Baxell correspondence, Ibid, p648
[6] Baxell, Ibid, p191, Baxell correspondence
[7] Hopkins, op cit., p150
[8] Stradling, op cit., p648, List of International Brigaders.

Williams

[1] Durgan, op cit., p8; South Wales Coalfield Collection, Urias Jones interview, op cit
[2] Alexander, op cit., p108
[3] South Wales Coalfield Collection, Urias Jones interview, op cit
[4] Orwell, op cit., p16-17, Durgan, op cit., p24, Thwaites, op cit., p54, Shelden, op cit., p281, Crick, op cit., p215, Taylor, op cit., p206-7
[5] Orwell, Ibid, p23, 38-39
[6] Cohen, op cit., p185, NL 02.12.38
[7] Cohen, Ibid, p182, Orwell, op cit., p190, Crick, op cit., p224, NL 26.02.37
[8] South Wales Coalfield Collection, Urias Jones interview, op cit
[9] Orwell and Angus, op cit., p408
[10] Crick, op cit., p232
[11] Tapsell Report states Williams was one of the volunteers who wished to leave the POUM militia. Marx Memorial Library, International Brigade Archive, Box 13/7a, op cit. But when he decided to join the International Brigade he missed Tapsell who had already returned to Albacete.
[12] South Wales Coalfield Collection, Urias Jones interview, op cit. Orwell and Angus, op cit., p408
[13] Cohen, op cit., p185
[14] NL 02.12.38
[15] NL 02.12.38

Wilton

[1] Stafford Cottman correspondence with Thwaites 07.12.86. Copy given to author by Michael Eaude. National Archives says he had a Communist International card.
[2] Correspondence with Jim Carmody.
[3] Stafford Cottman correspondence with Thwaites, op cit.
[4] Durgan, op cit., p24
[5] Orwell and Angus, op cit., p298
[6] NL 30.04.37
[7] Tapsell report, op cit.
[8] NL 24.09.37

FOREIGN VOLUNTEERS AND MEDICAL PERSONNEL

Levin
[1] Durgan, op cit., p22, correspondence with Jim Carmody, National Archives, op cit., Jim Fyrth, *The Signal was Spain: The Aid Spain Movement in Britain 1936-39* (Lawrence & Wishart, London, 1986) p183. Scottish Ambulance Unit was a non-political medical unit that tried to be independent of the Spanish Republican authorities. Although it treated many wounded Republican soldiers, it also caused a furore for helping right wing fugitives to leave the country. The unit was dogged with many changes of personnel and political arguments within its members.
[2] Orwell, op cit., p117, Spanish Revolution, op cit.
[3] Wadhams, op cit., p90

Martin
[1] http://ourhistory-hayes.blogspot.com/2007/03/notes-on-west-middle-sex-and-spanish.htm p3
[2] Thwaites, op cit., p52, McNair, op cit., p9, NL 02.10.36, Fyrth, opcit., p80
[3] Thwaites, Ibid, p52, Durgan, op cit., p6, Cohen, op cit., p179, Fyrth, ibid., p80. http://ourhistory-hayes.blogspot.com/2007/03/notes-on-west-middle-sex-and-spanish.htm p3
[4] NL 13.11.36
[5] NL 01.01.37
[6] Correspondence with Jim Carmody, MML Thomas letter.
[7] http://ourhistory-hayes.blogspot.com/2007/03/notes-on-west-middle-sex-and-spanish.htm p3

Milton
[1] Durgan, op cit, p8, Cohen, op cit., p180, Thwaites, op cit., p60. In the Tapsell Report Milton is listed as a Trotskyite who is not to be allowed to join the International Brigade. Marx Memorial Library, International Brigade Archive, Box 13/7a, op cit.
[2] Wadhams, op cit., p81
[3] David Jacobs, The Man who Saved Orwell, *Hoover Digest*, 2001 4, p2 http://orwell.ru/a_life/Spanish_War/english/e_harry
[4] Wadhams, op cit., p81-82
[5] Ibid, p85, Taylor, op cit., p215
[6] Ibid, p82
[7] Ibid, p88, NL 28.05.37
[8] Orwell, op cit., p124, Taylor, op cit., p221

[9] Ibid, p177, Shelden, op cit., p293, Taylor, Ibid, p226, 248
[10] Jacobs, op cit., p4
[11] Orwell, op cit., p207, Wadhams, op cit., p92, Imperial War Museum, Stafford Cottman interview, op cit., Felix Morrow, *Revolution and Counter-Revolution in Spain* (New York, Pathfinder Press, 1974), p193
[12] Jacobs, op cit., p3
[13] Davison, op cit., p228
[14] Durgan, op cit., p13, 21
[15] Crick, op cit., p231-232
[16] Taylor, op cit., p330, Jacobs op cit., p2

Ramon

[1] Orwell, op cit., p39. Also Orwell lists on p225 Spanish militiamen he particularly remembers from his time in Spain. Two of these men are named Ramon. One has the surname 'Fenellosa', the other 'Nuvo Bosch'. Because Fenellosa was the first name, and hence may have been known better to him, I have opted for that surname as the most likely for this Ramon.
[2] Ibid, p23
[3] Ibid, p103
[4] Orwell, op cit., p246.

Stearns

[1] Correspondence with Jim Carmody
[2] Marx Memorial Library, International Brigade Archive, Box 13/7a, op cit.

Wingate

[1] Michael Bor, *The Socialist League in the 1930's* (London, Athena Press, 2005), p151-152
[2] Bor, op cit., p299
[3] McNair, op cit., p12
[4] Ibid, p15-17, Durgan, op cit., p24
[5] McNair, Ibid, p17
[6] Bor, op cit., p323-324
[7] Ibid, p324
[8] Tom Buchanan, *The Spanish Civil War and the British Labour Movement* (Cambridge, Cambridge Univ. Press, 1991), p118, Fyrth, op cit., p286
[9] Buchanan, *The Spanish Civil War and the British Labour Movement*, op cit., p222, Fyrth, ibid, p265
[10] K. W. Watkins, *Britain Divided: The effect of the Spanish Civil War on British political opinion* (Thomas Nelson & Sons Ltd, London, 1963), p194.

Fyrth, op cit., p286

[11] www.historycooperative.org
The Commonwealth was a new left wing political party that was formed during World War II. It won several by-elections during the war but only managed to get elected a single MP at the General Election of 1945. After this setback it ceased taking part in elections.

[12] Paddy Fraser, G. S. Fraser: *A Memoir*
http://jacketmagazine.com/20/fraser.html
Correspondence with Andy Durgan.

Conclusion

ON DECEMBER 7th 1938 A LARGE CROWD greeted a group of about three hundred returning British and Irish anti-Fascist fighters at Victoria Station in London. Among the crowd of supporters were MPs, union leaders and two future Prime Ministers. Before being welcomed back home, some of these returning anti-Fascists had marched through the streets of Barcelona in the farewell parade of the International Brigades where hundreds of thousands of Spaniards had shouted their thanks. Spanish Communist Cortez Deputy Dolores Ibarruri - known as 'La Pasionaria'- praised their sacrifices in one of the great speeches of history, bidding them to return to Spain when it was once again at peace.[1]

Compare this with the return of the ILP volunteers to England, who returned home in disgrace and were shunned by most of the Left. The majority of the ILP volunteers were forced to flee Spain for their lives when the POUM was outlawed. A minority joined other military Republican units and were either invalided home or fled when Catalonia was falling to the Fascists in early 1939. There was no large crowd to greet the returning volunteers; in fact the reaction towards them was often one of hostility. The only place to offer any welcome was the 1937 ILP Summer School, at which some volunteers were speakers. The people who attended the Summer School supported the volunteers' stance of fighting in a unit that supported the Spanish Revolution.[2]

Throughout the Civil War the ILP supported the POUM and the Spanish Revolution. Many supporters of the Spanish Republic in the period 1936-39 accused the ILP of undermining the Republican Government's war effort by supporting the POUM and its rejection of the Republican government's policies. (The Republican Government wanted to centralise resources and set up and organise a trained Regular Army, which was anathema to the spirit of the Revolution.) They saw the ILP volunteers who fought in the military unit organised by the POUM as supporters of traitors and Fascists. Thus, any contribution made by the ILP to the anti-Fascist cause during the Civil War was either ignored or portrayed as damaging to the Republican Government because it was helping the POUM. This opinion of the ILP role in the Spanish Civil War has continued up to the present day in some quarters. I hope that my descriptions in this book of the anti-Fascist activities of the ILP during the Spanish Civil War have challenged this view.

40. Letchworth ILP Summer School 1937.
Back row left to right Stafford Cottman, George Orwell and John Braithwaite.
Front row left to right Douglas Moyle, Ted Fletcher and John McNair.
(Photograph lent to the author by Stafford Cottman)

At the outbreak of the Civil War in Spain the ILP was a party in decline, with barely four thousand members. The Spanish Civil War dominated party activity almost to the exclusion of domestic issues, which led to a further loss of members. The ILP raised thousands of pounds to help the anti-Fascist cause in Spain, providing medical supplies, an ambulance and a home for Basque refugee children. Individual ILP members supported non-ILP organisations like the 'Aid Spain' movement and helped to raised money for the Spanish Republic. They took part in demonstrations in favour of allowing arms

CONCLUSION

to be freely sold to the Spanish Republic and lobbied MPs and trade union leaders to break the arms embargo on the Spanish Republic. Some ILP members and ILP Contingent members also served in the International Brigades. The ILP's commitment to the anti-Fascist cause is best illustrated in its continuing support for the Spanish Republican Government even when it had declared the POUM an illegal organisation. In a similar vein, the death of Bob Smillie (the leader of the 'Guild of Youth', the ILP Youth wing) in a Spanish Prison was never used as a political weapon to condemn Communist Party policy in Spain.[3]

Like their fellow volunteers in the International Brigades the members of the ILP Contingent were mainly from a working-class background. Most of them were members of a trade union and worked in the manual or semi-skilled trades. A few volunteers had previous military experience either in World War I or in the Armed Forces in peacetime. Most of the volunteers were young single men. The majority were either members of the ILP or supported the ILP position on Spain. Unlike the International Brigades volunteers, the ILP Contingent had volunteered to fight to defend the new Revolution in Aragon and Catalonia, rather than the Republican Government. But both ILP and International Brigades volunteers saw themselves as fighters for anti-Fascism.

The ILP Contingent numbered around forty to forty-five men and included some Americans and a Spaniard besides Britons and Irishmen. They were issued with antiquated weapons and received almost no military training. The ILP volunteers served as a Section in the POUM militia on the Aragon Front from January to late April 1937. The Fronts they served on were generally very quiet, with the only significant action being occasional shelling, patrols and sniping. In winter the trenches and strong points they occupied were very cold - at times freezing - and later when the weather improved and became warmer, lice infested the volunteers' clothing. The ILP Contingent took part in one action where they performed bravely and were cited by their Commanding Officer. After the 'May Days' events about half the contingent decided they did not wish to go back to the Front. Most either stayed in Barcelona or returned home, while a minority joined other Republican units. The reduced ILP Contingent returned to the Aragon Front for a brief period in May with the odd volunteer staying on at the Front till July 1937 when the POUM 29th Division was disbanded.

At this point most of the ILP volunteers were forced to flee Spain to avoid arrest. Several ILP volunteers remained in Spain, serving in non-POUM units, one man was killed, most of the rest were wounded and the last man to leave Spain did not return to England until February 1939.[4]

The ILP Contingent's experiences in Spain cannot compare with the losses and sometimes ferocious actions in which the International Brigades were involved. While the International Brigades were suffering huge losses around Madrid, the ILP were on a quiet static Front until the summer of 1937. Indeed, the performance of the ILP Contingent has sometimes been compared to that of O'Duffy's Irish volunteers who fought briefly for the Nationalists. Nevertheless, the ILP Contingent was a group of anti-Fascists volunteers from these shores who volunteered to fight Fascism in Spain. On a quiet Front they did all that it was possible to do to support the anti-Fascist cause. They took part in patrols, volunteered for action when it occurred and were respected by neighbouring Spanish troops. If we include those ILP volunteers who later fought in other units, we find that approximately a third of the volunteers were killed or wounded while in Spain. This statistic refutes the argument that the ILP volunteers suffered little in Spain.

Throughout World War II and the Cold War period, and into the 1960's, the veterans of the International Brigades were mistrusted and viewed by the establishment as 'premature anti-Fascists'. However, by the time the fiftieth anniversary of the Spanish Civil War came around in 1986, Franco was long dead and the activities of the men and women who served in the International Brigades were being viewed in a different light. Books and articles have been written about many of the veterans' lives, and their experiences have been recorded before it was too late.[5] Many towns and cities throughout Britain have plaques and monuments commemorating the activities of local Civil War veterans, and in London there is statue near the 'London Eye' which celebrates the sacrifices and the ideals of those volunteers who served in the International Brigades.[6] Trade Union leaders, MPs, academics and artists are often present at commemorative events and more recently Spanish and British Government officials have even attended. In Spain the International Brigades have several monuments in their honour and are warmly accepted by the majority of Spaniards, with the Spanish Government granting International Brigades veterans honorary Spanish citizenship. The legacy and commemoration of the International Brigades anti-Fascist beliefs and sacrifices has come a long way from the days of the 'Cold War', when they were Anti-Fascist pariahs, to the situation today when their actions in Spain are openly celebrated by most people on the 'Left'.

The ILP volunteers returned to Britain to no hero's welcome and even, in some cases, persecution by the local Communist Party members.[7] The shadow of George Orwell has in some ways hindered research into the ILP volunteers. Attitudes to the ILP Contingent have been coloured by strong reactions to Orwell from biographers and academics: to some Orwell was a visionary; to others he was a fake.[8] Research about Orwell has usually covered his time in Spain and on occasions has included comments from fellow ILP veterans, but usually the material has always been focussed solely on Orwell.[9] Following on from Thwaites' work, this account of the ILP volunteers hopefully shows that the ILP Contingent's time in Spain deserves to be remembered. For the first time details of the ILP volunteers are now available to the reader. In the future I hope that this study will be expanded and who knows? Perhaps we will unearth more information on the ILP volunteers and possibly even add new names to the list of volunteers in chapter seven.

At one time International Brigades veterans were anti-Fascist pariahs, but are now rightly honoured and celebrated. The time has come for the story of the ILP volunteers in Spain to be made known. I hope that this study has started the process of showing that the ILP and its Contingent of volunteers were genuine anti-Fascist volunteers. In 2009 the first commemorative recognition of the ILP Contingent took place when a plaque was unveiled at the Salford Working Class Movement Library. This plaque hangs proudly on the wall of the Reading Room of the library. In 2011 in Manchester as part of the 75th anniversary of the Spanish Civil War a joint commemorative event took place in the Town Hall where both plaques honouring the International Brigades and the ILP Contingent were on show and both sets of volunteers were remembered. 2013 will see the 75th anniversary of the publication of Orwell's classic account of his experience of the Spanish Civil War, *Homage to Catalonia*, and many events will be taking place both in Britain and Spain. The International Brigade Memorial Trust is sponsoring one of these events. So interest in Orwell and his fellow volunteers is likely to be greatly increased. Like their comrades in the International Brigades the role of the ILP volunteers in Spain is now beginning to be commemorated and honoured and they are less and less being seen as the anti-Fascist pariahs of the Spanish Civil War.

41. Memorial plaque to the ILP Contingent volunteers
in the Reading Room of the Salford Working Class Movement Library.
(Design by Les Cartlidge)

CONCLUSION

42. The Author and Roma Marquez *(right)*, one of the last surviving militiamen of the 29th POUM Division who went to Zaragoza in August 1936, discussing the Huesca battlefield in October 2008.

43. Roma Marquez having a cup of coffee in Huesca on March 22nd 2009, almost 73 years late!

Notes

[1] Richard Baxell, *British Volunteers in the Spanish Civil War: The British Battalion in the International Brigades, 1936-1939* (Routledge, London, 2004, Abersychan, Warren & Pell, 2007), p107-108 (W & P p113-114)

[2] Gidon Cohen, *The Failure of a Dream: The Independent Labour Party from Disaffiliation to World War II* (Tauris, London, 2007), p185-186, Peter Thwaites, The Independent Labour Party Contingent in the Spanish Civil War, *Imperial War Museum Review*, 1987, p57-58

[3] Cohen, op cit., p176-191, Tom Buchanan, *The Impact of the Spanish Civil War on Britain: War, Loss and Memory* (Sussex Academic Press, Brighton, 2007), p98-121, Baxell, op cit., p12, 15, Jim Fyrth, *The Signal was Spain: The Spanish Aid Movement in Britain, 1936-39* (Lawrence and Wishart, London, 1986), p80-1, 210, 230, 245

[4] Thwaites, op cit., p50-61, Cohen, Ibid, p179-186, Hywel Francis, *Miners Against Fascism : Wales and the Spanish Civil War* (Lawrence and Wishart, London, 1984), p175, South Wales Coalfield Collection, Urias Jones interview (09.10.74) AUD/177, Swansea University.

[5] Imperial War Museum, The Spanish Civil War Collection: Sound Archive Oral History Recordings (Trustees of the Imperial War Museum, London, 1996). This lists over a hundred interviews with International Brigade veterans.

[6] International Brigade Association, *Memorials of the Spanish Civil War* (Alan Sutton, Stroud, 1996). Lists all memorials to the International Brigades in Britain, Ireland and Spain up to date of publication.

[7] Cohen, op cit., p139, 184

[8] Bernard Crick, *George Orwell: A Life* (Secker & Warburg, London, 1981) For a very favourable account of Orwell and his work. C. Norris (editor), *Inside the Myth: Orwell Views from the Left* (Lawrence and Wishart, London, 1984) For less favourable essays on Orwell, in particularly one hostile essay by the former International Brigade Commander, Bill Alexander.

[9] Stephen Wadhams, *Remembering Orwell* (Penguin, Harmondsworth, 1984) Includes several stories about Orwell, related by ILP volunteers.

Selected Bibliography

Works where the whole record is in *Italics* were sources that were consulted but not cited. Works not in Italics or only partly in Italics were cited in the chapter notes. The Bibliography has been organised by subject area rather than a straight alphabetic list.

INDEPENDENT LABOUR PARTY (ILP)

Brockway, Fenner *Inside the Left: Thirty Years of Platform, Press, Prison and Parliament* (George Allen & Unwin, London, 1942)

Cohen, Gidon *The Independent Labour Party from Disaffiliation to World War II* (Tauris, London, 2007)

Craig, F. W. S. (Compiler), *Minor Parties at British Parliamentary Elections 1885-1974* (MacMillan, London, 1975)

Dowse, R. E. *Left in the Centre: The Independent Labour Party 1893-1940* (Longmans. London, 1966)

__James, David, Jowitt, Tony__ and __Laybourn, Keith__ (Editors), The Centennial History of the Independent Labour Party: A Collection of Essays (Ryburn, Halifax, 1992)

__Joll, James__ The Second International 1889-1914 (Routledge & Kegan Paul, London, 1955)

Knox, William *James Maxton* (Manchester Univ. Press, Manchester, 1987)

McGovern, John *Neither Fear nor Favour* (Blandford Press, London, 1960)

__McKinlay, Alan__ and __Morris, R. J.__ (Editors), The ILP on Clydeside, 1893-1932: from foundation to disintegration (Manchester Univ. Press, Manchester, 1991)

__McNair, John__ James Maxton: The Beloved Rebel (George Allen & Unwin, London, 1955)

__Morgan, Kenneth O.__ Keir Hardie: Radical and Socialist (Phoenix Giant, London, 1997, first published 1975)

Pelling, Henry *Origins of the Labour Party* (Oxford Univ. Press, Oxford, 1965)

Ramsden, John (Editor) *The Oxford Companion to Twentieth-Century British Politics* (Oxford Univ.Press, Oxford, 2002)

Winter, Barry *The ILP: Past and Present* (Independent Labour Publications, Leeds, 1993)

WEBSITES

http://www.independentlabour.org.uk   *(Independent Labour Publications)*

BRITAIN IN THE 1930s

Branson, Noreen *History of the Communist Party of Great Britain 1927-1941* (Lawrence and Wishart, London, 1985)

Copsey, Nigel *Anti-Fascism in Britain* (MacMillan, London, 2000)

Croucher, Richard *We Refuse to Starve in Silence: A History of the National Unemployed Workers' Movement 1920-1946* (Lawrence and Wishart, London, 1987)

Fyrth, Jim (Editor), *Britain, Fascism and the Popular Front* (Lawrence and Wishart, London, 1985)

Hannington, Wal *Unemployed Struggles 1919-1936* (Lawrence and Wishart, London, 1975, first published 1936)

Jupp, James *The Radical Left in Britain 1931-1941* (Frank Cass, London, 1982)

Kingsford, Peter *The Hunger Marchers in Britain 1920-1939* (Lawrence and Wishart, London, 1982)

Kushner, Tony and **Valman, Nadia** (Editors), *Remembering Cable Street: Fascism and Anti-Fascism in British Society* (Vallentine Mitchell, London, 2000)

Laybourn, Keith *Britain on the Breadline: A Social and Political History of Britain 1918-1939* (Sutton, Stroud, 1990)

Mowat, Charles Loch *Britain Between the Wars 1918-1940* (Methuen, London, 1955)

Skidelsky, Robert *Oswald Mosley* (MacMillan, London, 1975)

Taylor, A. J. P. *English History 1914-1945* (Pelican, Harmondsworth, 1975)

Thurlow, Richard *Fascism in Britain: A History, 1918-1985* (Basil Blackwell, Oxford, 1987)

BRITAIN AND THE SPANISH CIVIL WAR

Alexander, Bill *British Volunteers for Liberty: Spain 1936-1939* (Lawrence and Wishart, London, 1982)

Baxell, Richard *British Volunteers in the Spanish Civil War: The British Battalion in the International Brigades, 1936-1939* (Routledge, London, 2004 and Warren & Pell, Abersychan, 2007)

Baxell, Richard *The Unlikely Warriors: The British in the Spanish Civil War and the struggle against Fascism* (Aurum Press, London, 2012)

Bell, Adrian *Only for Three Months: The Basque Children in Exile* (Mousehold Press, Norwich, 1996)

Bradley, Ken and **Chappell, Mike** *The International Brigades in Spain 1936-39* (Osprey, London, 1994)

Buchanan, Tom *Britain and the Spanish Civil War* (Cambridge Univ. Press, Cambridge, 1997)

Buchanan, Tom *The Spanish Civil War and the British Labour Movement* (Cambridge Univ. Press, Cambridge, 1991)

Edwards, Jill *The British Government and the Spanish Civil War, 1936-1939* (MacMillan, London, 1979)

Fyrth, Jim *The Signal was Spain: The Aid Spain Movement in Britain 1936-39* (Lawrence and Wishart, London, 1986)

Hopkins, James K. *Into the Heart of the Fire: The British in the Spanish Civil War* (Stanford Univ. Press, Stanford, USA, 1998)

O'Riordan, Michael *Connolly Column: The story of the Irishmen who fought in the ranks of the International Brigades in the national-revolutionary war of the Spanish people, 1936-1939* (New Books, Dublin, Ireland, 1979 and Warren & Pell, Abersychan, 2005.)

Rust, William *Britons in Spain: The History of the British Battalion of the XVth International Brigade* (Lawrence and Wishart, London, 1939 and

Warren & Pell, Abersychan, 2003)

Watkins, K. W. *Britain Divided: The Effect of the Spanish Civil War on British Political Opinion* (Thomas Nelson, London, 1963)

WEBSITES

www.international-brigades.org.uk (International Brigade Memorial Trust)

www.lacolumna.org.uk (La Columna Living History Group)

http://www.nojubilemlamemoria.cat/en/index.html (Catalan Spanish Civil War history group)

http://irelandscw.co/
(Site about Irish involvement in the Spanish Civil War)

www.mibnet.org.uk *(Site about Liverpool volunteers who went to Spain)*

SPANISH REPUBLIC AND THE SPANISH CIVIL WAR

Alpert, Michael A *New International History of the Spanish Civil War (Palgrave MacMillan, Basingstoke, 2004)*

Beevor, Antony *The Battle for Spain: The Spanish Civil War 1936-1939 (Weidenfeld & Nicolson, 2006)*

Carr, Raymond *Spain 1808-1975* (Clarendon Press, Oxford, 1982)

Cordery, Bob *La Ultima Cruzada: A Wargamers guide to the Spanish Civil War (Partizan Press, Leigh-on-Sea, 1989)*

Fraser, Ronald *Blood of Spain: The Experience of Civil War 1936-1939 (Penguin, London, 1979)*

Graham, Helen *The Spanish Republic at War 1936-1939 (Cambridge Univ.Press, Cambridge, 2002)*

Jackson, Gabriel *The Spanish Republic and the Civil War 1931-1939 (Princeton Univ.Press, Princeton, USA, 1967)*

Lannon, Frances *Essential Histories: The Spanish Civil War 1936-1939 (Osprey, Oxford, 2002)*

Payne, Stanley G. *Spain's First Democracy: The Second Republic, 1931-1936 (Univ. of Wisconsin Press, Wisconsin, USA, 1993)*

Preston, Paul *The Spanish Civil War 1936-39 (Weidenfeld and Nicolson, London, 1986)*

Thomas, Hugh *The Spanish Civil War* (Penguin, London, 1986)

SPANISH REVOLUTION AND THE POUM

Alba, Victor and **Schwartz, Stephen** *Spanish Marxism versus Soviet Communism: A History of the P.O.U.M.* (Transaction Books, Oxford, 1988)

Bateman, Don *Joaquim Maurin 1893-1973: Life and Death of a Spanish Revolutionary* (ILP, Leeds, 1974)

Brennan, Gerald *The Spanish Labyrinth: An Account of the Social and Political Background of the Spanish Civil War (Cambridge Univ. Press, Cambridge, 1988, second edition first published 1950)*

Broue, Pierre and **Temime, Emile** *The Revolution and the Civil War in Spain* (Faber and Faber, London, 1970)

Dolgoff, Sam *(Editor), The Anarchist Collectives: Workers' Self-management in the Spanish Revolution 1936-1939 (Montreal, Canada, Black Rose Books, 1990)*

Durgan, Andy *International Volunteers in the POUM Militias* http://libcom.org/history/international-volunteers-poum-militias

Hall, Christopher *Revolutionary Warfare: Spain 1936-37* (Gosling Press, Pontefract, 1996)

Low, Mary and **Brea, Juan** *Red Spanish Notebook: The First Six Months of the Revolution and the Civil War* (San Francisco, USA, City Lights Books, 1979, first published in 1937)

Orwell, George *Homage to Catalonia: And Looking Back on the Spanish War* (Penguin, London, 1988, first published 1938)

Paz, Abel *Durruti in the Spanish Revolution (AK Press, Edinburgh, 2007)*

Peirats, Jose and **Ealham, Chris** (Editor), *The CNT in the Spanish Revolution in 3 Volumes* (ChristieBooks, Hastings, 2006)

Revolutionary History, The Spanish Civil War: The View from the Left (Socialist Platform, London, 1992)

Solano, Wilebaldo *The Spanish Revolution: The Life of Andres Nin* (Independent Labour Party, London, ND)

Trotsky, Leon *The Spanish Revolution (1931-1939)* (London, Pathfinder Press, 1986)

WEBSITES

www.fundanin.org (Fundacion Nin, History of the POUM)

ILP/POUM VOLUNTEERS

Buchanan, Tom *The Impact of the Spanish Civil War on Britain: War, Loss and Memory* (Sussex Academic Press, Brighton, 2007)

Coward, Jack *Back From the Dead* (Merseyside Writers, Liverpool, ND)

Crick, Bernard *George Orwell: A Life* (Secker & Warburg, London, 1981)

Crossey, Ciaran *No Pasaran: "We intend to show the World"* (Belfast and District Trades Union Council, Belfast, 2007)

Darman, Peter *Heroic Voices of the Spanish Civil War: Memories from the International Brigades* (New Holland, London, 2008)

Davison, Peter (Editor), *Orwell in Spain: The Full Text of Homage to Catalonia with Associated Articles, Reviews and Letters from The Complete Works of George Orwell* (Penguin, London, 2001)

Diez, Antonio *Brigadas Internacionales. Cartas desde Espana* (Munoz Moya, Brenes, 2005)

Francis, Hywel *Miners Against Fascism: Wales and the Spanish Civil War* (Lawrence and Wishart, London, 1984)

Gray, Daniel *Homage to Caledonia: Scotland and the Spanish Civil War* (Luath Press, Edinburgh, 2008)

Hall, Christopher *'Disciplina Camaradas': Four English Volunteers in Spain 1936-39* (Gosling Press, Pontefract, 1994)

Hall, Christopher *'In Spain with Orwell': George Orwell and the Independent Labour Party Volunteers in the Spanish Civil War, 1936-1939* (Tippermuir Books, Perth, 2013)

Imperial War Museum The Spanish Civil War Collection: Sound Archive Oral History Recordings (Trustees of the Imperial War Museum, London, 1996)

Inglis, Amirah *Australians in the Spanish Civil War* (Allen & Unwin, London, 1987)

Jacobs, David The Man Who Saved Orwell , *Hoover Digest*, 2001, 4. http://orwell.ru/a_life/Spanish_War/english/e_harry

McNair, John *Spanish Diary* (Stockport, Independent Labour Publications, ND)

Meyers, Jeffrey Repeating the Old Lies, *The New Criterion*, 1999, p77 http://orwell.ru/a_life/Spanish_War/english/e_olies

Newsinger, John The Death of Bob Smillie, *The Historical Journal*, 41, 2, 1998, p575-578

Orwell, Sonia and **Angus, Ian** (Editors), *The Collected Essays, Journalism and Letters of George Orwell: Volume 1: An Age Like This 1920-1940* (Penguin, London, 1970)

Romilly, Esmond *Boadilla* (MacDonald, London, 1971, first published 1937)

Shelden, Michael *Orwell: Authorised Biography* (Politicos, London, 2006)

Stansky, Peter and **Abrahams, William** *Journey to the Frontier: Two Roads to the Spanish Civil War* (Constable, London, 1994, first published 1966)

Stradling, Robert *The Irish and the Spanish Civil War: Crusades in Conflict* (Mandolin, Manchester, 1999)

Stradling, Robert *Wales and the Spanish Civil War: The Dragon's Dearest Cause?* (Univ. of Wales Press, Cardiff, 2004)

Stradling, Robert *The Spies Who Loved Them: The Blairs in Barcelona, 1937*, Intelligence and National Security, Vol 25, No 5, October 2010, p638-655

Taylor D. J. Orwell: the life (Vintage Books, London, 2003),

Thwaites, Peter The Independent Labour Party Contingent in the Spanish Civil War, *Imperial War Museum Review*, 1987, p50-61

Toscano, Joseph Articles on Harvey Buttonshaw, *Anarchist Age Weekly Review*, 471, October 2001, 569, October 2003 www.takver.com/history/Buttonshaw_harvey.htm

Wadhams, Stephen *Remembering Orwell* (Penguin, Harmondsworth, 1984)

NEWSPAPERS

Guardian Obituaries **29.09.99**

Independent Obituaries **03.11.99**

New Leader 1936-1939

INTERVIEWS

Stafford Cottman (Imperial War Museum 9278)

Robert (Bob) Edwards (Imperial War Museum 4669)

Frank Frankford (Imperial War Museum 9308)

Urias Jones (South Wales Coalfield Collection AUD/177).

ARCHIVES

Bob Edwards Papers (Labour History Archive and Study Centre, 103 Princess Street, Manchester M1 6DD)

Marx Memorial Library International Brigade Archive Box C 13/7a 'Report on the English Section of the POUM' and 13/10 'Report on the position with regard to the ILP Group' both written by Walter Tapsell, May 1937. Box C 13/12 letters John Donovan and Harry Thomas to Communist Party Representative in Barcelona, May 1937.

National Archives, cat no KV/5/12 MI5 List of British Individuals who travelled to and from Spain 1936-39

Warwick University Spanish Civil War Collection: Trabajadores the Spanish Civil War through the eyes of organised labour
http://contentdm.warwick.ac.uk/cdm/landingpage/collections/scw

UCL Library Services Special Collections: George Orwell
http://www.ucl.ac.uk/library/special-coll/orwell.shtml

Lists of International Brigades Volunteers with annotations given to the author by Local History Group, Author unknown.

WEBSITES

See Jacobs, Meyers and Toscano above.

http://groups.msn.com/DundeeandtheSpanishCivilWar/homepage.msnw

Salford Working Class Movement Library: Spanish Civil War Collection
www.wcml.org.uk

CORRESPONDENCE

With authors / researchers Jim Carmody, Andy Durgan, Michael Eaude, Dan Payne, Antonio Diez and Richaerd Baxell

Index

Page numbers in **Bold** indicate illustrations.

Abyssinia 30
Adelante (newspaper) 47
Agnew, John, 117, **171**, 172, 227
Alcubierre **82**, **85**, **91**, 93, **95**, **96-7**, 106, 133, 145, 179, 183, 199-200, 208, 215, 218, 224
Alerta (newspaper) 47
Alfonso XIII 37
Allen, Clifford 12, 16
Antonov Ovsyeyenko, Vladimir (Russian Consul) 50, 58
Arquer, Jordi 88, 93, 100
Attlee, Clement 24, 31, 34
Auden, W. H. 155, 167
Avory, Lewis Ernest 117, 172, 227

Barbagal 93
Barbastro 93, 106, 212, 233
Basque refugees 66, 67, **68**, 186, 219, 246
Batalla, La (newspaper) 39, 41, 47, 52, 55, 56, 210
Baxell, Richard 1
Bennett, William 116, 172
Berenguer, Damaso 38
Blair, Eileen 63, 111, 133, 134-5, 151, 154, 218, 223
Blair, Eric (*see* also Orwell, George) 63, 113, 114, 117, 148, 150, 153, 154, 208
Bloc Obrer I Camperol (BOC) 39, 125-126
Braithwaite, John 117, **171**, 172-4, 228, **246**
Brandler, Heinrich 32-33, 36
Brandt, Willi 36, 184, 185
Bridgeton ward election 28

British Battalion, International Brigades 73-75, 118-19
British Union of Fascists (BUF) 21-2, 34, 71, 181, 190
Brockway, Fenner 7, 14, 15, 22, 32, 61, 68-71, 103, 105-6, 142, 150, 180, 195, 199, 206
Brown, George 138
Buchanan, George 23, 28, 31, 34
Buchanan, Tom 2, 211
Bulletin, The (newspaper) 26
Buttonshaw, Archie 116, 121, 122, 123, 124, 174-6, 228-9

Cable Street, Battle of **21**, 21-2
Camlachie ward election 28
Carmichael, James **30**
Carmody, Jim *vi*
Castle, Les 117, 176
Cerro de Aguila 98
Chambers, Bill 117, 156-7
Clarion Cycling Club 10
Clarke, William 117, 177-8
Clarks (family) 67
Clinton, Arthur 117, 178
Coles, Tom 117, 179
Coll, Josep 51
Committee for Militias 45-47, 49
Communist International (CI) 25, 28, 29, 30, 34, 141
Communist Party of Great Britain (CPGB) 19, 20, 21-32, 61, 76
Confederacion de Derechas Autonomas (CEDA) 38

INDEX

Confederacion Nacional Trabajadores (CNT) 39-40, 42, 45, 47, 48-53, 55, 58, 68, 70, 84, 157
Connor, Jock 79, 117, 180
Cook, Arthur 12, 16
Cope ('Tanky'), James Arthur 118, 125, 211-2, 238
Cornford, John 89, 92, 95
Cottman, Stafford *vi,* 2, 5, 112, 116-7, 121, 125, 154, 180-8, **181**, 204, 207, 231, 236, **246**
Cripps, Stafford 31, 36

Daily Mail 21
Daily Worker 75, 113, 183, 186, 190, 191, 194-5, 196, 212, 234
Donovan, John 'Paddy' 79, 117, 123, 124, 153, 157-60, 168, 189, 209
Doran, Charles 117, 124, 188-9, 232
Dutch Revolutionary Socialist Workers Party (RSAP) 32

Edwards, Bob 5, **24**, 61, 63, 104, 105, 106, 107, 109, 110, 111, 112, 114, 117, 138-48, 150, 152, 157, 158, 159, 160, 164, 172, 177, 178, 182, 194, 196, 198, 219
El Combatiente Rojo (newspaper) 47
Ermita Salas 94, 114, 129, 133, 137, 145, 152-3, 179, 184, 193, 196, 197, 198, 200, 201, 202, 204, 209, 212, 213, 220, 223, 224
Etchebehere, Hipolito 98
Etchebehere, Mika 92, 98
Evans 117, 123, 125, 189

Fagan, Thomas 75
Farrell, James 79, 117, 123, 124, 189-90
Federacio Obrero d'Unificacio Sindical (FOUS) 42, 47
Federacion Anarquista Iberica (FAI) 37, 45, 47, 49, 50, 53, 58, 84, 86, 189
Fletcher, Ted (Edward Joseph) 63, 65, **246**
Fourth International 27, 32, 35, 41
Frankford, Frank 117, 174, 190-6, 199, 206, 212, 233
Frankfort, Frank (*see* Frankford, Frank)
French Party of Proletarian Unity (PUP) 32

German Socialist Workers Party (SAP), 32

Gomez, Louise 92
Gordon, John 63
Gorkin, Julian 52, 55, 58, 63, 68, 92
Granen 93
Gross, George 118, 152, 196-7, 234
Grossi, Manuel 88, 93, 100

Hannington, Wal 23
Hardy, George 75
Hashomer Hatzair 32
Hemingway, Ernest 146
Hiddlestone, Reg 118, **171**, 197-8
Homage to Catalonia 2, 114, 135, 136, 148, 153, 155, 184, 249
Hotel Falcon 46, 47, 182
Huesca 63, 83, 91, 94, 95, 114, 116,128, 131, 133, 163, **171**, 173, 178, 183, 184, 189, 205, 221, 223185, 201, 208, 214, 216
Hunger Marches 19, 22, 23, 24, 25, 32, 34, 71, 72, 140, 206
Hunter, Philip 118, **171**, **198**, 198-9

ILP Guild of Youth 20, 21, 26, 73, 138, 173, 181, 184, 186, 206, 208, 247
ILP (Independent Labour Party) Contingent *vi*, 65, 72-7, 103-125
Independent Labour Party (ILP) *vi, xi, xii,* 1-36, 52, 61-80, 88, 92, 103-252
Independent Labour Publications *vi*
Italian Maximalist Socialists 32

Jellinek, Frank 134, 161, 196, 198
Jones, Jack 140
Jones, Uriah 118, 199-201
Jorge, Gregorio 117, 129-31, 137
Jose Arenillas, Luis 98
Joventud Communista Iberica (JCI) 43, 46, 52, 53, 56, 89, 130-1, 207
Julius 87, 118, 123, 201
Justesen, Charles 118, 201
Justessen, Charles (*see* Justesen, Charles)

Kareva, Olga 40
Kopp, Georges 110, 117, 130, 131-136, 144, 145, 147, 151, 158, 160, 175, 186, 194, 203, 207, 209, 218, 223, 224
Kupinski, Wolf (*see* Milton, Harry)

Landau, Kurt 54
Lecinena 93

Lenin Barracks, Barcelona 88, 92, 106, 107, **108,** 109, 144, 150, 157, 183, 221
Lesser, Sam 194, 212, 233
Levin, Louis 109, 118, 220-1
Levinski, Benjamin 117, 136-7
L'Hora (newspaper) 127
London Bureau 32-3, 35, 36, 41, 52, 61, 106, 138, 207, 210

MacDonald, Ethel 71
MacDonald, Robert 118, 202
McCartney, Wilfred 150
McGovern, John 23, 24, 28, **30, 61, 63, 69, 71-2**
McNair, John vi, 61-63, **64,** 65, 69, 74, 112, 144, 150-1, 158, 168, 173, 184, 185, 186, 195, 204, 207, 208, **208,** 210, 216, 225, **246**
McNeil, Hugh 118, 202, **202**
Manicomio, Huesca 91, 94, 133, 178
Martin, W. B. 63, 91, 111, 157, 221-2
Marxist Social Democratic Foundation 8, 29
Maurin, Jeanne 69
Maurin, Joaquim 39-43, 47, 56, 61, 62, 68-9, 89, 127
Maxton, James 7, 15, 19, 24, 28-9, **30,** 31-2, 61, 69, 71, 73, 75, 103, 206
Militias (Revolutionary) 81-102
Miller, Henry 150, 166
Milton, Mike (*see* Wilton) 99, 118, 219-20
Monzon 93
Morros, Doctor 63
Moscow Show Trials 36, 48, 189
Mount Oscuro 110
Mount Pocero 137
Moyle, Douglas 118, 123, 202-204, 209, 236, **246**

National Unemployed Workers' Movement (NUWM) 23, 140, 191
New Leader (newspaper) vi, 3, 12, 25, 28, 31, 62, 68, 92, 103, 104, 107, 113, 112, 113, 114, 134, 135, 137, 143, 144, 145, 147, 153, 154, 159, 160, 173, 174, 177, 182, 184, 187, 195, 198, 199, 200, 201, 202, 203, 205, 211, 212, 214, 215, 219, 221, 223
New Statesman (newspaper) 154
Nin, Andreu 33, 39, 40, 41, 42, 43, 45, 46, 47, 48, 50, 52, 55, 63, 71, 73, 216

Norwegian Labour Party 33

O'Duffy, Eoin 158, 168, 248
O'Hara, Patrick 118, 124, 204-5
Orwell, George (*see also* Blair, Eric) 2, 63, 90, 93, 95, 96, 99, 113, 114, 117, 123, 124, 129, 130, 131, 133, 134, 135, 136, 137, 144, 145, 143, 148-156, 157, 158, 159, 160, 161, 171, **171,** 172, 173, 174, 176, 178, 179, 184, 185, 186, 187, 188, 190, 192, 193, 194, 195, 196, 198, 199, 201, 202, 203, 204, 209, 210, 215, 216, 218, 219, 220, 221, 222, 223, 224, **246, 249,** 252
O'Shaugnessy, Eileen (*see* Blair, Eileen)
O'Shaugnessy, Gwen 135

Parker, Buck 117, 124-5, 160-161, 172
Partido Communista Espana (PCE) 39, 84
Partido Obrero de Unificación Marxista (*see* POUM) vi, 2, 3, 4, 5, 33, 36, 37-59, 61, 62, 65, 66, 68, 69, 70, 71, 72, 73, 74, 75, 76, 77, 81-102, 103, 104, 106, 107, 109, 110, 112, 113, 114, 115, 116, 118, 119, 120, 127, 128, 129, 130, 131, 132, 133, 134, 137, 142, 145, 146, 150, 151, 152, 154, 159, 160, 161, 172, 173, 174, 175, 176, 177, 178, 179, 180, 182, 185, 186, 187, 188, 189, 190, 191, 192, 194, 195, 198, 199, 200, 201, 202, 203, 204, 205, 206, 207, 208, 210, 213, 214, 216, 218, 219, 220, 221, 223, 224, 227, 235, 240, 245, 246, 247, 248
Partido Socialista Obrero de Espana (PSOE) 37, 39
Paton, John 27
Peters, Evan 75
Pinar de Humera 98
Pivert, Marcel 33
Pollitt, Harry 213, 217, 238
Popular Front 30, 31, 36, 38, 41, 42
Pravda (newspaper) 48

Ramon 118, 218, 224, 242
Red International of Labour Unions (RILU) 39, 43
Revolutionary Policy Committee (RPC) 25, 139
Richards, Vernon 156, 167
Ritchie, John 118, 123, 204-5

INDEX

Robinson, Sydney *vi, xi*
Robres 93
Robson, R. W. 157, 168
Rogers, Lance *vi*, **60**, 75
Romanian Independent Socialist Party 32
Rovira, Josep 46, 88-89, 93, 94, 100, 116, 123, 127-129

Sandham, Elijah 27
Sarinena 93
Scottish Ambulance Unit 220, 241
Second International 11, 16, 33
Seven Seas Spray 146
Silvert, Sydney 92, 101
Sinclair-Loutit, Kenneth 154, 167
Skidelsky, Robert 29
Smillie, Bob *vi*, 2, 63, 73, 74, 112, 118, 125, 136, 153, 157, 186, 188, 191, 201, 206-211
Smith, C. A. 26
Smith, John Mileno 75
Smith, John Milnes Alan 118, 211
Social Democratic Foundation (SDF) 9
Socialist League 19, 30, 31, 36, 177, 217, 225
Socialist Movement of Catalunya (MSC) 129
Solano, Wilebaldo 46
Spain Campaign Committee (SCC) 226
Spanish Medical Aid 63, 77, 217, 239
Spender, Stephen 155, 167
Sproston, Walter 75, 80
Stearns, Douglas Clark 118, 121, 123, 208, 225
Stephen, Campbell, Reverend 35, 61
Stewart, James 75
Swedish Socialist Party 32

'Tanky' *see* Cope, James Arthur
Tapsell, Wally 74, 79, 113, 122, 154, 168, 185, 201, 206, 211, 221, 227, 235, 240
Telefonica, Barcelona 53
Teruel 98
Texidor, Greville 92
The Grange, Street (Basque refugee colony) 66, **67**
Third International 32, 34, 39, 40, 41
Thomas, Harry Parry 213-4, 221, 238
Thompson, Douglas 118, 214
Trades Union Congress (TUC) 9, 15, 27, 138

Trench, Chalmers 92
Trench, Patrick 92
Tribune (newspaper) 155
Trotsky, Leon 26, 34-5, 40, 41, 48, 52, 55, 58, 93, 138, 189, 222
Trotskyite Communist League 26

Union General de Trabajadores (UGT) 37, 39, 42, 47, 48, 58, 71, 84
United Front Congress 20, 24
Unity campaign 22, 28, 30, 31

Vidal, Germinal 46

Wallhead, Richard 27
Warnotte, Germaine 136
Webb, Harry 118, 124, 216
Whalley, Eric 140
Wickes, David 217-8
Wilding, George 75
Wilkinson, Ellen 24
Williams, Bob 118, 123, 125, 218-219
Wilton, Mike (*see* Milton) 99, 118, 123, 219, 220, 240
Wingate, Sybil 63, 118, 225-7
Woman's Social and Political Union (WSPU) 11
Workers' and Peasants' Bloc (BOC) 39
Young Communist League (YCL) 26, 74, 119, 181, 186, 206, 207
Zamora, Alcala 42

Illustration taken from an Independent Labour Party Card, 1927.
(Glasgow Caledonian University)

The International Brigde Memorial Trust

The International Brigade Memorial Trust (IBMT) was formed in 2002 from the veterans of the International Brigade Association, the Friends of the International Brigade Association, representatives of the Marx Memorial Library, and historians specialising in the Spanish Civil War.

Its aims are:

To educate the public in the history of the men and women who fought in the International Brigades and in the medical and other support services in the Spanish Civil War; in particular, by preserving and cataloguing valuable historical material relating to and by making such material available to the public.

To foster good citizenship by remembering those who have fallen in the Spanish Civil War by preserving, maintaining and assisting in the construction of war memorials.

The IBMT produces a newsletter twice a year, holds a public lecture once a year, an annual general meeting at a different city in October, and a memorial meeting every July at the International Brigade Memorial by the London Eye. The IBMT has its own travelling exhibition called 'Antifascistas'.

For further information on the IBMT visit
www.international-brigades.org.uk
or contact its Secretary Jim Jump, 6 Stonells Road,
Battersea, London SW11 6HQ.

The ILP Past and Present

For further information about the modern ILP (now Independent Labour Publications) and their pamphlet on the Spanish Civil War, Land and Freedom, email info@independentlabour.org.uk, or write to ILP, PO Box 222, Leeds LS11 1DF, or visit http://www.independentlabour.org.uk/main/.

Ruta Orwell
La Guerra Civil en Los Monegros

In 2006 to commemorate the 70th anniversary of the outbreak of the Spanish Civil War the Comarcal of Los Monegros has implemented a project to restore trenches in the Los Monegros area connected with George Orwell's experiences described in *Homage to Catalonia*. In addition to the reconstructed trench systems with interpretative panels a new museum in Robres has been opened covering the history of the Spanish Civil War on the Aragon Front.

For further information on the Ruta Orwell go to
www.guerracivil.losmonegros.com

Tippermuir Books Limited
is a 'not-for-profit' publishing companybased in Perth, Scotland.
It was founded in 2009 by two historians,
Rob Hands and Paul Philippou.

IN SPAIN WITH ORWELL
is the company's fifth title to date. The other four are:

BATTLEGROUND PERTHSHIRE (2009),

SPANISH THERMOPYLAE (2009),

PERTH: STREET BY STREET (2012), and

BORN IN PERTHSHIRE (2012)

All titles are available from bookshops and from most
online booksellers. Alternatively, contact Tippermuir Books Limited
by electronic mail at

tippermuirbooks@blueyonder.co.uk

for details of direct ordering.

Spanish Thermopylae is the story of the fifty-seven Cypriots who served in the International Brigades during the Spanish Civil War, 1936-39. It is also the story of a war that defined the lives of a generation and whose outcome decided the fate of hundreds of millions of people across the world. Drawing on recently-released records from the Comintern Archive in Moscow, *Spanish Thermopylae* will appeal both to the reader interested in the experiences of the Cypriot volunteers, and to anyone looking for a concise history of the Spanish Civil War.

Spanish Thermopylae is written by Paul Philippou.